A CONQUERED CITY IN STILL LIFE

In George Barnard's magnificent image, Atlanta sl
peacetime after its taste of war's ravages. The cause
suffering lies in the foreground, the railroad track
with the Confederacy east and west

The South Besieged

VOLUME FIVE OF

The Image of War
1861–1865

A Project of

The National Historical Society

Gettysburg, Pennsylvania

ROBERT H. FOWLER, Founder

EDITOR

WILLIAM C. DAVIS

SENIOR CONSULTING EDITOR

BELL I. WILEY

The South Besieged

VOLUME FIVE OF

The Image of War 1861-1865

DOUBLEDAY & COMPANY, INC.
GARDEN CITY, NEW YORK
1983

OVERLEAF: The flagging South's blood, men who could not be spared. Prisoners captured in Virginia in 1864 can do nothing more for their country now, and can only stare at the camera for posterity. Lean and weathered, worn and starved like their infant nation, their war is done. (RINHART GALLERIES, INC.)

Library of Congress Cataloging in Publication Data
Main entry under title:

The South besieged

(The Image of war, 1861–1865; v. 5)
"A project of the National Historical Society"
Includes index.
1. United States—History—Civil War, 1861–1865—Campaigns—Pictorial works. 2. United States—History—Civil War, 1861–1865—Photography. I. National Historical Society. II. Title.
E470.S76 1983 973.7'3'0222
ISBN: 0-385-18281-3
Library of Congress Catalog Card Number 82-45399

PRINTED IN THE UNITED STATES OF AMERICA
FIRST EDITION
DESIGNED BY PAUL RANDALL MIZE

Contents

A NOTE ON THE SOURCES: A credit line accompanies each photograph in this volume. Each source is written out in full when first cited, but those that contributed many photographs are thereafter abbreviated. A list of abbreviations is included at the end of the book, and we would especially like to acknowledge the generosity of the sources on this list.

Introduction

WILLIAM C. DAVIS

THERE HAS ALWAYS BEEN a timeless quality to the images that survive from the American Civil War. More than seventy years ago, in 1911, as the first rumblings of unrest in Europe gave hint to the threat of a global conflict, William Short, secretary of the New York Peace Society, viewed a collection of Civil War photographs and was moved by them. "They are the greatest arguments for peace that the world has ever seen," he declared. "Their mission is more than to record history; it is to make history—to mold the thought of the generations as everlasting witnesses of the price of war."

It is not a point to argue. Francis Trevelyan Miller, as he was editing his monumental *Photographic History of the Civil War* (10 vols.), found himself forced to agree despite all the romanticism that he felt. "The hand of the historian may falter, or his judgment may fail," he wrote in introducing his first volume in 1911, "but the final record of the American Civil War is told in these time-dimmed negatives." More than that, he said, "It is in these photographs that all Americans can meet on the common ground of their beloved traditions . . . here the generations may look upon the undying record of the valor of those who fought to maintain the Union and those who fought for independence from it." Yet beyond all those high-toned phrases and the patriotic rhetoric of the times, Miller, too, saw something more in the images. "These photographs are appeals to peace," he said. "They are the most convincing evidence of the tragedy of war." It was not mere chance that, with the world about to leap into a war "to end all wars," Miller closed his introduction with the words of U. S. Grant: "Let us have peace." As so often in the history of human endeavors, it was a plea that would have to wait for another time.

We cannot say with certainty just which of the thousands of images of the war they were that so impressed Miller and Short so vividly—and which apparently failed to impress their generation sufficiently to keep it from another conflict. But if we had to hazard a guess, we might not go far off the mark to suggest that they were many of the images presented here in this fifth volume of *The Image of War: 1861–1865*. For this is the volume of 1864 for the most part, when the war's ferocity and the cameramen's ability combined to produce truly the most eloquent and horrifying pictures of the cost and waste caused by the whirlwind sweeping over the divided nation.

Here in this volume, we see at last the war from ocean to ocean, virtually engulfing the entire continent from Maine to California. Here is the Volunteer State—Tennessee—torn from border to border by the greatest and bloodiest battles west of the Alleghenies. Here is already beleaguered Virginia, about to be blooded yet again as never before when Grant and Lee meet in the Wilderness and grapple inexorably onward toward Richmond. Here is the campaign that failed up the Red River, where politics so affected strategy that the two were inseparable. Here is the war off the deep Southern coastline, as the Yankee blockaders kept tight their stranglehold on the dwindling Confederate ports. Here is war on the most costly and ravishing level, as Sheridan scours the once-beautiful Shenandoah, to leave it a place where carrion birds could not find a meal. And here is mighty Sherman, the dread angel of destruction, paying visit to Georgia as only he could.

Following them all were the men with their lenses and wet plates. Their craft had become both an art and a highly professional business by now. Tempered by three years of the war, they were hardened to the rigors of campaign, knew how to protect themselves and their apparatus from the disrespectful wear and dangers of the field, and could work quickly and effectively. More than that, they knew what to photograph, and it is apparent that they, too, were increasingly preoccupied with the waste and tragedy of it all. To be sure, they still portrayed the strutting generals, the simple grinning soldiers, and armies on the march and in camp. Yet increasingly their lenses focused on the dead, the wounded, the bits and parts of men and machines, and the battered landscape they left behind. Perhaps the artists themselves, like Miller and others a half-century later, had finally come to their own realization of what their work meant—or could mean. After three seemingly endless years of peering through their cameras, they had seen as much death and destruction as any soldier. It did not matter that, when they looked through their lenses, the images appeared upside down—by 1864 the whole country seemed upside down.

It was a year that would produce some of the most eloquent imagery of the war, as several photographers matured into premier chroniclers of the conflict. Down in Baton Rouge, Louisiana, now firmly in Yankee grasp, Andrew D. Lytle continued the work that he had carried on without interruption since the war began. With ever greater frequency, he took his wet-plate camera outside, exposing his large 6½″ by 8½″ glass negatives with scenes of the Federals in camp and field. Most of all, he turned his equipment toward the great Mississippi, always the best source of interest and news for a river town. There he caught, one after another, the mighty Federal gunboats and ironclads that maintained their viselike grip on the waterway, splitting the western and eastern Confederacy. There, too, he photographed the men and vessels that would embark on the ill-fated Red River Campaign, photographing them again and again, never satisfied with one image when two or three more would complete the record. Years later his son would claim that he made all these images as an agent for the Confederacy, secretly spiriting his pictures to Rebel authorities to give them information on their enemy. It is hardly likely. The Confederates already knew what a Yankee gunboat looked like. They had seen altogether too many of them on the western rivers these past three years. Nothing Lytle could show them would be new—only a reprise of images they would just as soon forget. No, A. D. Lytle was simply one of many with a vision that there was something happening here that was worth saving—perhaps as a curiosity, perhaps as a lesson, perhaps as a warning. Whatever it was, he went out of his way to save it all.

So did photographers in San Francisco; Denver; New Mexico Territory; Missouri and Arkansas; Brownsville, Texas; and more places than we can yet ascertain. All through the West, the cameramen used their precious materials to record what they could. Mostly the profitable portraits, to be sure, but now and then some enterprising fellow went outdoors: in Little Rock to photograph the city in Yankee hands in 1864; in Brownsville to capture the scenes of the Confederate evacuation in 1863.

And they were out in force in the East, where always their numbers and their works were the greatest. Samuel Cooley was doing great service in South Carolina, as were the partners Haas & Peale, recording the scenes of Hilton Head and Beaufort; the siege of Charleston; the occupation of pretty St. Augustine, Florida; and more. Off the coast, they captured the images of the mighty blockading fleets, and along the shore they turned their lenses to the brave blockade runners who tried and failed to pass the cordon of steel unharmed. In Virginia there were several, their names unknown to us for the most part, who ventured into the Shenandoah to record the few scenes we have of the fighting amid that lush breadbasket. Everywhere, the artists and the year had come together, ready for one another, ready for the greatest of the nation's trials, and for the greatest of the image-makers' achievements.

None of them surpassed the Scotsman Alexander Gardner. Long since broken free of his onetime mentor and employer Mathew Brady, Gardner had assistants and equipment of his own covering the armies in Virginia. The body of work he was creating, he said, "is designed that it shall speak for itself." All of these artists felt and wrote of their works as things that would "speak" to those who looked. "As mementoes of the fearful struggle," said Gardner, the images "will possess an enduring interest." How right he was when he went on to declare that "localities that would scarcely have been known and probably never remembered, save in their immediate vicinity, have become celebrated, and will ever be held sacred as memorable fields, where thousands of brave men yielded up their lives a willing sacrifice for the cause they had espoused."

And as if to forecast the words of Francis T. Miller half a century later, Gardner declared in 1866 that "verbal representations of such places, or scenes, may or may not have the merit of accuracy; but photographic presentments of them will be accepted by posterity with an undoubting faith." Indeed, so they would be accepted for generations until Americans of a later time discovered that the photographers, Gardner included, were not above tampering with a scene a bit before making an exposure. Posing the dead just so, rearranging their weapons, staging soldiers like actors in a tableau. They were not falsifying history —just framing it a bit better on the wet plate.

Gardner hardly needed to pose and alter most of the views that came before him, and especially in 1864 as Grant and Lee met in death grapple in Virginia. These generals and their armies fighting in the Wilderness, at Spotsylvania, along the North and South Anna rivers, at Cold Harbor, and on toward Petersburg were themselves creating scenes so eloquent of the majesty and tragedy of a brothers' war that Gardner and the others need only follow and photograph.

But of all of the camera artists abroad in the land in 1864, it was the year of George N. Barnard. None of them created or left behind as magnificent a record of a great movement in history as did this Connecticut-born artist who had worked for a time for Brady, as had so many others. Then forty-four, Barnard had been a professional photographer for over twenty years as the year dawned. He and his craft were old friends, ready for the challenge of making him the premier photographer of the Civil War in Tennessee and Georgia.

That was no small achievement or task, for the premier battles of the war were being fought out there, battles that equaled in size and ferocity the great conflicts in Virginia. In 1863 Barnard attached himself to the Military Division of the Mississippi, commanded by Major General William T. Sherman. The great battles in Tennessee of that year were already done, but Barnard turned his lens to at least a few scenes of the great fighting around Chattanooga. Then he was off with Sherman as together they marched through Georgia, to Atlanta and the sea. Just how many photographs Barnard made during 1864 we cannot say, but within months of the end of the war he was back in Georgia capturing what still remained of the scenes of the great campaign. The mountain passes, the railroad bridges hastily thrown up, the battlefields and earthworks of New Hope and Resaca and Kennesaw Mountain, and most of all the defenses and ravaged streetscapes of Atlanta. Sherman himself—he who had made war hell, yet whoever after reviled warfare—heartily approved of Barnard's intention to preserve for all time the scenes of the great march that split and crippled the Confederacy. Perhaps Sherman, too, like Gardner and Miller and so many more, felt that if only people could see the face of war, then perhaps they would turn away from it the next time their passions made men think of rushing to their guns. "I approve highly your purposal [*sic*]," said Sherman, when Barnard suggested doing a book of his views. "They will be very interesting and instructive," wrote the general, and indeed they are.

When the public saw Barnard's images of the scenes of 1864, of the days of the South besieged, they agreed. "For the care and judgment in selecting the point of view, for the delicacy of execution, for scope of treatment, and for fidelity of impression," wrote a reviewer in 1866, "they surpass any other photographic views which have been produced in this country—whether relating to the war or otherwise."

Of course, these most noted artists were not the only ones following the armies that year. Men lesser known turned their instruments toward the scenes of the war. McPherson and Oliver of Baton Rouge continued making the series of views of the Mississippi and the ships that plied its waters. They, like Lytle, photographed some of the men and ships that embarked on the Red River Campaign. Indeed, one or both of them went along on the expedition, taking their camera to record the scenes of near-disaster as Banks' army and Porter's fleet were trapped at Alexandria by low water.

Then there were Haas & Peale, so obscure that we do not yet know their given names. What we do know them by is their superb work, done in a rather unusual 5″ by 7″ format that showed far greater detail than the stereo and *carte de visite* views most prevalent among photographs produced for public consumption. Thanks to this pair, most of the scenes of Morris Island, James Island, and the siege of Charleston survive with wonderful quality. And they did not pose their images so much as the others. They let the voice of the war speak for itself.

Alas, we know so little about their comrades in the West. It was a J. Leonard who made the marvelous series of views of Yankee ironclads off the Mound City, Illinois, naval station, showing them under construction and then afloat. But any more of him we do not know. We know so little of J. W. Petty, the New Orleans photographer whose series of images of the men of the Washington Artillery represent the most complete coverage extant of a Confederate unit in the field. Lawrence and Houseworth's entire Civil War photographic career consisted of making their stereo views of the sunken *Aquila,* its raising, and the reassembly of the cargo in its hold, the Yankee monitor *Camanche.* Missouri could boast several artists whose contribution consisted of but a single image or two. O. D. Edwards; J. A. Scholten of St. Louis; E. E. Henry of Fort Leavenworth, Kansas; and so many more now entirely lost to history made but a few trips outside their studios to record fading images that are now their only remembrance. Texas was particularly blessed with such daring men—for they made these images using precious supplies, with little hope of economic reward. F. B. Bailey of Navasota captured the quiet scene of Huntsville. An unknown photographer of Ellis County made a remarkable image of new Texas recruits in 1864 wearing new uniforms, something by now unheard of in the armies. And most unusual of all was A. G. Wedge, who took his camera out into the streets of Brownsville in November 1863 to record the Confederate evacuation and the Yankee occupation. To him, as to so many other unsung artists, the preservation of the look of war in the Trans-Mississippi West is a lasting memorial.

What is most evident in the pages that follow is that the war had taken a decided turn. Perhaps the outcome of the conflict was always preordained, even before the first gun was fired. Veterans and later historians would—and will—argue that for generations to come. Yet certainly in these images there begins to gel a picture of a Confederacy pushed to the wall, of a Union conscious of its transcendent might and confident that, though the battle was not yet done, the outcome was secure. Somewhere in all those photos of the wrecked blockade runners, of the miles of ruined railroad track, the burned bridges, the devastated cities, the trail of wreckage and debris left by the retreating armies—somewhere in all of that is the mournful fetch, the foretelling of final doom. The people of the besieged South were living through the most intimate association with war that any Americans have ever known, and staring them in the face from their ravaged landscape and in the visages of their tired and hungry soldiers was the same picture of exhaustion, of impending defeat, that stares at us still from the fading negatives. Here in the images of 1864, we begin to see at last the look of inevitability, of a climax that might be delayed for a time yet, but which, like the "great death" in Stephen Crane's *The Red Badge of Courage,* would come "when it would come."

Yet it is not wholly a somber picture. For here, too, are the beginning scenes of the peace that is just as certain as defeat. Somehow, for all their eloquent picture of death and destruction, still the men like Gardner and Barnard had so perfected their craft that even in their most ghastly images there is as well the quality of hope. The landscape shows to its best in their pictures of Virginia and Georgia. The trees look alive, the streams flow clear and clean; America, for all its scars, is still beautiful, and promises to grow in beauty when the guns grow silent. For every scene of bloated ruin, there is one of hope.

That is what these artists have left us in their picture of the South besieged. Thousands of timeless, priceless images of men marching to victory or defeat, in a dance as old as history itself, all of them on their way to a denouement that would lift them above themselves. It is our happy fortune that through these images, we can see them still.

As in the previous four volumes of *The Image of War: 1861–1865, The South Besieged* seeks to bring together the best of all this, capitalizing upon the eight years of research and untold dollars and man-hours that went into locating these rare old images. Perhaps half of what appears in this volume is published here for the first time, and much more is only now correctly identified. It would be a fruitless dream to expect that all that is good has now been found and included here. Just as this volume goes to the publisher, a new collection of several hundred Civil War images has emerged down in Virginia, and already the editor has had the heartbreaking task of saying no to himself when another good image comes to light, for want of space.

Happily, there is a sixth and final volume in *The Image of War* series still to come, and it will include more unusual and little-known scenes. Happily, too, the whole project continues to enjoy the universal support and encouragement of the host of professional historians, libraries and archives, and private collectors who have played such a major role in the success of this enterprise. Many have already been mentioned in previous volumes, but it would be remiss not to offer special thanks here to others not previously recognized, to collectors like Gary Wright for his precious Brownsville images, to old friend Robert J. Younger, to Charles Schwartz and Terence P. O'Leary, and to Michael Hammerson in faraway England. Thanks, too, to Craig Symonds of the U.S. Naval Academy for the invaluable assistance of himself and his fine book on the Charleston blockade.

Their assistance, after all, is but continuing testimony to the lasting interest Americans feel for what happened over a century ago. We know now that this was a special time, of something great in our past that lasts in our spirit. They knew it at the time, too. That is why the cameramen made their images, and that is why we still treasure them.

The War for Tennessee

EDWIN C. BEARSS

The endless, bloody battles for the state called "Volunteer"

CIVIL WAR PHOTOGRAPHERS recorded the soldiers and scenes of the sweeping military operations that dashed Confederate expectation in America's heartland and shattered a mighty Southern army. During the six months following the struggle at Stones River, December 31, 1862–January 2, 1863, Union Major General William S. Rosecrans' Army of the Cumberland regrouped and built up strength in and around Murfreesboro in Middle Tennessee, 30 miles southeast of Nashville. Confederate General Braxton Bragg's Army of Tennessee fortified a line covering Duck River barring the direct route to Chattanooga.

Geography and the "iron horse" dictated that Chattanooga, with only 2,545 people in 1860, play a key role in the Civil War. The town was on the south bank of the Tennessee, where the great river knifed its way through a mountain barrier. Possession of Chattanooga, "Gateway to the deep South," was vital to the Confederacy, and a strategic necessity Union leaders could not ignore.

Railroads focused the armies' attention on Chattanooga. It was the terminus of major railroads leading northeast to Knoxville and Richmond, southeast to Atlanta, and northwest to Nashville and Louisville. At Stevenson, Alabama, 40 miles to the southwest, the railroad to Memphis joined the tracks of the Nashville & Chattanooga.

On June 24, 1863, Rosecrans, in response to goading from Washington, took the offensive. There ensued, on the part of the Federals, a brilliantly planned and executed ten-day campaign. After stubborn but brief fights at Hoover's and Liberty Gaps, the bluecoated columns forged ahead. Satisfied that his Middle Tennessee position had become untenable, Bragg determined to abandon the region. Rosecrans' soldiers entered Tullahoma on July 1, capturing a few prisoners, and the Confederates retreated across the Cumberland Plateau and took position behind the Tennessee River. Rosecrans now called a halt, sent his troops into camp, and began stockpiling supplies for a thrust across the Tennessee and on to Chattanooga.

By mid-August, Rosecrans resumed the offensive. His army had regrouped, and ripening corn promised forage for his thousands of horses and mules. His immediate goal was Chattanooga. As in the Tullahoma Campaign, Rosecrans hoped to maneuver the Confederates out of their stronghold by hard marches and an indirect approach.

General Bragg, pending arrival of reinforcements, massed his army in and around Chat-

Mr. Lincoln's army was on the move in Tennessee. In a brilliant campaign, Rosecrans had feinted Bragg out of Tennessee's heartland. Now he prepared to drive him into Georgia, and here at Stevenson, Alabama, the right of the advancing Federals established Redoubt Harker to guard rail supply lines. (U.S. ARMY MILITARY HISTORY INSTITUTE)

tanooga. Yankee artillery, north of the Tennessee, opened fire on the town, and Bragg, to counter this threat, recalled most of his troops guarding the downstream crossings. Rosecrans took advantage of Bragg's miscalculations, and divisions crossed and bridged the Tennessee. Pressing rapidly forward after what Rosecrans believed to be a broken and dispirited foe, the XIV and XX Corps entered mountainous northwest Georgia. Thus by September 10 some 45 miles of rugged country separated the wings of Rosecrans' army.

Meanwhile, General Bragg had been reinforced. Major General Simon B. Buckner's 8,000-man corps joined him, and 11,500 troops arrived from central Mississippi. On September 6, Bragg had evacuated Chattanooga and massed his army near La Fayette, 26 miles to the south.

Bragg now moved to take advantage of Rose-

Here around the Stevenson railroad depot the Yankees built up their supplies for the campaign to come. Mountains of boxes of "army bread" and row after row of salt beef and pork barrels wait on the siding. (BEHRINGER-CRAWFORD MUSEUM, COVINGTON, KENTUCKY)

crans' blunder and defeat the Federals in detail. On September 10 he moved to crush Major General George Thomas' advance—Major General James S. Negley's division of the XIV Corps in McLemore's Cove. Plans were frustrated by the inaction of the principal subordinates involved, Lieutenant General Daniel H. Hill and Major General Thomas C. Hindman, and Thomas pulled back. Bragg then turned to assail Major General Thomas Crittenden. Again, a senior corps commander failed and Bragg's plans misfired.

Rosecrans now realized that his army was imperiled. Thomas' XIV Corps and Major General A. M. McCook's XX Corps were recalled and ordered to join Crittenden at Lee & Gordon's Mills, 12 miles south of Chattanooga. Nightfall on September 17 found Rosecrans' infantry corps within supporting distance: Crittenden's at Lee & Gordon's Mills, Thomas' nearby, McCook's in McLemore's Cove, and Gordon Granger's Reserve Corps, called up from near Bridgeport, Alabama, in position at Rossville, guarding the road into Chattanooga.

General Bragg, fuming over his subordinates' failures, marched his columns northward on the east side of Chickamauga Creek. He planned to cross the Chickamauga north of Lee & Gordon's Mills, block the road to Chattanooga, and turn on

A magnificent image of an unidentified Federal regiment drawn up for the camera near Stevenson. Hard-bitten Westerners like these would take the war to the enemy wherever they found him. (BEHRINGER-CRAWFORD MUSEUM, COVINGTON, KENTUCKY)

and either crush Crittenden's XXI Corps or hurl it back on Thomas. By mauling Rosecrans' left, Bragg could reoccupy Chattanooga and possibly destroy the Union Army before it recrossed the Tennessee.

On September 18 three brigades of Lieutenant General James Longstreet's corps detrained at nearby Ringgold. These Army of Northern Virginia veterans, vanguard of a famed corps, had left Virginia nine days before. The Confederacy had employed its interior position and warworn railroads to give Bragg a numerical advantage in the impending struggle.

One of Longstreet's brigades reinforced Brigadier General Bushrod R. Johnson's division as it pressed toward Reed's Bridge. Johnson's column, in Bragg's plan, was to cross the Chickamauga at this bridge and wheel left. Other Confederate divisions and corps, in turn, were to cross at upstream bridges and fords, their movements facilitated by Johnson's advance.

Union cavalry and mounted infantry, guarding the crossings, engaged the Confederates. Alexander's Bridge, upstream from Reed's, was broken down by the horse soldiers, and Major General W. H. T. Walker's corps, advancing on Johnson's left, was compelled to proceed to a downstream ford, where it crossed and reinforced Johnson. The Federals pulled back. By daybreak on the 19th, all of Bragg's army, 66,000 strong, except three divisions, was west of Chickamauga Creek.

General Rosecrans took advantage of time bought by his mounted troops to redeploy his 58,000-man army to counter Bragg's threat to the Union left. Thomas' corps was called up during the night, and two of his divisions took position on Crittenden's left, covering the roads leading to Reed's and Alexander's bridges.

On September 9, 1863, Rosecrans also obtained a valuable prize well north of Bragg. Cumberland Gap fell to Federals, thus closing that passage to the enemy and giving the Yankees a back door into eastern Tennessee. (LINCOLN MEMORIAL UNIVERSITY)

Early on September 19, General Thomas sent Brigadier General John M. Brannan to reconnoiter the Confederate forces that had crossed the Chickamauga. Feeling their way ahead, the Federals, as they neared Jay's Mill, clashed with Brigadier General Nathan B. Forrest's dismounted cavalry, screening Bragg's right. The Yanks pushed Forrest's people and their supporting infantry back. The Confederates brought up reinforcements, Walker's corps, and the Federals, in turn, recoiled.

As the day progressed, Bragg and Rosecrans continued to call up and commit fresh units. By midafternoon savage combat raged along a three-mile front. Around 2:30 the Confederates began advancing successfully. By 4 P.M. the situation looked bleak for the Army of the Cumberland. Bragg's Confederates, if allowed to exploit this success, were in position to block the Dry Valley road —Rosecrans' only remaining link with Chattanooga. Desperately, the Federals held on.

Although darkness closed in, close combat flared for several more hours before the firing and shouting ceased. During the night General Longstreet arrived from Ringgold with two fresh brigades.

George N. Barnard's image of the pass in Raccoon Mountain near Whiteside, Georgia. An important trestle bridge of the Memphis & Chattanooga Railroad passed through here, and both Confederates and Federals vied for it. These blockhouses are only part of its defenses. (USAMHI)

Bragg then reorganized his army into two wings preparatory to resuming the attack. Lieutenant General Leonidas Polk was to command the right wing and Longstreet the left.

Bragg called for resumption of the battle at daybreak on Sunday, September 20. Major General John C. Breckinridge's division on the right was to open the attack, which would be taken up by successive divisions to his left. Misunderstood orders and difficulties in effecting dispositions resulted in several hours delay. It was 9:30 before Breckinridge advanced, and as he did his brigades gained ground and threatened to envelop Thomas' left. A Union counterattack blunted and threw back Breckinridge's grim fighters, mortally wounding one of President Lincoln's Confederate brothers-in-law, Brigadier General Ben Hardin Helm.

Patrick R. Cleburne's division now struck, closing on the Union breastworks. His brigades were mauled as General Thomas called up more reinforcements. After two and a half hours of savage fighting, Polk's wing, having frittered its energy in futile piecemeal attacks on Thomas' barricaded line, recoiled.

It was now 11:15, and Longstreet massed a three-division column under hard-hitting Major General John B. Hood opposite Rosecrans' center. Through a misunderstanding, Rosecrans had just

Barnard's camera also caught some of the men who manned those defenses.
(WESTERN RESERVE HISTORICAL SOCIETY)

then created a huge hole in his own line opposite Longstreet.

Longstreet's thunderbolt now struck, his column surging through the gap that had opened in the Union line because of Rosecrans' blunder. It shattered their foe. Whole divisions fled the field. Among the dead was the brilliant and beloved Brigadier General William H. Lytle. Rosecrans, McCook, and Crittenden, caught up in the panic, abandoned the field. The right wing of the Union Army, except Colonel John T. Wilder's brigade, which advanced and battered one of Hindman's brigades, was in wild retreat.

General Thomas did not panic. He pulled back and re-formed his right along the crest of Snodgrass Hill. Unwilling to bypass Thomas, Longstreet's troops repeatedly charged up the slopes only to be repulsed. They next moved to envelop Thomas' right and were succeeding when General Granger, marching to the sound of the guns, arrived with two reserve brigades on Snodgrass Hill. Attacking, Granger hurled the Confederates back.

Undaunted, Longstreet returned to the attack, vainly committing his reserve, General William Preston's division. About 4 P.M., Polk's wing resumed battering Thomas' left, and at dusk Thomas withdrew most of his troops to Rossville Gap. On that grim Sunday afternoon Thomas saved the Army of the Cumberland and earned the *nom de guerre* "The Rock of Chickamauga."

They were all commanded by the smiling Major General William S. Rosecrans, "Old Rosey," whose prospects in the campaign ahead took a decidedly less rosy turn. (USAMHI)

Losses in the battle, the war's bloodiest two-day fight, which the Confederates won but failed to follow up, were staggering. Bragg listed 2,312 dead, 14,674 wounded, and 1,468 missing. Rosecrans reported 1,657 dead, 9,756 wounded, and 4,757 missing.

On the night of September 21, 1863, the defeated Union Army was back in Chattanooga. Here, between Confederates in front and natural obstacles to the rear, it was trapped. Bragg's troops advanced and invested the Union forces, occupying Missionary Ridge, Chattanooga Valley, Lookout Mountain, and Lookout Valley.

News of Rosecrans' defeat at Chickamauga had far-reaching repercussions. Two corps, the XI and the XII, were detached from the Army of the Potomac, placed under Major General Joseph Hooker, and rushed west as fast as the railroads could move them. Four divisions were detached from Major General Ulysses S. Grant's Army of the Tennessee, then based at Vicksburg, and sent up the Mississippi by steamboats to Memphis. These units were led by Major General William T. Sherman.

Then Grant, overall commander in the theater, relieved Rosecrans, elevating General Thomas to command the Department and Army of the Cumberland. Grant promptly learned something of Thomas' character. Replying to a telegram from Grant to hold Chattanooga at all hazards, Thomas answered, "We will hold the town till we starve."

The most immediate task facing Grant and Thomas was supplying Chattanooga. Rosecrans began work on a route using the Tennessee River, and now they completed it. While mechanics built the steamboat *Chattanooga,* and other vessels were repaired for service, the generals went about taking and holding Lookout Valley, vital to their supply route. It took secrecy and desperate fighting at Wauhatchie, but by November 1 the route was open. The "cracker line" they called it, bringing vital supplies from the railhead at Bridgeport, Alabama, up the river to Kelley's Ferry aboard the *Chattanooga* and several other ships like her, and then overland to Chattanooga.

Grant now confronted the enemy in his front. But Bragg immediately blundered by allowing Longstreet to take his corps on an ill-advised campaign into East Tennessee toward Knoxville. Learning of this, Grant began to plan an attack on the remaining Confederates.

Early on November 23, to confirm the reports of deserters and spies that two divisions of Buckner's corps were en route to East Tennessee to reinforce Longstreet, Grant directed Thomas to make a forced reconnaissance of the Rebel lines. The Army of the Cumberland—Granger's corps on the left and John N. Palmer's on the right—moved out at 2 P.M., as if on parade, and formed lines of battle in view of watching Confederates. Taking up the advance, the Federals drove in Bragg's pickets and routed the Rebels from a line of rifle pits, capturing more than 200. On the afternoon of the 24th, Sherman's army moved out from its bridgehead in three columns. They overpowered several outposts and, by four o'clock, occupied the north end of Missionary Ridge.

To hinder Rosecrans' advance, the Confederates had destroyed the Howe Turn bridge over the Tennessee River at Bridgeport. Engineers are building a temporary bridge to span the stream. (MINNESOTA HISTORICAL SOCIETY)

Meanwhile, at 4 A.M. on the 24th, General Hooker put his three divisions in motion. While his pioneers bridged Lookout Creek, Hooker sent Geary's division, reinforced by Brigadier General Walter C. Whitaker's brigade, upstream to cross at Wauhatchie. Screened by a morning fog, Geary's people forded the creek and swept down the slope overlooking the right bank, routing Confederate pickets. Covered by this movement, Hooker's main column bridged and crossed the stream. Supported by enfilading fire of cannon emplaced on Moccasin Point, Hooker's divisions forged ahead, driving a Confederate brigade around the face of Lookout Mountain to the Cravens farm. Though ordered to halt and re-form, Geary, seeing he had the Rebels on the run, pushed ahead until checked by Confederate reinforcements posted behind breastworks beyond the Cravens house. By 2 P.M. the fog had thickened and it was impossible for the combatants to see more than a few yards. This, along with an ammunition shortage, caused Hooker to halt and consolidate his gains. The "Battle Above the Clouds" had ended in a Union success.

During the night of the 24th the Confederates

The commander of those Confederates, General Braxton Bragg, was on the verge of winning the most shattering triumph in the career of Southern arms. (VALENTINE MUSEUM)

He would win that victory along the banks of Chickamauga Creek in northwestern Georgia. Some of the first skirmishing prior to the battle took place near Lee & Gordon's Mills on the creek. (LIBRARY OF CONGRESS)

withdrew from Lookout Mountain and reported to Bragg on Missionary Ridge. Next morning, a patrol from the 8th Kentucky scrambled up the mountain and at sunrise, the fog having lifted, unfurled the U.S. flag from the point, to the cheers of bluecoated onlookers.

Grant's November 25 program called for Sherman to assail Tunnel Hill, at the north end of Missionary Ridge, at daylight; Hooker to march at the same hour on the road to Rossville, storm Rossville Gap, and threaten Bragg's left and rear; and Thomas to hold his ground until Hooker and Sherman had accomplished their missions.

Sherman began his attack as scheduled. Strong battle lines advanced and occupied a wooded crest within 80 yards of rifle pits held by Cleburne's division. A savage fight ensued. The outnumbered Confederates held firm and stood tall in the face of Sherman's blows. About 2 P.M. two of Sherman's brigades effected a lodgment on the slope of Tunnel Hill but were counterattacked and driven back in disorder.

Hooker was also in trouble, not with the foe, but with Chattanooga Creek. Reaching that stream at 10 A.M., he found the bridge destroyed and the Rossville road obstructed by retreating Confed-

The water of Chickamauga Creek would soon be stained with the blood of thousands as the battle commenced. Scores of dead floated peacefully past Lee & Gordon's. (NATIONAL ARCHIVES)

erates. Hooker lost three hours crossing his lead division, which then advanced and seized Rossville Gap. His other divisions followed, and, deploying them in line, Hooker pushed ahead.

Grant, at his Orchard Knob command post, knew that Sherman had been rebuffed at Tunnel Hill and that Hooker had been delayed. To assist Sherman, Grant told Thomas to send his four center divisions to carry the Confederate rifle pits at the foot of Missionary Ridge and there halt and await further instructions. At 3:30 P.M. signal guns on Orchard Knob boomed, and the divisions, covered by a powerful skirmish line, swept forward. The Federals, though subjected to a storm of shot and shell from Confederate batteries emplaced on the commanding heights, routed the Rebels from the rifle pits. After a brief halt and without orders to continue, first one regiment and then others scrambled to its feet and surged up the ridge. They followed so hard on the heels of the Confederates fleeing the rifle pits that the Rebels posted in the works on the crest at many points hesitated to fire for fear of hitting their comrades. Units from Major General Philip H. Sheridan's division reached the crest first, routing Confederate soldiers from their breastworks near Bragg's headquarters. Regiments from the other three divisions ripped the line at other points, and the brigades holding Bragg's center panicked. Many prisoners and cannon were captured. Though the Confederate center was shattered, Lieutenant General William J. Hardee's corps, on the right, grimly held its ground till dark and then retired with Cleburne's division, successfully screening the army's retreat to winter camp at Dalton, Georgia.

Coincident with the November 25 orders for pursuit of Bragg's defeated Army of Tennessee, Grant directed Thomas to send General Granger with 20,000 men to the relief of the force led by Major General Ambrose Burnside, then besieged in Knoxville. In late summer of 1863, Burnside, at the head of the Army of the Ohio, had advanced from bases in central Kentucky. Bypassing heavily fortified Cumberland Gap, Burnside's troops entered Knoxville on September 2. On September 9 the 2,100 Confederates under Brigadier General John W. Frazer, left to "wither on the vine" at Cumberland Gap, laid down their arms.

Burnside was expected to join Rosecrans near Chattanooga, but he moved slowly, and Rosecrans' defeat at Chickamauga doomed plans for a rendezvous of the two armies. Then, in early October, 1,500 Southern horsemen led by Brigadier General John S. Williams, advancing from Jonesboro, came down the road paralleling the railroad to the vicinity of Bulls Gap. Burnside reinforced his men in that quarter, and, on October 10, at Blue Springs mauled Williams' column and drove it back into southwestern Virginia.

Following the Battle of Wauhatchie, General Bragg had divided his army, sending Longstreet and his corps, reinforced by four brigades of Wheeler's cavalry, to assail Burnside and recapture Knoxville. Longstreet's 10,000 infantry and artillery were shuttled by rail from the Chattanooga area to Sweetwater. General Joseph Wheeler and his cavalry, 5,000 strong, were to cut Burnside's communications and seize high ground at Knoxville. Longstreet, with Lafayette McLaws' and Micah Jenkins' infantry divisions and E. Porter Alexander's reinforced artillery battalion, would cross the Tennessee and make a direct approach on Knoxville.

Wheeler failed. Meanwhile, Longstreet's columns had crossed the Tennessee on November 13 and 14. Spearheaded by a strong vanguard, the Rebels vigorously pushed ahead in a vain effort to force Burnside to fight before he could mass his forces within the Knoxville fortifications. To gain time and enable Burnside's infantry and artillery to strengthen their earthworks, Brigadier General William P. Sanders and his horse soldiers engaged and delayed the Confederate vanguard. With 700 men, he manned and stubbornly held a position covering the Loudon road, about a mile outside the perimeter. The bluecoats held the Rebels until mid-afternoon on the 18th, when the roadblock was smashed by the South Carolina brigade and Sanders mortally wounded.

Next morning, the Confederates appeared in force. Longstreet, ignoring the need for haste, invested the city, and his soldiers began digging in. "The earthworks on each side seemed to grow like

The bulk of the real battle will be fought on the right, where Lieutenant General Leonidas Polk commands Bragg's right wing. The bishop-turned-general will repeatedly disappoint Bragg, as he does almost everyone except his old friend Jefferson Davis. An unpublished portrait. (COURTESY OF TED YEATMAN)

It was chiefly divisions of the corps of Lieutenant General Daniel H. Hill of North Carolina that set the scene for the Confederate victory. It was his attacks on Rosecrans' left wing that forced the Federal to weaken his center. (VM)

It came at a heavy price. Leading his brigade in one of Hill's attacks, Brigadier General Ben Hardin Helm of Kentucky fell, mortally wounded. He was the brother-in-law of President Abraham Lincoln. (USAMHI)

magic," recalled one soldier. Sharpshooters banged away, and several successful sorties buoyed the defenders' morale.

On the night of the 23rd, Longstreet received a message from General Bragg stating that if it was practicable to defeat Burnside it must be done immediately. The sector selected by Longstreet's chief engineer to be assailed was shielded by Fort Sanders. Longstreet scheduled the attack for sunrise on the 25th, but, on being apprised of the approach of two infantry brigades sent by Bragg as reinforcements, he postponed the assault to await their arrival. With these troops came Brigadier General Danville Leadbetter, an officer of engineers, presumably familiar with the area. Leadbetter's advent resulted in a new reconnaissance and vacillation on the part of Confederate leaders and, as Porter Alexander recalled, "cost us three as valuable days as the sun every shone upon."

Meanwhile, Longstreet had changed his battle plan. Instead of jumping off at sunrise and being preceded by a savage bombardment by Alexander's massed artillery of Fort Sanders, a surprise thrust by four infantry brigades was programmed. The night of November 28–29 was miserable. Temperatures went below freezing and it misted. At 10 P.M. Confederate skirmishers advanced, captured or drove in the enemy pickets, and took possession of abandoned rifle pits within 150 yards of the fort.

The firing alerted the Federals, particularly the 440 soldiers garrisoning Fort Sanders, and the works to the strongpoint's right and left. Cannoneers manning the 12 guns emplaced behind the fort's embrasured parapets stood by their pieces and, during the remaining hours of darkness, fired harassing charges of canister.

At dawn Confederate signal guns barked; several of Alexander's batteries roared into action briefly; and in two columns McLaws' veterans scrambled to their feet and rushed forward. As they neared the fort the van encountered a nasty surprise, telegraph wire entanglements stretched a few inches above ground and secured to stumps and stakes. Though this obstacle was soon passed, it disordered the ranks and caused wild rumors to circulate among supporting units as to impenetrable barriers and a slaughter of the attackers.

From inside the fort and adjoining rifle pits grim Union soldiers blazed away at the oncoming mass with rifle muskets and cannoneers got off several charges of canister. The Confederates rushed on and crowded into the ditch fronting Fort Sanders' northwest bastion. The men lacked scaling ladders, and the parapet slope was frozen and slippery. Soldiers shot through embrasures, causing the Yanks to keep their heads down and to slacken their fire. This enabled some of the Confederates to claw their way up the icy slope and plant three battle flags on the parapet. Men seeking to reach and rally on the colors were killed or captured, and one of the standard bearers was dragged into the fort by the neck.

Confederates milling in the ditch now found themselves under a deadly flank fire of musketry and canister, as well as shells rolled into the moat as hand grenades. To advance or retreat was equally hazardous, and a number of soldiers began to wave their handkerchiefs. Many of their comrades, however, pulled back slowly at first, but the retreat quickly became disordered and rapid. As McLaws' men withdrew, one of Jenkins' brigades, though Longstreet sought to have it stopped, rushed the fort. Striking the ditch east of the scene of McLaws' repulse, this brigade suffered a similar fate. The assaulting columns were rallied by their officers under cover of the Rebel works, some 600 yards in front of Fort Sanders, and rolls were called. The charges had cost the Confederates 813 casualties: 129 killed, 458 wounded, and 226 missing. Union losses in Fort Sanders were about a score.

Plans for a new and better-organized attack were discussed, but before it could be launched dispatches were received confirming rumors of Bragg's defeat and retreat beyond Ringgold and ordering Longstreet to end the siege and reinforce Bragg.

In the confusion behind Rosecrans' lines, his chief of staff, Brigadier General James A. Garfield, was too busy to write an order for his commander. Rosecrans dictated it to another, and inadvertently it cost him the battle. Garfield, however, would win promotion for Chickamauga and eventually become President. (USAMHI)

Preparations were accordingly made to withdraw the troops and, as soon as it was dark, begin the march south. But, after meeting with his generals and being apprised that General Sherman was en route to Knoxville with a powerful column, Longstreet determined to hold his ground in front of Burnside and compel Sherman to continue his march. Longstreet held firm until December 3, when he learned that Sherman's vanguard was

There was confusion enough in the Federal army without bungled orders. Major General James S. Negley unaccountably wandered away from the battle line with most of his division and did not heed orders to return. He would never command again, though he claimed for the rest of his days that his disgrace had been engineered by jealous West Point trained officers who despised a man never educated at the Military Academy. (COURTESY OF RONN PALM)

A man who obeyed orders to the letter, however, was Major General Thomas J. Wood. Rosecrans' dictated order told him to move to the left, and Wood obeyed, even though it left a massive hole in the Union line just as . . . (USAMHI)

within a day's march. During the night the trains started rolling northeastward. Longstreet's troops followed as soon as it was dark on the 4th, retreating to Rogersville. Sherman entered Knoxville on the 6th to be welcomed by General Burnside and his troops, victors in the 16-day siege. The soldiers soon went into winter quarters, and the year's campaigning in Middle and East Tennessee ended.

ONE YEAR LATER, in November 1864, Middle Tennessee again became a focal point in the struggle. General John B. Hood, in the weeks following his evacuation of Atlanta, had succeeded in securing President Jefferson Davis' approval of a plan fated to lead his army deep into Tennessee. Boldly crossing the Chattahoochee, Hood lunged at the Western & Atlantic, the single-track railroad over which General Sherman supplied his "army group." Sherman, detaching a corps to hold Atlanta, hounded Hood's columns across the ridges and hollows of northwest Georgia and into Alabama. Despairing of overtaking and bringing Hood to battle,

Major General Bushrod R. Johnson and his division spearheaded the attack of a Confederate corps aimed precisely at the gap. Johnson, a native of Ohio, was yet one of the most able generals in the Southern service. (COURTESY OF WILLIAM A. ALBAUGH)

Some of the attacking soldiers in that Confederate assault were hardly more than children, like this youngster of the 9th Mississippi. (COURTESY OF PAUL DE HAAN)

Sherman was delighted to learn, on November 8, that General Grant had approved Sherman's proposal to return to Atlanta, where preparations would be completed for evacuation of that city and the "March to the Sea."

When Hood failed to turn and follow the Union columns on their return to Atlanta, Sherman directed Major General John M. Schofield and his XXIII Corps to join Thomas in Middle Tennessee. Schofield soon reached Nashville by rail, and part of his corps rushed westward to bolster troops routed from the Johnsonville supply depot by now Major General Nathan B. Forrest's cavalry. Schofield, accompanied by two divisions of his corps, traveled to Pulaski, where, as senior officer, he took command of the troops assembled there to oppose Hood's advance.

Also ordered to join Thomas were Major General Andrew J. Smith and his three divisions that had helped smash the Confederates at Westport, near the Kansas border, on October 21–23. Low water on the western rivers delayed the transfer of Smith's "ten wandering tribes of Israel," and the vanguard did not disembark at Nashville until November 30.

General Hood had sought to cross the Tennessee River at Decatur, Alabama, but an aroused defense by the garrison frustrated his plans. Hood then pushed on to Tuscumbia, where by the end of October his men crossed the river and occupied Florence.

On Monday, November 21, Hood put the 50,000-man Army of Tennessee in motion. Screened by Forrest's cavalry, the three infantry corps traveled different roads. Vital days had been lost, and the weather was frightful. There were continuous snow, sleet, and ice storms.

Apprised of the Confederate advance, General

Yet others were experienced and battle-hardened veterans, like Brigadier General John Gregg of Alabama, shown here in an unpublished portrait. He led his brigade into the attack right behind Johnson, taking a wound for his effort. (COURTESY OF LAWRENCE T. JONES)

Schofield sent his supplies to the rear and evacuated Pulaski. Union infantry reached Columbia on the 24th, in time to reinforce the cavalry and check a dash by Forrest's horse soldiers. Some 48 hours elapsed before all of Hood's infantry arrived in front of Columbia, and by then Schofield had perfected his dispositions for defense of the Duck River crossings.

Hood, seeing that a frontal assault on the Duck River bridgehead could be suicidal, sought to slip across the river and outflank Schofield. On the 28th, Forrest's cavalry hammered backward Thomas' cavalry, who retired toward Franklin, uncovering the Columbia pike.

Leaving Lieutenant General Stephen D. Lee and two divisions of his corps and the army's artillery to entertain Schofield in front of the Columbia bridgehead, Hood, at daybreak on the 29th, began crossing Duck River via a pontoon bridge positioned at a ford uncovered by Forrest's surge. Several of Forrest's brigades spearheaded the Confederate thrust toward Spring Hill, a village on the Columbia pike, eight miles north of Columbia. If the Rebels blocked the road Schofield's army would be confronted by a disastrous situation. By a hair's breadth, they failed. Schofield, informed that he was outflanked, held Spring Hill long enough to get his army marching safely toward Franklin.

The Confederates, the night being very dark, did little to impede the Union retrograde, though Schofield's columns marched by in view of Hood's campfires.

Except for several dashes by Forrest's cavalry, Schofield's 14-mile retreat to Franklin was not disturbed. General Jacob D. Cox's division was first to reach Franklin on a cold last day of November, and Cox established his command post at Fountain

The attack isolated most of Major General Alexander McCook's XX Corps, and McCook himself, with two of his divisions, fled the battlefield in rout. He never led troops again in the war, and in 1866 was serving as a lowly captain. (USAMHI)

Major General Thomas L. Crittenden fared no better. The Confederate attack shattered one of his divisions and cut him off from the other two. He joined McCook and Rosecrans in following the rout and never held important command again. (WRHS)

B. Carter's house. The brick dwelling fronted on the west side of the Columbia pike south of town. Schofield arrived and told Cox to deploy the XXIII Corps' two divisions to hold a bridgehead south of Franklin and shield the army as it crossed to the north of the Big Harpeth River on two improvised bridges. Combat veterans all, the soldiers needed no encouragement as they strengthened the earthworks erected some year and a half earlier. More divisions arrived, including General James H. Wilson's cavalry.

An angry and bitter Confederate Army marched north following the Spring Hill fiasco. General Hood was in a foul humor, convinced that failures by subordinates had permitted the Federals to es-

Yet there were heroes. Brigadier General William H. Lytle of Ohio was best known then and later as a poet. Here at Chickamauga his division was just moving to the left when the Confederate attack struck. To protect the moving columns of Federals, he turned his brigade back to meet the attack and try to stall it. One brigade faced more than a division of the enemy. In the desperate fight, Lytle was hit by four bullets and died soon thereafter. The Confederates who later found him placed a guard over the body to prevent its being robbed, and gave him an honored burial. That night many Confederates sadly recited the lines of Lytle's most famous poem, Antony and Cleopatra. *It began, "I am dying, Egypt, dying."* (USAMHI)

It was good ground for a battle, and even after the Confederate breakthrough, the remnants of the Federal army could hold out on hills like this. (NA)

cape a frightful mauling. He was determined to make a final effort to destroy Schofield's army before it gained the security afforded by the Nashville defenses. Hood called for a frontal attack.

It was 4 P.M. when the Rebel battle lines, flags unfurled, stepped out. Few Civil War combat scenes were as free of obstructions to the view. As 15 brigades swept forward at quick step, Union troops posted behind the perimeter anxiously waited. Cleburne's and Brown's people momentarily recoiled when they hit George D. Wagner's advance division, and then stormed ahead. Wagner's brigades broke and bolted for the rear. Confederates raised a shout, "Let's go into the works with them," and the race was on. A number of Cleburne's and Brown's men entered the works to the left and right of the pike hard on the heels of panic-stricken bluecoats.

Colonel Emerson Opdycke hurled his brigade into the breach. Reinforced by two of Cox's regiments, Opdycke's men, in furious fighting centering about the Carter house and gin, drove back the Confederates. General Cleburne was among those killed in this savage fighting.

The Rebels attacked with reckless abandon. Brigadier General John Adams led his brigade, and, jumping his horse over a ditch, his steed was killed astride a parapet, and the general pitched

Leading those holdouts was Major General George H. Thomas. Today he would become the "Rock of Chickamauga," valiantly fighting on while nearly surrounded in order to cover the withdrawal of the rest of the army. (LC)

Regiments like the 44th Indiana, cut off from their brigades, wandered to Thomas' aid as he built a hasty defense against the ceaseless enemy attacks. (WRHS)

headlong among the defenders, mortally wounded. Brown's division assailed the Union center in concert with Cleburne's and grimly clung to a toehold in the ditch fronting the works. Here, Brigadier General Otho F. Strahl stood directing the fire of his men. And here he fell. As darkness, which came quickly, closed in, the combatants, separated by little more than the parapet, banged away, aiming at the flash of the enemy's rifle muskets. Brown had been wounded; two of the division's four brigade commanders, Strahl and States Rights Gist were dead; George W. Gordon had been captured; and John C. Carter was mortally wounded. Battered but still victorious, the Federals withdrew at 11 P.M. when threatened yet again by Forrest on the flank.

The Confederate charge at Franklin, pressed with a savage ferocity, left the field strewn with dead and wounded. Losses among the Rebel leaders were staggering. General Hood reported 6,300 casualties. Five generals were killed, six wounded, one mortally, and one captured. Union losses were 189 killed, 1,033 wounded, and 1,104 missing, of whom more than a thousand were in Wagner's two unnecessarily exposed brigades.

Schofield's tired but confident army reached Nashville on the morning of December 1, where it merged with the forces General Thomas was massing. General A. J. Smith had finally arrived from the Kansas-Missouri border with his three divisions, about 12,000 strong. Major General James B. Steedman had rushed up from Chattanooga by

So heavily did the Confederates batter the Yankees that William Preston's division was not even needed until late in the day. He delivered the last major attack on Thomas, with fearful casualties. The general would later be appointed Confederate minister to Mexico. (DEPARTMENT OF ARCHIVES AND MANUSCRIPTS, LOUISIANA STATE UNIVERSITY)

At last relief came to Thomas when a division of Major General Gordon Granger's Reserve Corps arrived in time to help repulse Preston. (USAMHI)

rail, bringing two brigades of blacks and a provisional division of casuals organized from soldiers belonging to Sherman's army group, who had returned from leave too late to participate in the March to the Sea. Most of Steedman's 5,200 officers and men reached Nashville on the evening of the 1st. But one train, having been delayed, was attacked on the 2nd by Forrest's cavalry five miles southeast of Nashville. The locomotive and cars were captured and destroyed. Most of the soldiers, however, cut their way through to Nashville.

Protecting the approaches to Nashville, a vital Union supply base and communications center since February 1862, were a formidable belt of fortifications. These included redoubts, redans, lunettes, and star forts sited on knobs and hills commanding the roads entering the city from the region south of the Cumberland. These strongpoints were connected by rifle pits.

Thomas positioned his rapidly increasing army in the defenses, while General Hood, despite the Franklin mauling, boldly closed on the southern approaches to Nashville. His reasons for doing so have been challenged, but Hood, however, was a confident man and undoubtedly hoped that a blunder on Thomas' part might yet give the desperate Confederates a victory.

As he closed in on Nashville, Hood deployed S. D. Lee's corps in the center, across the Franklin

Leading the first brigade to arrive was Brigadier General Walter C. Whitaker, who marched "to the sound of the guns." (COURTESY OF BARBARA CHEATLY)

pike, A. P. Stewart's corps formed on the left, holding the Granny White and Hillsboro pikes, and Cheatham's corps to the right, its flank anchored near the railroad and Murfreesboro pike. One of Forrest's divisions, James R. Chalmers', was detached and guarded the several miles of countryside between Stewart's left and the Cumberland River. Forrest, with the rest of his corps, to effect a partial investment of Thomas' army, swept through the counties to the southeast and guarded the army's right.

Now Hood weakened his army by sending Forrest and William B. Bate's infantry division to harass Thomas' rail communications. Though partially successful, their absence gave the Federals an opportunity. General Grant and the Lincoln administration urged Thomas to take the offensive. On December 2, Grant telegraphed from City Point, Virginia, advising Thomas to attack Hood immediately. Thomas, desirous of boosting the strength of Wilson's mounted arm, which had experienced difficulty coping with Forrest, decided to wait several days. But, on the 8th, the weather, which had been fair with moderate temperatures for more than a week, changed. Sleet and snow blanketed the area, all but paralyzing both armies. Thomas and his generals determined to wait for a thaw before moving out. His situation was not appreciated by Grant and the Administration, and, on the 13th, Major General John A. Logan was ordered to proceed from Washington to Nashville for the purpose of replacing Thomas. Grant, himself, was preparing to leave the nation's capital for Middle Tennessee when apprised of the successes scored by Thomas' troops on December 15. This news caused Grant to cancel the orders relieving Thomas and to return to City Point.

On the morning of the 15th, the snow and ice having melted, Thomas' troops moved out. A thick fog hid their march, but the mud slowed their deployment. Thomas' plan called for a feint against Hood's right, to be followed by a powerful thrust designed to envelop the Confederate left.

Advancing via the Murfreesboro pike, Steedman with two brigades, one of them black, attacked Hood's right—Cheatham's corps—between the railroad and pike. Steedman's demonstration focused Hood's attention on this sector. Spearheaded by Wilson's cavalry corps, A. J. Smith's powerful columns trudged out the Charlotte and Harding pikes and assailed Confederate forces guarding Hood's left. Chalmers' outnumbered Rebel horse soldiers were brushed aside and a supporting brigade of infantry mauled. In the fighting, as the battle lines wheeled southeastward, Wilson's cavalry to the right and Smith's infantry on the left, the Federals stormed Redoubts Nos. 4 and 5. Smith's divisions next approached a stone wall paralleling the Hillsboro pike and defended by men of Stewart's corps. Coincidentally, Schofield's XXIII Corps, which had supported the attack on Hood's left, took position of Smith's right.

Meanwhile, General Thomas Wood had committed his IV Corps to Smith's left. At 1 P.M. one

Before their successful withdrawal, the last Federal volley fired by Thomas' troops came from the 9th Indiana. Men of Company A pose here. Perhaps their most illustrious private was young Ambrose Bierce, who would later become one of America's most popular essayists and humorists. (NA)

of Wood's brigades had carried Montgomery Hill, a Rebel outpost midway between the lines in his sector. Wood's battle formations then closed on the rifle pits held by Stewart's people to the right and east of the stone wall. The Confederate line at this point formed a right angle. Assailed by Wood's men coming in from the north and Smith's from the west, Stewart's grim fighters were routed from the salient. Simultaneously, Schofield crossed the Hillsboro pike on a broad front.

Hood, his left shattered, hastened to occupy and hold a new and shorter front. Too late, Hood recognized the folly of the overconfidence that had led him to extend his lines in the presence of an enemy possessing superior numbers. Orders were sent recalling Forrest, but it would be many hours before he could rejoin the army. Sixteen cannon and 1,200 prisoners had been captured, Hood's main line of resistance broken, and his divisions rolled back two miles.

General Thomas met with his corps commanders that evening and made plans for a continuation of the offensive. The night and morning of the 16th were spent by the Federals adjusting their lines and perfecting connections between units.

Then Union skirmishers advanced and found the foe either strongly entrenched or posted behind stone walls. Wood directed the fire of his artillery against Peach Orchard Hill, while Smith's and Schofield's cannoneers swept Shy's Hill with a deadly crossfire. Wilson's cavalry, having dismounted, pushed back Chalmers' outnumbered

Rosecrans retreated to Chattanooga, and there began to fortify himself. Viewed here from Lookout Mountain, the city appears nearly a year later, with Moccasin Point in the Tennessee River in the foreground. Here for nearly two months the Federals sat and waited. (USAMHI)

division. About 3 P.M., while Union artillery pounded the Shy's Hill salient and Wilson's cavalry threatened to sweep Chalmers from the field and turn Hood's left, Wood and Steedman attacked Peach Orchard Hill. Covered by a host of skirmishers, four brigades ascended the slopes. Some of the Yanks gained the Rebel rifle pits, only to be dislodged by a slashing counterstroke by S. D. Lee's troops. The Union brigades recoiled, suffering heavy casualties, including one brigade commander and a number of officers.

Four o'clock was approaching and darkness would soon put a stop to the day's fighting. In the hollow fronting Shy's Hill, Brigadier General John McArthur of Smith's corps had massed one of his brigades. Coincidentally, Wilson's dismounted cavalry continued to gain ground, outflanking Govan's brigade, forcing back Chalmers, and threatening to envelop Cheatham's left. McArthur's brigade now stormed the steep slopes of Shy's Hill. In a short but desperate struggle, the bluecoats routed the Southerners from the rifle pits. Among the slain

Rosecrans, disgraced, was to be replaced. Now commanding the Army of the Cumberland would be Thomas, his headquarters here in Chattanooga. (USAMHI)

was Colonel William M. Shy, of the 20th Tennessee, who gave his name to the hill. Shy's Hill was the key to Hood's position. Cheatham had no reserves to plug the breakthrough. Schofield's corps and Wilson's cavalry and other units of Smith's corps drove ahead. Abandoning their artillery, the Confederates posted west of Granny White pike fled.

As night fell, a drenching rain set in, adding to the confusion, darkness, and misery. Thomas ordered Wood to pursue by the Franklin pike and Wilson via the Granny White pike. Few, if any, Confederates retreated by the latter because of the proximity of Wilson's people. Hurriedly organized and defended roadblocks in the Brentwood Hills gaps and at Hollow Tree Gap, four miles north of Franklin, enabled a few dedicated units to delay Wilson's horse soldiers long enough for the shattered army to cross the Big Harpeth. At Columbia, Forrest rendezvoused with Hood's columns and with his cavalry, and five infantry brigades covered the army's retreat to the Tennessee River. Hood crossed the Tennessee at Bainbridge, Alabama, on December 26 and 27, the campaign done.

Hood had played hell with the Army of Tennessee. A number of units would fight again in North Carolina and others in the defense of Mobile, but the once proud army had been destroyed as a feared fighting machine. Hood had lost the confidence of his officers and men, so, at his request, he was relieved of command by President Davis.

Thomas listed his losses in the decisive two-day Battle of Nashville as 387 killed, 2,562 wounded, and 112 missing. Hood failed to file a return of his casualties, but Thomas' provost marshal listed the number of prisoners captured and deserters received in November and December as more than 13,000. In addition, 72 cannon and 3,000 stands of arms were captured by the Federals. It was an altogether bloody and decisively fitting end to the fight for Tennessee, scene of some of the bloodiest and most decisive combat of the Civil War.

And on October 23, 1863, the new overall commander in the theater arrived, Major General U. S. Grant. This image was made in Nashville around this time by T. F. Saltsman. (COURTESY OF WILLIAM C. DAVIS)

With Grant's arrival there was no question that the siege would be broken. He would not sit and wait here in his headquarters for long. (NA)

Reinforcements came in, among them Major General William T. Sherman with two corps. He made his headquarters here. (NA)

George N. Barnard's photograph of Union soldiers camped at Monument Garden near Chattanooga shows some of the hard-boned Westerners who will fight their way out of Chattanooga. (LC)

Grant's first chore was to break the strangling hold that Bragg had on his supplies. The "cracker line" is what they called the circuitous route by which Grant re-established his supply. It depended upon the Tennessee River. (USAMHI)

Supply steamers like the Missionary *sometimes had to be towed through the shallows as they went upstream.* (NA)

But still they came to tie up at the banks and disgorge their precious cargo. (USAMHI)

They came, like the Chickamauga, *loaded with barrels of salt pork.* (NA)

Or like the Chattanooga, *piled high with sacks of grain.* (MHS)

There was usually a cannon aboard, and sometimes even a woman, as here on the Wauhatchie. (LC)

And here the Missionary *stands empty but for firewood, ready to return for more. The boiler parts in the foreground give evidence that the Federals had to be prepared for makeshift repairs and spare parts for these vital vessels.* (USAMHI)

Then they were off on the return voyage to get more of the food and material that kept Chattanooga supplied during the siege. Soldiers and civilians were there to watch them go, and to look anxiously for the next steamer. (NA)

It was a tenuous lifeline, always in danger of attacks from Confederate raiders, particularly cavalry led by intrepid soldiers like General Nathan Bedford Forrest. He so loathed Braxton Bragg that he called him "a damned scoundrel" and declared that "if you were any part of a man I would slap your jaws." (USAMHI)

To protect against men like Forrest, Grant had gunboats such as the USS Peosta *patrolling the Tennessee, sometimes convoying the supply ships.* (USAMHI)

Some months after the siege, special gunboats would be commissioned to continue this duty after the armies had left Chattanooga. Here at her moorings sits the USS General Grant. (USAMHI)

Long a landmark in Chattanooga, this old Indian mound became a military office during the siege. "Visitors are requested to register their names at the office," reads the sign at the foot of the steps. (NA)

Life during the siege was at first a hardship for the scantily provisioned Federals, and then, once the "cracker line" was operating, the enemy became boredom. Here a jaunty band of neckerchiefed officers pose at the Western & Atlantic Railroad terminal. (COURTESY OF JOSEPH H. BERGERON)

Their musicians relieved what they could of the doldrums. Here the regimental band of the 4th Minnesota, taken at Huntsville, Alabama, soon after the siege. (MHS)

And as soon as the supplies could get in, the "robbers' rows" and sutlers' shops appeared to relieve the soldiers of their pay. They were barely more than shacks behind their facades. (USAMHI)

There was drill aplenty to keep the men in shape. Here several companies stand in double ranks during skirmish drill, their skirmishers and sharpshooters thrown forward as if on the advance. There would be plenty of this work for them before long. (USAMHI)

That work would come when Grant decided to take Lookout Mountain. Up these steep and rugged slopes some Federals had to climb and fight on November 24. (MHS)

It was bloody and costly fighting. Brigadier General John W. Geary led a division that included his own son. In the battle just west of Lookout, in "Wauhatchie's bloody glen," his son was killed while his father was driving the Confederates off the mountain. (USAMHI)

In command of the attack on Lookout Mountain was a veteran of the Virginia campaigns, Major General Joseph Hooker. Here he stands with his staff with Lookout in the background. Hooker stands at the right, a head taller than the rest, while just behind him, looking away, is General Daniel Butterfield, often erroneously credited with composing "Taps." (USAMHI)

Hooker proudly sits atop his conquest, Point Lookout on the mountain's summit. (USAMHI)

Photographer R. M. Linn captured this view of the Confederate defenses and quarters atop Lookout Mountain. Fortunately, the Federals did not have to attack these directly, but moved around them. (COURTESY OF T. SCOTT SANDERS)

It was a fight in a dense fog much of the time, and some orders could be transmitted only by bugle call. A Confederate cornetist. (COURTESY OF CLYDE E. NOBLE)

The Lookout House on Lookout Mountain, high over the slopes overlooking Chattanooga and the battle that raged for the summit. A lone Federal sentry now stands vigil at its base. (MHS)

The day before the assault on Lookout, Grant sent Thomas forward to take Orchard Knob, the bald rise of ground seen between the two trees. George N. Barnard made this image from the crest of Missionary Ridge, providing the viewer with precisely the view that Bragg's Confederates had as they watched Thomas advance to take the knob. Two days later, from this same vantage, the Confederates watched in awe as the Army of the Cumberland swept across the intervening ground and up the slopes to the very spot where Barnard placed his camera. (USAMHI)

Here Barnard captured the view in reverse. The camera is now on Orchard Knob, and this is what Thomas' Federals saw as they began their assault up Missionary Ridge. (WRHS)

Barnard made this panoramic blending of images at Rossville Gap, the southern end of Missionary Ridge. Here Hooker attacked the left wing of the Confederate line, rushing past the John Ross house at the right and up the slope at left onto the ridge. (BOTH USAMHI)

Men of Gordon Granger's IV Corps practice forming for an assault, sharpshooters and skirmishers in front, artillery in place to give support fire, and the infantry drawn up in wave after wave of double-ranked soldiers. There may be as many as two full brigades in this remarkable image, made at Blue Springs, Tennessee. Granger's corps, including these men, struck at the very center of the Confederate line on Missionary Ridge. (USAMHI)

It was lean and tough Westerners like these who swept up the ridge to drive Bragg's Confederates from the summit. An unidentified regiment. (RP)

In Barnard's view of part of the main run of Missionary Ridge, the lines of Confederate defenses are faintly visible at the crest. Thomas' army marching in full view up that slope unnerved many Southerners and helped lead to the rout that followed. (USAMHI)

Another part of the five-mile line of summit that Bragg tried to defend. His army was so thinly spread that there was only one man for every seven or eight feet in places. (USAMHI)

Yet the men that he had were good ones. Men like the Washington Artillery of New Orleans, shown here in an unpublished image made in New Orleans in 1861. The officer seated is probably Colonel James B. Walton. (CONFEDERATE MUSEUM, NEW ORLEANS)

The men Walton led were hardy Louisianians like these, photographed in 1861 by J. W. Petty of New Orleans. The lines drawn on the image were probably made by designers in 1911 when they defaced the original photo in using it in Francis T. Miller's Photographic History of the Civil War. (USAMHI)

At the northern end of Missionary Ridge another attack was under way while Thomas and Hooker assaulted the center and southern ends. Here General William T. Sherman struck. (USAMHI)

Barnard captured the rugged and difficult terrain over which Sherman had to advance. The crest of Missionary Ridge runs off on the left, while in the distance rises Lookout Mountain. (USAMHI)

Assisting Sherman in his attack were artillerymen such as these, men of Battery B, 1st Illinois, the Chicago Light Artillery. They appear here at war's outset, at Bird's Point, Missouri, in May 1861. They will be battle-seasoned by the time they shell Bragg. (CHICAGO HISTORICAL SOCIETY)

Sherman's objective was Tunnel Hill, where the Chattanooga & Cleveland Railroad passed through this tunnel in Missionary. (NA)

Opposing Sherman was Lieutenant General William J. Hardee. When the rest of the Confederate line on Missionary gave way to Thomas and Hooker, still he held out for a time, covering the retreat. Bragg never had a better subordinate. A heavily retouched prewar portrait taken when Hardee was in United States service. (CIVIL WAR TIMES ILLUSTRATED COLLECTION)

Major General John M. Palmer commanded the XIV Corps in the November 25 attack, virtually covering the entire battle line. One of his divisions held Thomas' right, another was the center division in the attack up Missionary, and yet a third of Palmer's divisions was with Sherman at Tunnel Hill. (CWTI)

When the Confederates fled in rout from Missionary Ridge, they left behind them not only a signal Federal victory but also forty-two pieces of artillery. Here some 19 of the captured guns stand in line for the conqueror's camera. (USAMHI)

After the victory there was rest for a time, and a sense of revenge for the humiliation of Chickamauga. Federal generals like Brigadier John H. King established their headquarters in comfortable surroundings such as this Italianate masterpiece on Lookout Mountain. (COURTESY OF TERENCE P. O'LEARY)

There was time to lounge and relax once again. (TPO)

Once again they could sight-see, here at Saddle Rock, for instance. "By sitting on this rock under a hot sun," they joked, "you can get a 'Saddle Rock Roast.'" (TPO)

And in Chattanooga now the trains could come and go freely once more, taking men home for furloughs and bringing more back to continue the drive into the Confederacy. (MHS)

Though Grant did not pursue Bragg into Georgia after Missionary Ridge, the Federals did begin even then gathering information for the next campaign in the spring. Out of Chattanooga they sent W. J. Lawton, an intrepid Federal scout who often traveled in the uniform of a Confederate colonel, as he is seen here. In mid-December he penetrated deep into the Confederate lines, learning that after their defeat the Southerners were "low-spirited and demoralized and said they had lost all hope of ever gaining their independence." (USAMHI)

Even while the Chattanooga operations were under way, there was another campaign brewing in Tennessee, and it, like Chattanooga, brought another former commander from Virginia. Hooker fought for Lookout Mountain, and Major General Ambrose Burnside, the loser at Fredericksburg, defended Knoxville. Here he poses, seated, with his former chief of staff, Major General John G. Parke, standing at left. (COURTESY OF BRUCE GIMELSON)

Burnside occupied Knoxville in September, freeing much of eastern Tennessee and allowing thousands of pro-Union Tennesseeans like these refugees to return home. These men were photographed in Knoxville just after their return, and the tattered condition of their clothing testifies to the hardships of their exile. (NA)

Soon after Burnside took Knoxville, Confederate Brigadier General John S. Williams came out of southwest Virginia to harass the Federals. (VM)

Williams fought with elements of Parke's IX Corps here at Blue Springs in October, but was forced back, ending any threat to Burnside for several weeks. Here portions of Parke's corps are encamped, protecting Knoxville's northeastern flank. (LC)

George N. Barnard's view of the bridge of the East Tennessee & Virginia Railroad crossing the Holston River at Strawberry Plains. It was a major approach to Knoxville and well guarded, as the earthwork fort on the hill attests. One of Barnard's assistants—perhaps it is Barnard himself—stands behind an instrument at right. (LC)

This panoramic view, blending two images, shows Knoxville as it appeared during the siege. It is taken from Fort Byington, west of the city, and looks across it. The Holston flows past at right, with Fort Stanley rising above the river at the south end. At the left center rise two hills containing important defensive works, Fort Huntington Smith at the left and Fort Hill to its right in the distance. (BOTH NA)

Knoxville appears here in the spring of 1864, looking much the same as during its siege. Taken from the heights below Fort Stanley, this view looks north across the Holston. The Knoxville jail is at left. (LC)

Looking farther to the west, the camera shows the jail at right and, at far left, the University of Tennessee building. In the distant background just to its right is Fort Sanders. (LC)

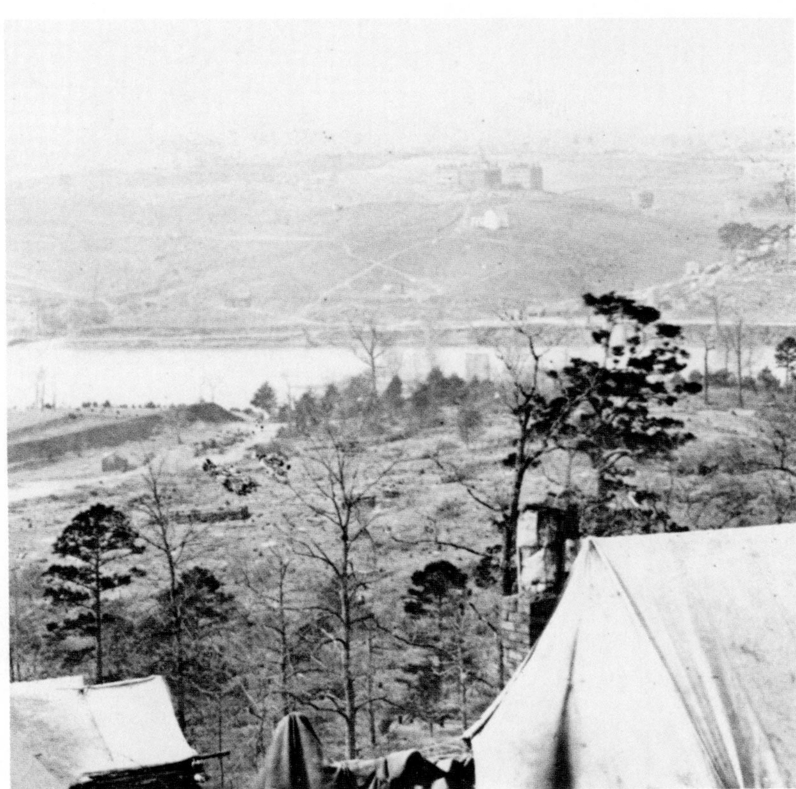

Another view of the university, this image made at the time of the siege. (USAMHI)

One of the defensive ditches on the perimeter of Fort Sanders, the Union bastion that withstood Longstreet's desperate assault. The university stands in the distance. (LC)

Fort Sanders not long after the siege. A lone soldier stands now where thousands struggled. (LC)

The Confederate chief of ordnance in the Knoxville siege was Lieutenant Peyton T. Manning, but for advice on the best use of his artillery, General Longstreet was more apt to turn to his devoted subordinate . . . (PRIVATE COLLECTION)

. . . Colonel E. Porter Alexander, chief of artillery. Through the entire campaign he lost only four guns, thrown into the Holston during the retreat. (TULANE UNIVERSITY LIBRARY, NEW ORLEANS)

Less successful was Major General Lafayette McLaws, one of Longstreet's division commanders. His commander severely censured him for failing to take Fort Sanders, even though McLaws had fought well at Chickamauga. This portrait of McLaws was taken in Augusta, Georgia, in September 1863 during a brief stop in the trip from Virginia to join Bragg at Chickamauga. (TU)

One of the first to die in the siege of Knoxville, Major William M. Gist of the 15th South Carolina was instantly killed on November 19 as he prepared to lead his regiment in a charge. A Federal sharpshooter's aim was true, and a fine Confederate officer lay dead. (MUSEUM OF THE CONFEDERACY)

Silent Fort Sanders after the siege was done. Burnside's chief engineer, Brigadier General Orlando M. Poe, sits at left, facing Lieutenant Colonel Orville E. Babcock, chief engineer of the IX Corps. The success at Knoxville was largely due to their efforts. (USAMHI)

Tennessee was relatively quiet for almost a year, until November 1864 when one last Confederate invasion came out of Georgia. General John Bell Hood planned to leave Sherman behind in Georgia and meet and defeat Thomas and his army around Nashville. Then he could invade Kentucky. It was a bold plan, but boldness was in the character of the one-legged general, shown here around the end of the war. (CHS)

Hood and the Federals met first around the little town of Franklin, shown here in an early postwar image. (USAMHI)

Commanding the three Union divisions in the fight at Franklin was Major General John M. Schofield, just thirty-three years old. Many years later he would recommend that the United States acquire Pearl Harbor in Hawaii. Schofield Barracks, near Pearl Harbor, is named for him. (USAMHI)

Hood's attacks at Franklin were brutal, costly to both sides, and in the end he almost wore out his army. Major General Benjamin F. Cheatham, often accused of drunkenness by Bragg, led one of Hood's corps. He was already under severe censure by Hood for allowing Schofield to retreat to fortified Franklin. (CHS)

Cheatham led his corps in an assault up the Columbia Pike against Federals placed behind the stone wall in the center of the photograph. (USAMHI)

Then the Confederates came up against Schofield's main line, part of it on the Carter farm, just in front of this gin house. (USAMHI)

Brigadier General John C. Brown led his division in attacks on the Carter farm until seriously wounded. (CHS)

Half of Schofield's small army was the IV Corps, commanded by Major General David S. Stanley, seated second from the right. Nathan Kimball, seated at right, led the division that held Schofield's far right. General Thomas J. Wood, of Chickamauga fame, seated second from the left, stayed in reserve in the rear. The other generals are: seated at left, Samuel Beatty; standing, left to right, Ferdinand Van Derveer, Washington L. Elliott, Luther P. Bradley, and Emerson Opdycke. All except Van Derveer were in the battle. (USAMHI)

Opdycke, in particular, was outstanding. His brigade spent thirty minutes bitterly defending a gap that had opened in Schofield's line near the Carter house. He sits in the center here with his regimental commanders. The young officer at far right is only nineteen years old and already lieutenant colonel of the 24th Wisconsin and a Medal of Honor winner. He is Arthur MacArthur, future father of General Douglas MacArthur. (USAMHI)

Some of the bitterest fighting of the war rages around the Carter house, and it tells in the casualties. (USAMHI)

Colonel George A. Smith of the 1st Confederate Georgia Infantry was killed. (VM)

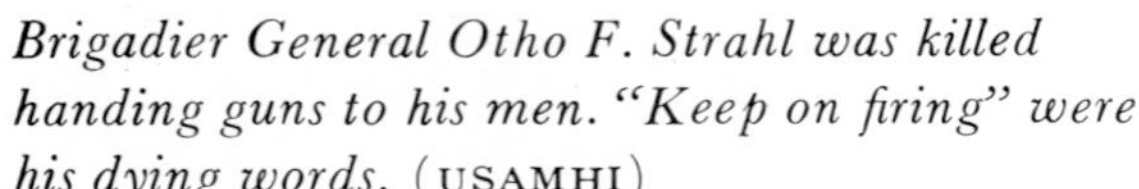

Brigadier General Otho F. Strahl was killed handing guns to his men. "Keep on firing" were his dying words. (USAMHI)

Brigadier General States Rights Gist, like Strahl, led a brigade in Brown's division. He was killed instantly in the attack. (USAMHI)

The cost to Hood's high command was devastating. Besides Strahl and Gist, Generals Hiram Granbury and John Adams were killed, and John C. Carter mortally wounded. But surely the most telling loss of all was the death of the premier division commander in the Army, Major General Patrick R. Cleburne. His was a loss that could never be replaced. (VM)

While Schofield battled Hood at Franklin, General Thomas readied the defenses of Tennessee's capital . . . (USAMHI)

. . . Nashville. George N. Barnard made this image several months after the Battle of Nashville, but it still reveals Federal soldiers encamped on the state house grounds. (KEAN ARCHIVES, PHILADELPHIA)

The state house in Nashville, with the Nashville & Chattanooga Railroad in the foreground. (NA)

The view looking west from the capitol. The log breastworks hastily erected on the capitol building are still in evidence, with loopholes for firing. They were not used, but give evidence of Thomas' determination to hold every inch of ground. (USAMHI)

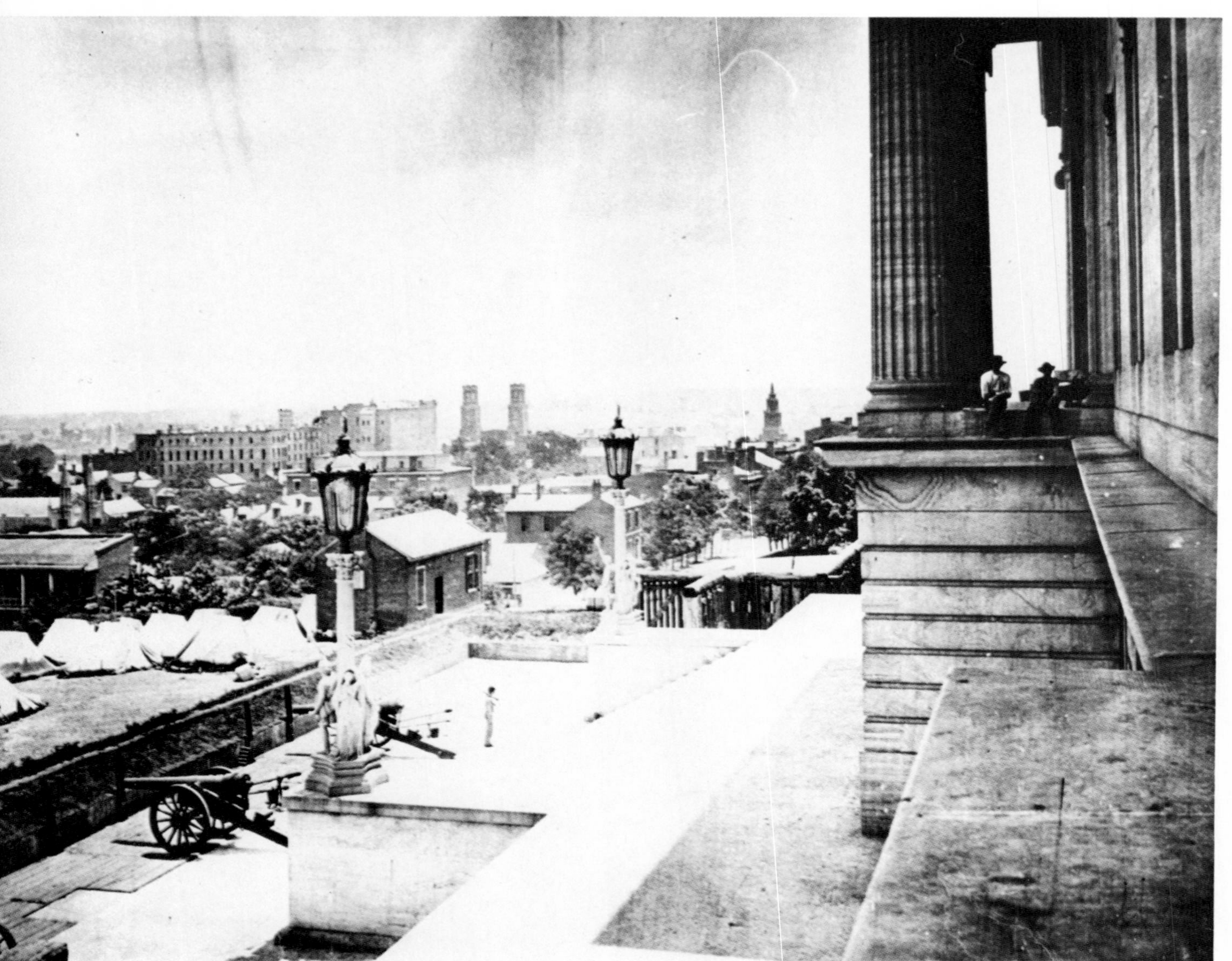

Looking south from the capitol across the city. Cannon and earthworks still surround the building. (CWTI)

Market Street, off the public square, in downtown Nashville. (USAMHI)

With Hood weakened after Franklin, Grant ordered Thomas to leave his defenses and attack him. But Thomas would not do so until his cavalry was properly mounted. Mounts were always a problem for the cavalry. Here in Nashville, mechanics and smiths work at shoeing horses and keeping wagons in running order. (USAMHI)

It presented a deceptively peaceful picture prior to the fury that was released when Thomas finally did attack on December 15. (USAMHI)

The next day, December 16, while the battle raged south of Nashville, soldiers left in the outer defenses of the city listened to and watched what they could of the battle. (MHS)

George Barnard captured much of the Nashville scene that day including, here, another view along the outer defense perimeter. Somewhere in the distance Hood's army was being virtually destroyed. (LC)

It was Brigadier General John McArthur's division that attacked and routed Hood's left flank on the first day of fighting. Hood never recovered, and McArthur won another star. (LC)

Lieutenant General Stephen D. Lee had missed the debacle at Franklin, but reached Nashville in time to command the corps holding the right of Hood's deteriorating line. His was the last Confederate command to hold its position as Thomas continued his attacks. (USAMHI)

Brave Confederates like these enlisted men of the Washington Artillery were no match for the greater numbers and fresh troops under Thomas. When New Orleans artist J. W. Petty photographed them in 1861, they were jaunty. After Nashville, they and their army were devastated. (USAMHI)

Everyone was a spectator on those two December days. (USAMHI)

Federal Fort Negley, south of Nashville. Hood never got close enough to attack it. (CHS)

Another view of Fort Negley, its gun embrasures glaring, like a smile with missing teeth, toward the Confederates. (USAMHI)

A casemate inside Fort Negley. The light is gleaming on a gun tube inside the ironclad casemate, but the gun will never fire. With the repulse and destruction of Hood, the last threat to Tennessee is at an end. For three years North and South bitterly contested the Volunteer State. Now at last it is decided, and with it rests much of the fate of the Confederacy. (USAMHI)

Squadron of the South

FRANK J. MERLI

Of ships and sea and suffocating the Confederacy

WHEN PRESIDENT ABRAHAM LINCOLN announced his intent to blockade the Confederate coast, he set on foot a host of problems for his Administration. For one thing, he violated a fundamental maxim of the American view of naval war—that there be no paper blockades. From the days of the Founding Fathers, Americans had insisted that in order for a blockade to be recognized in law it had to be maintained by forces sufficient to prevent entrance to and exit from the ports under blockade. However, in April 1861 the Union Navy simply did not possess enough ships to seal off the 3,500-mile shoreline of the South.

Of course, the President asserted his intent to post a competent force "so as to prevent entrance and exit of vessels from the ports aforesaid." But obviously, with only eight warships in home waters at war's outset, that was bold talk. And before the North could build or buy the ships that would demonstrate its determination to close the South to foreign trade, the European powers would monitor the blockade and assess its impact on their interests.

In the opening weeks of the war—about the time foreign officials started sorting out their responses to conditions in America—a talented Washington naval administrator began devising means to subdue the South by way of its vulnerable seacoasts. Alexander Dallas Bache, great-grandson of Benjamin Franklin, promoter par excellence of technological and scientific innovation, superintendent of the coastal geographic survey, and a supremely gifted political infighter, saw and grasped an opportunity to merge his interests with those of the navy and the nation.

Bache's suggestion for a naval planning board to develop a comprehensive strategy for implementing the blockade therefore found a sympathetic hearing, especially after John C. Frémont, a prominent Republican then in London, warned of "very active" and well-financed Confederate efforts to buy up large numbers of steamers in British shipyards. Secretary of the Navy Gideon Welles and his assistant Gustavus V. Fox remembered the proposal for a centralized naval coordinating committee and set about establishing it. Fortunately, they had at their disposal a number of talented men for the task. In addition to Bache, the Strategy Board, as it came to be called, consisted of Commander Charles H. Davis, Major John C. Barnard, representing the Army Corps of Engineers, and Captain Samuel F. Du Pont, a capable, if sometimes controversial, naval officer who acted as the board's president. Less than a month after its inception, it had pre-

As with the origins of the North Atlantic Blockading Squadron, its Southern counterpart had to depend at war's start upon ships already in service, and often of checkered careers. The USS Niagara, *shown here in September 1863 at Boston, was the steam frigate that helped lay the first transatlantic cable. In 1860 she carried Japan's first diplomatic mission to the United States, then returned to America in April 1861 to find civil war. Immediately she went on the blockade.* (LC)

pared a number of important reports, suggesting division of the Southern coastline into four commands, the North Atlantic, South Atlantic, East and West Gulf Squadrons. The navy must seize a base in each, which, besides providing convenient supply and repair facilities for the fleets would also discourage European intervention for the South. They must show Europe that they could control their coastline.

In the autumn of 1861, as Captain Du Pont began massing his Federal armada for its assault on Port Royal, South Carolina, and began assembling and deploying the forces that would become the South Atlantic Blockading Squadron, the chief of Confederate naval procurement in Europe, Captain James D. Bulloch, started planning a challenge to that squadron. Bulloch decided to buy a ship, stock it with much-needed war material, and

Warships were not available in abundance to begin Mr. Lincoln's stranglehold on the Southern coastline. This wooden side-wheel tugboat, USS O. M. Pettit, *was purchased by the Navy at the war's start and sent south. She appears here in 1862 off Hilton Head, South Carolina.* (USAMHI)

run it through the blockade. He set about that task with the flair and skill that marked all he did—and he succeeded brilliantly. The *Fingal* was loaded in Scotland, Bulloch and other passengers did not board until after she cleared customs, and after a slow passage the *Fingal* reached Bermuda on November 2. Now she prepared for the final, most perilous steps in the journey to the American coast.

Meanwhile, Union countermeasures began to yield results. On the same day that newly promoted Rear-Admiral Du Pont issued his General Order No. 1 to the commanding officers of the blockading vessels under his command, on October 24, 1861, Secretary of the Navy Welles sent him a warning that the *Fingal* was coming, loaded with supplies for the rebellion. Further, Welles had learned that a Confederate firm in London had purchased the vessel, making her "in reality a Confederate ship." That made her fair game.

After circumventing efforts of the American consul at Bermuda to deplete his crew and deprive him of coal, Bulloch set out for the southern coast on the afternoon of November 7. At a deck conference Bulloch took the men into his confidence, explained his mission, and asked for volunteers. To the question "Will you go?" he received unanimous assent. He then explained his intention to defend the ship against the Savannah blockaders. In the event of an encounter with a blockader, Bulloch intended to take control of the ship and fight it. Would the crew help? Again, to a man, they answered, "Yes."

After settling affairs with the deckhands, Bulloch looked to the most important preparation for a successful dash past the blockaders, the steam engine. As Bulloch explained his plan, Chief Engineer McNair told him that "he had been putting aside a few tons of the nicest and cleanest coal," that if

Ships that accompanied the first offensives directed at the Confederate coast then stayed on post to do blockade duty. The USS Unadilla *was with the Federal fleet that attacked and occupied Beaufort, South Carolina, in November 1861. Thereafter she patrolled those waters, her hearty crew denied another real fight until war's end.* (USAMHI)

Bulloch could arrange for him to clean his flues and fireboxes, the engines might be made to drive the ship, overloaded as she was, at 11 knots for a brief period.

The last night out, soon after midnight, "as nice a fog as any reasonable blockade-runner could have wanted" enveloped the ship, and under its protection the *Fingal* edged toward land, so as to be inshore of patrol boats. With lights out, engines silent, nerves taut, the crew waited for daybreak. Suddenly, an eerie wail, a sound like an "unearthly steam whistle" threatened to reveal their presence to every Federal vessel for miles around. Then it came again. The offending chanticleer, that bird of morning, did not greet the sun, for it met quick and violent death at the hands of an irate sailor.

At daybreak all was in readiness for the final dash into the harbor. The engineer's preparations proved their worth, as the engines now propelled the ship northward at a steady 11 knots. Even the elements helped, for the fog moved out to sea, forming a curtain between the shore and any patrol boats in the vicinity. Soon the *Fingal* sighted the massive brick walls of Fort Pulaski, crossed the bar, hoisted the Confederate flag, and acknowledged the waving hats and inaudible cheers of the men lining the parapets of that ill-fated fort. Then, close to safety, the *Fingal* ignominiously ran

The first commander of the South Atlantic Blockading Squadron upon its creation on September 18, 1861, was Rear Admiral Samuel F. I. Du Pont, standing second from the left aboard his flagship USS Wabash *in 1863. He enjoyed a notable career during the Mexican War, then began the Civil War by planning and executing the attack on Port Royal and Hilton Head.* (USAMHI)

aground. Some hours later, with the help of a rising tide and local tugs, the *Fingal* completed her voyage upriver to Savannah at 4 P.M., November 12, 1861. She brought with her, by Bulloch's estimate, the greatest military cargo ever imported into the Confederacy. Bulloch himself modestly noted that probably "no single ship ever took into the Confederacy a cargo so entirely composed of military and naval supplies." In this, as in so much else connected with his Civil War career, he makes a reliable witness, though his contribution to the Confederate cause is vastly underrated all too often.

The original Confederate plan called for Bulloch to stock the *Fingal* with cotton for the credit of the Navy Department abroad and to "return to Europe with her to carry out the further purposes of the government there." But from about November 25, 1861, until February 5—when Bulloch returned to Europe by an alternative route—it proved impossible for the *Fingal* to slip past the blockaders of the Union Squadrons.

During his enforced idleness at Savannah, Bulloch studied the strength and movements of units of the South Atlantic Squadron and assessed Confederate defenses and possibilities of keeping the port open to foreign commerce. His starkly professional reports make grim reading. At the Wassaw

Du Pont's mighty ship, the Wabash, *taken in Port Royal Harbor in 1863, from the deck of the monitor USS* Weehawken. *Ironically, the only known image of the* Weehawken *that survives is the stanchion and rope that appears in the lower left of this image.* (USAMHI)

outlet Union forces consisted of anywhere from four to seven ships, "frequently as many as eleven"; the enemy seemed fully informed of the *Fingal*'s position and of Southern plans to get her out to sea: "Unless there be some changes in the political relations of the United States with the courts of Europe, I consider the port of Savannah as completely closed to commerce for an indefinite time. There are . . . five ships-of-war at the entrance to the Romerly Marsh, a force too powerful for the simple blockade of the *Fingal,* and this assembling of the enemy's fleet can only be regarded as preliminary to an attack in force upon the city."

But of all of Bulloch's commentaries on conditions in Savannah and of his attempts to get the *Fingal* out past enemy blockaders, one has a particular poignancy. On November 25, 1861, Bulloch told Secretary of the Navy Stephen R. Mallory:

> I have the honour to report that the steamship *Fingal* has been discharged, and now lies in the Savannah River ready to receive freight. . . . I cannot refrain from urging the necessity of getting the ship off without delay. Yesterday five of the enemy's gunboats stood cautiously in, and after throwing a number of shells upon and over Tybee Island, a force was landed without opposition. This morning the Federal flag is flying from the lighthouse, and they will doubtless soon have a battery upon the point of the island. The only egress left for the *Fingal* is through Warsaw [*sic*] Inlet, and it can scarcely be supposed that the enemy will permit it to remain open many days.

Perhaps his pressing concern for getting the *Fingal* back to England and for resuming the vital tasks assigned to him by the Navy Department prevented the usually astute Bulloch from assessing the larger significance of that Federal flag on Tybee Island's lighthouse.

From the USS *Savannah,* at anchor off Tybee Bar at 1 P.M. on November 25, Commander J. S. Missroon reported to Flag Officer Du Pont that at 3 P.M. the previous evening Commander John Rodgers "hoisted the flag of the Union on the martello tower and light-house . . . [on Tybee Island]." Du Pont lost no time in conveying this good news to his superiors in Washington. "I have," he told Welles, "the honor to inform the Department that the flag of the United States is flying over the territory of the State of Georgia. . . . I am happy now to have it in my power to inform the Department that the *Flag,* the *Augusta,* and the *Pocahontas* are at anchor in the harbor abreast of Tybee beacon and light, and that the *Savannah* has been ordered to take the same position. The abandonment of Tybee Island on which there is a strong martello tower, with a battery at its base, is due to the terror inspired by the bombardment of Forts Walker and Beauregard, and is a direct fruit of the victory of the 7th." Then Du Pont added a strategic prediction of some importance: "By the fall of Tybee Island, the reduction of Fort Pulaski, which is within easy mortar distance, becomes only a question of time."

An unpublished portrait of a black seaman aboard the Wabash. *Hundreds of Negroes served in the Union Navy and aboard the blockading ships.* (PAUL DE HAAN)

Given the supposed impregnability of the massive masonry walls of Pulaski, few, especially among the local Southern military commanders, would have agreed with that assessment. But in early 1862 steps were already under way to reduce the sentinel of Savannah.

In its first report of July 5, 1861, the Strategy Board had called for the capture of "a convenient coal depot on the southern extremity of the line of Atlantic blockades, and . . . if this coal depot were suitably selected it might be used not only as a depot for coal, but as a depot of provisions and common stores, as a harbor of refuge, and as a general rendezvous, or headquarters, for that part of the coast." The place selected by the board for these functions was Fernandina, roughly on the Florida-Georgia border. In addition to the many advantages Fernandina offered as a supply depot, its possession would afford Union forces considerable opportunities to cut off rail and water trade with other parts of the South—it would, in short, serve much the same function at the southern terminus of the blockade that Port Royal and Hampton Roads served in the North. It would give the Squadron effective control over the Georgia coast. "And," as the board noted, "the naval power that commands the coast of Georgia will command the State of Georgia."

Although Du Pont wished to commence the Fernandina offensive as soon as the Port Royal operation was completed about mid-November 1861, a number of factors combined to delay the start of that operation until early in 1862. Toward the end of 1861 the naval and military commanders, Du Pont and Brigadier General Thomas W. Sherman, had agreed "to some kind of offensive against Savannah," but the ambitious undertaking, requiring logistical resources (especially supplies of coal) and coordination of command facilities not then available, proved "too intricate and hazardous," and it had to be curtailed. As a sort of compromise, the navy set out for Florida, and the army set about preparing for the task of reducing Fort Pulaski, a major obstacle to control of the en-

Commander C. R. P. Rodgers was captain of the Wabash *while Du Pont flew his flag in that ship, commanding it in the attack on Port Royal. In the later siege of Fort Pulaski, Rodgers led the naval force that fought on land in the trenches, and in 1863 took the helm of the ironclad* New Ironsides. (USAMHI)

Fort Pulaski was the next major move for the Southern squadron, but first there was extensive preparatory work. Ships like the Coast Guard schooner Arago *did hydrographic work along the shore and in the channels, making some 60,000 casts of the lead in sounding over 300 miles of coastline. Only armed with this knowledge could Du Pont's ships brave the Confederate shores and inlets.* (USAMHI)

trances to Savannah. While Sherman set his plans in motion, Du Pont assembled his armada for the assault on what would become the southern depot of the South Atlantic Squadron.

The long-awaited attack on Fernandina when it came proved an anticlimax. On March 4, Du Pont reported himself in complete possession of the objectives of his mission, having achieved that goal merely by defending his forces against "a few scattered musket shots . . . from the town." Du Pont's report of the expedition to Secretary Welles contains a capsule comment on the affair that would be difficult to improve upon: "We captured Port Royal, but Fernandina and Fort Clinch have been given to us." If he knew the reason for the "gift" he did not mention it in his report.

After the loss of Port Royal, General Robert E. Lee and other Confederate leaders had reluctantly concluded that the defense of the Atlantic seaboard was impracticable and beyond the capabilities of military and naval forces of the South. Except in a few special cases, as, for example, Charleston, Confederate forces would withdraw inland, out of range of Union naval bombardment. In early February 1862, General Lee wrote to General James M. Trapier, commander of the Florida military district, that Fernandina might have to be abandoned unless sufficient guns could be found to command the entrance to the Cumberland Sound, "the back door" to the island. By February 24 the Confederate high command realized that no guns could be supplied to the Cumberland forts, and

The first goal was Tybee Island, which controlled access to Fort Pulaski. Ships like the USS Savannah . . . (USAMHI)

. . . *and the steam sloop* Pocahontas *mustered for the November 24, 1861, attack.* (USAMHI)

The officers of the Pocahontas . . . (USAMHI)

Trapier was authorized to evacuate his defenses. The logic of Southern strategy, not overpowering Union strength, gave Du Pont control of the South Atlantic Coast at no cost. The navy subsequently played only a minor, token role in the later attack on Fort Pulaski, which was predominantly an army operation. Federal troops had occupied Tybee Island, about a mile from the fort, in late 1861, and by early April 1862 they had constructed eleven batteries, including ten 9-inch Columbiads, heavy rifled guns, and emplacements of 13-inch mortar.

Although the attack on Fort Pulaski did not lead to the surrender of Savannah, it did demonstrate another lesson of "modern" war—that walls, however massive and well constructed, could not withstand the pounding of heavy rifled cannons, especially those equipped "with these wonderful projectiles which we now possess," as one Union gunner summed up the encounter. In fact, so poorly defended was the fort that it took Federal forces a mere 30 hours and about 5,275 shots on April 10–11 before the Confederate commander, twenty-six-year-old Colonel Charles H. Olmstead, surrendered. But he raised the white flag only after the fort's flagpole, flying the Stars and Bars, had been shot away three times and the fort's magazine stood exposed to the danger of imminent explosion

. . . and the men . . . (USAMHI)

from enemy fire. His seven and one-half-foot thick walls crumbled under Yankee bombardment.

A reporter for a local newspaper visited the shattered fort soon after its surrender and left this account: ". . . all the parapet guns were dismounted. . . . Every casemate gun, except one, [was] dismounted and the casemate walls breached in almost every instance to the top of the arch —say between five and six feet in width. The moat outside was so filled with brick and mortar that one could have passed over dry-shod. . . . The parapet walls on the Tybee side were all gone, in many places to the level of the earth. . . . The protection to the magazine in the northwest angle of the fort had all been shot away; the entire corner of the magazine next to the passageway was shot off, and the powder exposed, while three shots had actually penetrated the chamber."

The role of the South Atlantic Blockading Squadron was limited and of minor significance. For a time the naval component of the expedition camped on the beach, without being allowed into combat, for all the guns had been manned. Then, after an insubordinate colonel had been relieved of his command and his German troops refused to fight without him, the sailors of Du Pont replaced them and served with distinction. The naval battery, firing three 30-pound Parrott rifled guns and one 24-pound James rifle, proved to be one of the two deadliest components of the Union attack. Commander C. R. P. Rodgers later reported that his rifled guns bore "into the brick face of the wall like augurs," while the columbiads were "striking like trip hammers and breaking off great masses of masonry which had been cut loose by the rifles." The general in command recognized the services of the Navy by including Naval Lieutenant John Irwin in the party that accepted the Confederate surrender of the fort.

This left the *Fingal* trapped in Savannah, and

. . . and the boat's crew of the ship's cutter were all ready for the attack on . . . (USAMHI)

now that presented the Confederate defenders with a glorious opportunity to augment their naval forces. In the spring of 1862 the vessel was turned over to a local shipyard for conversion into an ironclad. In time the blockade runner *Fingal* became the ironclad CSS *Atlanta,* and her story is very much part of the adventures of the South Atlantic Blockading Squadron.

First, the ship was cut down to her deck, which was slightly widened and overlayed with a thick layer of timber and iron. "A casemate was built, the sides and ends inclining at an angle of about 30°." The sides and ends of the casemate were covered with about four inches of iron plate, secured to a backing of three inches of oak over 15 inches of pine. She was armed with two 7-inch rifled guns on bow and stern pivots, and two 6-inch rifled guns in broadside.

As soon as the ship was completed, a public clamor "to do something" with so magnificent a weapon arose, and the public political pressure prevailed over the calmer, more prudent plans of the naval authorities charged with the defense of the city. "Although the [city] council considered the Confederate armorclad to be competent to almost any achievement," Tattnall knew better. His experience with the *Virginia,* plus his knowledge of the *Atlanta*'s deficiencies, convinced him that she would not stand a chance. "I considered the *Atlanta* no match for the monitor class of vessel at close quarters, and in shoal waters particularly." Despite his considerable misgivings about the wisdom of trying to run past the Union guardships, Tattnall agreed to make the attempt. But Union reinforcements of the outlets with the new class monitor *Passaic* stymied Southern plans, at least for the moment.

After several shake-ups in the Savannah naval

. . . Tybee Island. They took it without opposition, thus gaining a foothold at the mouth of the Savannah River and a perfect base for the attack on Fort Pulaski, which defended the city. (USAMHI)

command, Mallory found a man anxious for action. The new commander, William A. Webb, had a reputation with fellow seamen as "a very reckless young officer," one who received his appointment primarily because "he would at once do something." His plans included, among other things, to "raise the blockade between here and Charleston, attack Port Royal, and then blockade Fort Pulaski"—all this without assistance, if need be!

Union intelligence about the maneuvers and plans of the *Atlanta* were "uncanny." When, on the night of June 16, she attempted to surprise the Union forces, a lookout on the monitor *Weehawken* spotted her approach and sounded the alarm at 4:10 A.M. Captain John Rodgers, commander of the Union monitor, was a member of one of America's most illustrious naval families and an experienced officer in his own right, with a reputation for courage and audacity. He commanded an experienced crew that knew its business, cleared for action, and took their ship downstream ready for any contingency, though they and their captain were a bit puzzled by the opening gambit in this game.

Upon entering the Wilmington River, Webb had sighted his quarry, and in his enthusiasm to attack he left the narrow channel and ran aground, a perfect target for the gunners on the *Weehawken*.

Approaching the grounded ship to a range of about 300 yards, Rodgers opened fire with his 11-

It was a place that had been defended before, 304 years before to be exact. The Spaniards erected this martello tower on Tybee in 1557. No longer are there halberds and burnished breastplates, but the soldiers are much the same, like the tower itself, eternal. (USAMHI)

and 15-inch Dahlgrens, and four out of five shells fell with devastating impact on the near-helpless Southern ship. One shot wounded as many as 40 or 50 men. Other shots disabled guns, shot away the pilot house; and Webb's immobility and list prevented him from bringing any of his own guns into effective play. He fired some seven shots, none of them effective. Fifteen minutes of battle—if it can be called that—convinced Webb that he had no choice but to surrender.

Rodgers got a vote of confidence from Congress and a promotion to commodore; the Navy Department believed that its faith in the new monitor class had been vindicated at the bar of history; and Admiral Du Pont could turn over command of the South Atlantic Blockading Squadron to Admiral John A. Dahlgren with a measure of contentment, that, while sweet, did not quite erase the bitterness of his failure to capture the cradle of the Confederacy at Charleston, South Carolina.

From the beginning of the war, Charleston, South Carolina, "the cradle of the Confederacy" and "the hotbed of secession," had possessed a peculiar fascination for Union military and naval planners. Consequently, Washington devoted more resources and time to the subjugation of the city than its military importance justified. However splendid the city might be as a symbol of Confederate defiance, it had no war industries of importance, and its comparatively inadequate rail network with the rest of the South deprived it of any great utility as a way station for blockade-runners.

Yet, Federal naval administrators, especially Assistant Secretary of the Navy Gustavus V. Fox, regarded capture of the city as "the ultimate propaganda prize" for the United States Navy; further, capture of the city would enhance the department's reputation and demonstrate its worth by "attaining a spectacular psychological victory," and in addition a Union victory at the heart of rebeldom would mute press and congressional criticism of the department and confirm the Administration's faith in the invincibility of the newer class of monitors, then coming off the stocks of northern naval yards.

Du Pont wished a carefully prepared and coordinated attack on the city, not because it had any military value, but because failure at so prominent a place might have disastrous domestic and international repercussions. Impressed by some of the technological improvements in Union ships and guns, Du Pont nonetheless retained substantial reservations about the plans outlined to him by his superiors. More important, he was made to believe that the Navy was expected to take the city: he had "to recognize that this operation was of no consequence to the Army" and no troop reinforcements could be expected for the raw recruits that had been sent to the region. And Du Pont made an important mistake: he never fully convinced his superiors that in fact "he was fundamentally opposed to the *method* of attack" rather than to merely this or that tactical aspect of the plan.

At noon on April 7, 1863, Du Pont ordered his offensive, with the *Weehawken* in the van, pushing a raft to clear mines and torpedoes from the column's line of approach. The Confederates had not only heavily obstructed the channels but they had marked them with range finders, which greatly increased the accuracy of the fire with which they were able to rake the Union ships as they advanced into range. The *Weehawken,* for example, engaged the enemy for some 40 minutes, sustaining over 50 hits, and as she disengaged she was taking water through a shot hole in her deck. The *Passaic* was hit about 30 times; *Patapsco* became a kind of sitting duck for the Confederate gunners in Forts Moultrie and Sumter and sustained nearly 50 hits; *New Ironsides* escaped certain destruction when an electric torpedo with a ton of gun powder miraculously failed to go off. The last ironclad in line, the *Keokuk,* spent 30 minutes under the undivided attention of the guns of the Confederates, sustaining some 90 hits, many of which lodged below the waterline. Calm weather allowed her to stay afloat overnight, but the next day a roughening of the sea sent her to her grave, but not before the captain and 15 survivors were able to save themselves.

Now came Brigadier General Quincy A. Gillmore, and with him came a plan. He placed heavy batteries of rifled cannon on Tybee Island, and from there would bombard Fort Pulaski into submission. It was the first time that rifles were used against masonry, and the results were devastating. (USAMHI)

The severe battering that his ironclads had sustained led Du Pont to call off the attack, and though he originally expected to resume it the next

Starting on April 10, 1862, Gillmore began to pulverize Fort Pulaski. Shell after shell burrowed into the brick face of the bastion. (USAMHI)

By the end of the day very few Rebel cannon still stood ready to continue the fight. (USAMHI)

day, the reports of his captains changed his mind. As he told Welles, "I was fully convinced that a renewal of the attack could not result in the capture of Charleston, but would, in all probability, end in the destruction of a portion of the ironclad fleet and might leave several of them sunk within reach of the enemy. I therefore determined not to renew the attack, for in my judgement it might have converted a failure into a disaster."

Perhaps Du Pont anticipated some of the northern response to the repulse of his forces, for on April 8 he wrote to Henry Winter Davis and let some of his bitterness show. He told Davis, "Of course, I am ready for the howl—but I never was calmer in my life and never more happy that, where I thought a disaster imminent, I have only had a failure." In letter after letter Du Pont bitterly complained of the monitor mania of his superiors in Washington and of the greed of those civil contractors who pressed the Navy for immediate use of a weapon of unproven effectiveness. In an outburst of anger he once told Davis that "eight musical boxes from Germany off Ft. [Sumter] would have brought about the same effect upon the rebel cause."

Public and departmental dissatisfaction with the results at Charleston led to a shake-up in the naval chain of command. On June 3, 1863, Secretary Welles informed Du Pont that because of his opposition to a renewal of the attack on Charleston the department was relieving him of his command of the South Atlantic Blockading Squadron. The new commander, Andrew Foote, an officer admired by Du Pont, despite the former's advocacy of monitors, unfortunately died before he could assume his new command. His replacement was, from Du Pont's point of view, a less happy one. Admiral John Dahlgren had long intrigued for command of the South Atlantic Squadron, and in his quest he had the advantage of being a favorite of President

More were out of action, like this mortar caught by photographer Timothy O'Sullivan, who made most of the Fort Pulaski views taken that April. (LC)

Lincoln, who much appreciated the loyal support that Dahlgren had tendered in the uncertain early days of the war. In his new post, the armchair admiral hoped to add seagoing laurels to his impressive record of some 20 years as chief of the Bureau of Ordnance. Earlier Du Pont had told another correspondent that "Dahlgren [had been] made an admiral, in part for a gun which is a greater failure than the monitor which carries it."

Dahlgren's repeated attacks on Charleston in the months that followed his appointment fared no better than had Du Pont's, and resulted in greater loss of life and material. Dahlgren launched a series of well-organized but vain attacks on the city but could make no substantial progress in reducing it into submission. It has been estimated that in the course of the Union attacks in a few days of the summer of 1863 over 5,000 Federal shells, weighing well over a half million pounds, had rained down on the defenders of Charleston—and still

Inside the casemates was a shambles, the rubble so choking the embrasures that even functioning guns could not be reloaded. (LC)

The next day Gillmore resumed his bombardment against weakening resistance. These two gaping holes appeared in the wall, leaving the fort vulnerable to an assault at any time. Its commander had little choice but to surrender.
(NEW-YORK HISTORICAL SOCIETY)

they held out; it is also said that the Union bombardment of Sumter on September 1–2, 1863, was one of the heaviest ever recorded in the annals of war up until that time. Yet the beleaguered city continued to hold out against the best the Union could throw at it, and when the end came, it did not come from the sea.

It is extremely difficult to judge with any precision the impact that the blockading squadrons had on the defeat of the South. The need for secrecy and the danger of capture led to the falsification and destruction of records; the intricacies of international law and the ramifications of British neutrality regulations led to some really imaginative efforts at subterfuge and disguise. Nor is it always possible to unravel the complicated skein of secrecy that the Confederacy wove to cover its operations.

Most important, blockaders had to contend with

In time the industrious Yankee engineers and workmen rebuilt Pulaski into a powerful link in the blockade chain that constricted Savannah. (CHS)

By 1863 the Federals had built up a mighty arsenal and restored much of the fallen masonry, making Pulaski again one of the more attractive casemated forts on the Atlantic coast. (USAMHI)

The 3d Rhode Island Heavy Artillery came to man the mighty seacoast guns that faced Savannah and the ocean. (USAMHI)

the greed of those who saw golden opportunities in evading it. "Moreover, once the blockade was in effect, the inflated prices that provisions and war supplies commanded in the Confederacy made it profitable for British shipbuilders to construct fast vessels designed exclusively for blockade-running," and most of these benefited from the technological improvement that steam gave the runner over the blockader. The ports of the South seemed a cornucopia of profit, and even as late as 1864 it is estimated that as many as two of every three ships eluded the most vigilant blockaders. One careful assessment of the efficiency of the blockade of the Carolina ports from 1861 to 1865 estimates that of the more than 2,000 attempts to breach the blockade about 85 percent were successful.

No one has ever calculated the profits of foreigners who entered the Confederate trade. Successful captains cleared £1,000 on a round trip from Nassau to Wilmington, and their crews were proportionately well paid. It is reported that one ship earned nearly £85,000 for about three weeks work; and conservative estimates say that profits of £30,000 on each leg of a journey into and out of the Confederacy were not uncommon. It is well known that throughout the war profits remained high, with one Liverpool firm reported to have cleared over £4 million in the trade. Unfortu-

The giant smoothbores dwarf a smaller siege gun as the Rhode Islanders go at their gun practice. Two men at front left strain under the weight of a projectile while others pass a powder cartridge from the open chest. (USAMHI)

nately, most of these profits accrued to middleman profiteers, for it was late in the war before the Confederate Navy Department established its own system of supply under government sponsorship—and by that time it was too late to have much of an impact on the course of the war.

But the blockade may have cost Lincoln more than it was worth, for it tied up warships that might have been more effective elsewhere. America's greatest naval historian, Alfred Thayer Mahan, reflected upon the naval lessons of the Civil War, and in an all too infrequently quoted passage he observed, "But as the Southern coast, from its extent and many inlets, might have been a source of strength, so, from those very characteristics, it became a fruitful source of injury. The great story of the opening of the Mississippi is but the most striking illustration of an action that was going on incessantly all over the South. At every breach of the sea frontier, warships were entering. The streams that had carried the wealth and supported the trade of the seceding States turned against them, and admitted their enemies to their hearts. Dismay, insecurity, paralysis, prevailed in regions that might, under happier auspices, have kept a nation alive through the most exhausting war. Never did seapower play a greater or more decisive part than in the contest which determined that the course of the world's history would be modified by the existence of one great nation, instead of several rival states, in the North American continent."

Possibly the blockade was a waster of resources and opportunities. Certainly the lessons of history are wasted if we recount the story of the South Atlantic Blockading Squadron without asking whether the Federal ships engaged in that duty could have struck a more decisive blow if they had abandoned the coasts for the rivers.

Some of their guns they named for popular generals and, like "Burnside," the not so popular. His fellow Rhode Islanders here were perhaps more forgiving than others in the North. (USAMHI)

Governor William Sprague found this namesake at the southwest corner of Pulaski's parapet, commanding a scene that inspired confidence in Union might. (USAMHI)

Officers of the 48th New York garrisoned the fort and posed for the camera along with their colonel, W. B. Barton, standing with his wife. Beyond them lay the mouth of the Savannah River and, in the distance, Tybee Island. (USAMHI)

Inside, on the parade ground, the band of the 48th New York and, on dress parade . . . (USAMHI)

. . . the 48th New York itself, complete with seldom seen white gloves. (USAMHI)

But always in the distance, just ten miles away to the northwest, lay Savannah, and Fort Pulaski must be, like the sentinel, ever vigilant. (USAMHI)

For the sea-based elements of the Southern squadron, there was much more to blockade duty than looking for runners. Army generals like Benjamin F. Butler might live in the plush cabins of their headquarters boats like the transport Ben DeCord *. . .* (USAMHI)

. . . but the Navy men had constant work to do. Maintaining the fleet in those Southern waters required extensive on-site facilities, like the machine and carpenters' shops in Station Creek, near Port Royal. (USAMHI)

Machine shops at Bay Point performed repairs, such as replacing the smoke stack of the monitor Passaic *after it was severely damaged in the April 7, 1863, attack on Charleston.* (USAMHI)

Most of the fleet repairing took place at this floating shop in Machine-Shop Creek, near Port Royal, where two old whaling ships, Edward *and* India, *were converted for the purpose.* (USAMHI)

A constant flow of ships passed into and out of Port Royal, ships like the monitor at center, the transport at left, and James Gordon Bennett's yacht Rebecca *at right.* (USAMHI)

Old ships of the line like the Vermont, *too aged for active service, came south to act as receiving and store ships.* (NAVAL HISTORICAL CENTER)

Captain John Rodgers, standing fourth from left in the center group, commanded the Vermont *at Port Royal and chafed that her massive array of guns remained silent.* (USAMHI)

For officers who had trained for active service, their—perhaps their only—war seemed to be merely one of watch and wait. Even the ship's dog seems bored with the blockade service. (USAMHI)

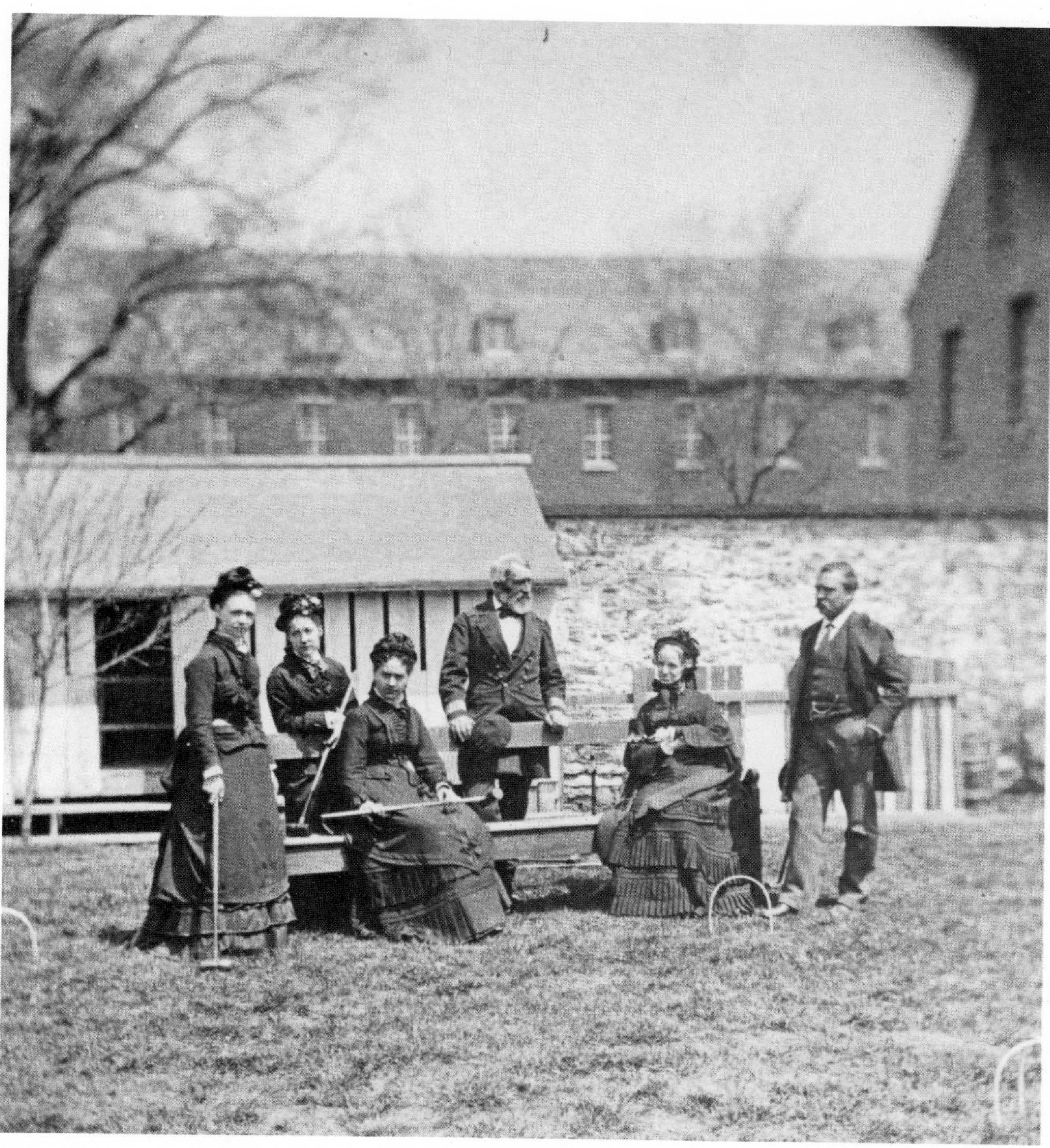

But certainly some were not bored. Poor Commander George Preble, standing center at the Philadelphia Navy Yard in this early postwar image, was dismissed from the service in 1862 for allowing a Confederate cruiser to run the blockade into Mobile, but then was restored to his rank and sent to Port Royal. He commanded the coal depot for a time, and near the end of the war actually led a "fleet brigade" in fighting on shore. (USAMHI)

Real action came to the squadron in 1863, as blockaders, enemy ironclads, and attacks on Charleston kept the fleets busy. On April 7, Du Pont, against his better judgment, attacked Charleston and saw his ironclad fleet severely battered. Ships like the Passaic *visibly displayed their damage.* (USAMHI)

The officers even posed beside their dented turret. (NA)

The USS Nahant *took 36 hits on its turret, which was completely disabled during the fighting. She appears here shortly afterward in Machine-Shop Creek, with the floating machine shops barely visible in the distant background to the left. The powerful 15-inch Dahlgren and 11-inch Dahlgren smoothbores peering out of the turret were useless to her in the attack.* (USAMHI)

Yet the Nahant *was revenged a bit. She joined the* Weehawken *in June 1863, with Captain John Rodgers now commanding the latter.* (USAMHI)

The two of them passed the Frying Pan Shoals Lightship and steamed to Wassaw Sound. The Nahant *is the monitor in the right background.* (USAMHI)

Together they battled and captured the formidable Confederate ironclad Atlanta, *shown here after she was converted to Federal service and sent to the James River in Virginia.* (NA)

Captain W. A. Webb was the Atlanta*'s luckless commander. He spent the next several months in Fort Warren Prison.* (MC)

So did Lieutenant George H. Arledge. (WA)

And 1st Assistant Engineer W. J. Morell. (WA)

And Gunner T. B. Travers. (WA)

And poor Midshipman J. Peters. (WA)

And soon after the capture of the Atlanta *there came a new face to the South Atlantic Blockading Squadron, Rear Admiral John A. Dahlgren, shown here at center with his staff aboard his flagship, the USS* Pawnee. (NHC)

When it was first decided to replace the hapless Du Pont, Washington opted for a naval hero from the West, Admiral Andrew Hull Foote, who relinquished his command of the Mississippi flotilla after the successes at Forts Henry and Donelson and Island No. 10 due to a wound. On June 4, 1863, he received orders to relieve Du Pont, but three weeks later, before he could assume command, he died. (CWTI)

Once again the crews and their guns readied for an attack. The after 10-inch Dahlgren smoothbore aboard the Wabash, *the gun designed by the new squadron commander.* (USAMHI)

The Wabash'*s forward pivot gun, a mammoth 200-pound rifle. Captain H. B. Lowrey, commanding the ship's Marine contingent, stands bearded in the center, while one of his Marines brandishes a much smaller rifle at the far left.* (USAMHI)

Another great Dahlgren aboard the Wabash, *dubbed the "Truth Seeker."* (USAMHI)

The USS Pawnee, *ready for battle.* (NA)

Dahlgren's signalmen aboard the Pawnee *will transmit his orders to the fleet during the impending attack on Charleston.* (LC)

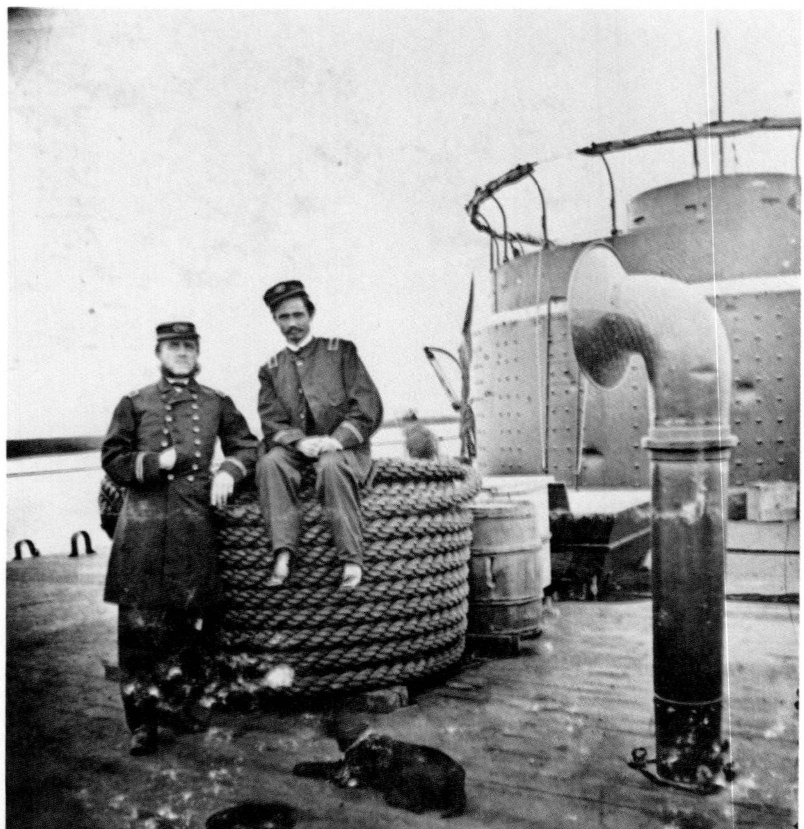

Yet Dahlgren's attacks are no more successful than Du Pont's. The monitor Patapsco's *turret shows the beating it takes.* (USAMHI)

The USS Dai Ching *is no more successful, though later in the year she will go on to capture a blockade-runner before being ordered to Florida.* (USAMHI)

But for the Dai Ching *the war will end on February 3, 1865, when she goes down off Savannah.* (USAMHI)

Again in September, Dahlgren sends his monitors against Fort Sumter, and again without success. For the Patapsco *there are only more dents in the turret.* (USAMHI)

Dahlgren himself went aboard the Montauk *for his September bombardment, but its most famous passenger would come nineteen months later, when the body of John Wilkes Booth was brought here briefly before its burial. Here, too, some of the other conspirators in the Lincoln murder were imprisoned.* (DAM, LSU)

After the attacks of the summer of 1863, the squadron settled down to the routine of hunting blockade-runners, and effectively at that. The USS Nipsic *captured the runner* Julia *on June 27, 1864.* (USAMHI)

The fragile runners could not hope to match powerful guns aboard gunboats like the Nipsic. *If they were unable to get away, they surrendered without a fight.* (USAMHI)

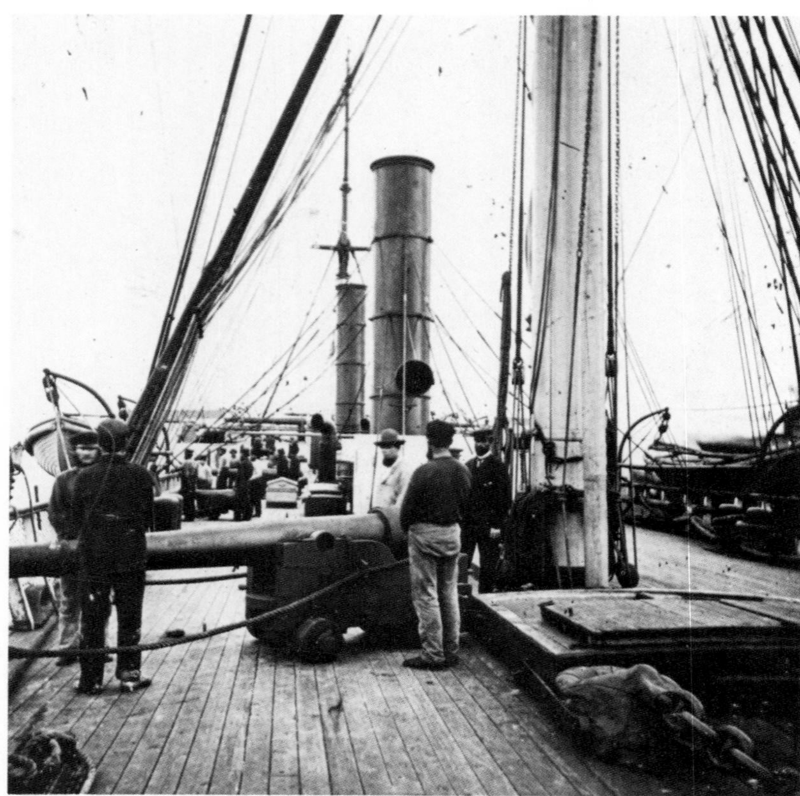

Sometimes even lightly armed transport ships like the Arago *managed to effect a capture or two.* (USAMHI)

The Arago, *shown in this Samuel A. Cooley view, took part in the celebrated capture of the runner* Emma, *loaded with cotton, turpentine, and resin.* (NA)

The mortar schooner USS Para *lent a hand in taking the* Emma, *though this mighty mortar, "Old Abe," was not called on in the fight, for there was no fight.* (USAMHI)

Gentlemen like this blockade-runner captain, posing calmly with a Confederate banner in Havana, were the wary quarry. (HP)

And their ships were the coveted prizes. Frequently they ran them aground rather than surrender, only to see the vessels battered by the waves. Here, on Morris Island, near Charleston, lie the remains of the Ruby. (USAMHI)

And here the wreck of the blockade runner Colt, *near Sullivan's Island, in 1865. It was a sad end for these greyhounds of the sea.* (USAMHI)

The squadron extended down to Florida as well, and there Commander John R. Goldsborough patrolled in his USS Florida, *helping in the 1862 capture of Fernandina.* (USAMHI)

While for others the age-old game of wait went on. The old ship of the line Alabama *was laid down in 1819, but was never launched until April 23, 1864, forty-five years later! She hit the water with a change in name, now the USS* New Hampshire, *and went south to Dahlgren.* (USAMHI)

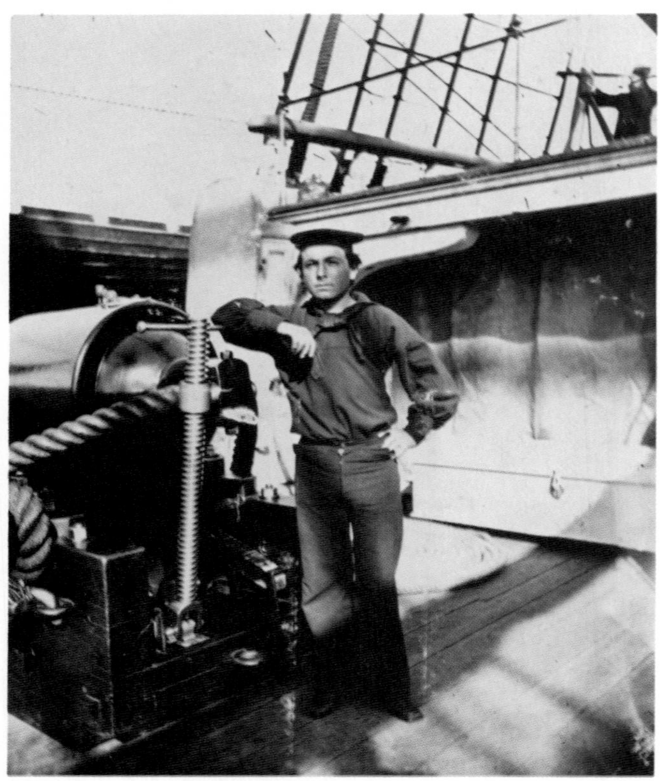

There her crew would not see action but simply relieve the Vermont *as a stores and depot ship. It was an ignominious end for these mighty ships of oak.* (USAMHI)

And so the work went on. Work done by a hundred forgotten vessels and thousands of unsung men. Little armed transports like the Nelly Baker *did their share.* (NA)

So did the giant transports like the Cahawba, *shown here in June 1864, probably in Hampton Roads.* (USAMHI)

There was little the Confederates could send against them except their innovative but ineffective little "Davids," the cigar-shaped torpedo boats that Southerners hoped might sink a few of the Goliaths strangling their ports. One rests here at the Bay Point machine shop, captured by the Federals and photographed by Cooley. (WRHS)

While the "Davids" were not too successful, the Confederate submarine CSS H. L. Hunley *managed to sink the USS* Housatonic *in Charleston Harbor before she went down herself in mysterious circumstances. The USS* Canandaigua *shown here swooped in to pick up the survivors from the first ship in history to be sunk by a submarine.* (GLADSTONE COLLECTION)

Another "David" appears, beached near Charleston, its propeller broken, its torpedo spar extending from its nose. They were makeshift vessels, little better than coffins. (NA)

And at war's end they seemed everywhere along Charleston's waterfront. (NA)

Even in Washington's navy yard they were to be seen tied up next to Yankee monitors. They were the last tangible evidence of the vain efforts of the Confederacy to combat the power of the South Atlantic Blockading Squadron. (NHC)

Partners in Posterity

A PORTFOLIO

Haas & Peale and their incomparable record of siege in South Carolina

IN 1863, AS FEDERAL MINIONS sought relentlessly to take Charleston, their major obstacle was Fort Sumter and the ring of earthwork forts built around the South Carolina city. In a chapter in Volume IV of this series, *Fighting for Time,* the story of the Siege of Charleston was told. However, there were a pair of photographers there who told much of the story themselves in images far better than words. They were Haas & Peale of Morris Island and Hilton Head. Their 1863 images depicting General Quincy Gillmore's efforts to take Charleston represent almost the total corpus of their Civil War work. Except for a few portraits and random images, Haas & Peale seem to appear in Civil War photography with their arrival at Morris Island, and then disappear again when they have done. Little more is known of them.

Yet if any artists of the war can rest securely knowing that their fame depends upon a single series of images, then surely Haas & Peale have safely made for themselves a niche in posterity with their Charleston views. They are somewhat unique in Civil War photography. Mathew Brady, Alexander Gardner, Samuel Cooley, and others attempted to create and market series of images showing battle and campaign scenes, yet they offered them to the public only in oversized "imperial" prints too unwieldy for casual collecting, stereo views that required a stereo viewer, or else in the small *carte-de-visite* format that offered little detail for large outdoor scenes. Haas & Peale, however, created a series of over 40 serially numbered views around Charleston in a medium-sized format that offered the advantages of size, chiefly quality, without the disadvantages attendant to the oversize prints.

Alas, it remained for others to gain public acceptance of this new photographic style in the years after the war when the cabinet photograph enjoyed its vogue. But though their innovation did not last, still the work of Haas & Peale has lasted, a reminder of perhaps the most accomplished photographic partnership of the war.

Here on Morris Island, spread out toward the horizon, sprawls the camp of the 9th Maine Infantry. (USAMHI)

They made a virtual tent city, huddled along the shoreline to catch the ocean breezes in the hot, humid summer. (USAMHI)

Undaunted by the heat, General Gillmore and his staff posed in reasonably full uniform for the partners. Gillmore sits at center striking a contemplative pose as he ponders an enormous map captioned "Charleston, South Carolina." Arrayed here and there are a variety of shells and solid projectiles to lend a suitable warlike atmosphere. (USAMHI)

Still, Gillmore, too, could seek some relief from the sun and heat in his tent headquarters on Folly Island. (USAMHI)

There was less relief for the men manning the siege guns that pounded Fort Sumter and the other Charleston forts, however. Here are three 100-pounder Parrott rifles in Battery Rosecrans, all trained on Sumter. (HUGH LOOMIS COLLECTION, KA)

Things do not always go as planned, including cannon shells. One of those 100-pounders had a shell burst before it cleared the muzzle, creating a considerable curiosity for men and officers of the battery. (USAMHI)

An equal curiosity were men from the webfoot service doing shore gun duty. This naval battery of two 80-pounder Whitworth rifles threw its shells, too, at Fort Sumter. Just so no one would forget where they came from, the naval deck carriage of the rifle at right carries the legend "Rear Admiral S. F. Du Pont, Port Royal, S.C." It also carries a pair of boots and some laundry drying in the sun. (USAMHI)

The mammoth 300-pounder Parrott rifle in Battery Strong. (NYHS)

In some places Gillmore built his batteries on artificial islands made of pilings driven into the swamps, or else on little more than built-up sand spits. Here in Battery Hays sat one such gun emplacement, this one for an 8-inch Parrott rifle that is, at the moment, dismounted. (CHS)

The rest of the guns in Battery Hays, however, these 30-pounder Parrott rifles, are more than ready to do service in the bombardment of Confederate Fort Wagner at the end of Morris Island. (SOUTH CAROLINA HISTORICAL SOCIETY, CHARLESTON)

This 300-pounder Parrott in Battery Brown got a bit carried away. (USAMHI)

Its neighbor manages to seem coolly indifferent. (NYHS)

Gillmore peppered Fort Sumter with everything, including these 10-inch siege mortars in Battery Reynolds, here aimed at Fort Wagner. One of the mortar shells can be seen dangling between the two soldiers at extreme left. (NYHS)

These two 100-pounder Parrotts in Battery Meade are attempting to blast a breach in the masonry walls of Sumter. All that they and their fellow batteries will succeed in doing, in fact, is in reducing the fort to a shapeless mound of rubble that will never surrender. (SOUTH CAROLINA HISTORICAL SOCIETY)

Here at the headquarters of the field officer of the trenches, almost anything might be found, stretchers, beer bottles, spare shells, even an "infernal machine," a torpedo or mine. (HUGH LOOMIS COLLECTION, KA)

The telegraph operator, relaying orders and messages back and forth, really needed protection, and here in this bombproof he got it. (NYHS)

Everywhere those who did not live in tents went underground. Here in Fort Wagner, after its fall to Gillmore's army, Federals occupied the bombproofs once used by the Confederates. Earth and sand were happily neutral in this war—they would shield blue and gray alike. (USAMHI)

Life in the lens of Haas and Peale was a little better for the men at sea, even those serving aboard converted Staten Island ferry boats like the Commodore McDonough. *At least they could move a bit now and then, steam up to within range of one of the forts, throw a few shells, and then put back out to sea where the breezes cooled the guns and the men.* (USAMHI)

The gunboats could not count on navigational assistance from the Charleston lighthouse on Morris Island. In 1863 this is all that was left of it. (USAMHI)

And this is all that is left of a 300-pounder Parrott after a shell burst just inside the muzzle. Yet this gun could still be fired, and was. (USAMHI)

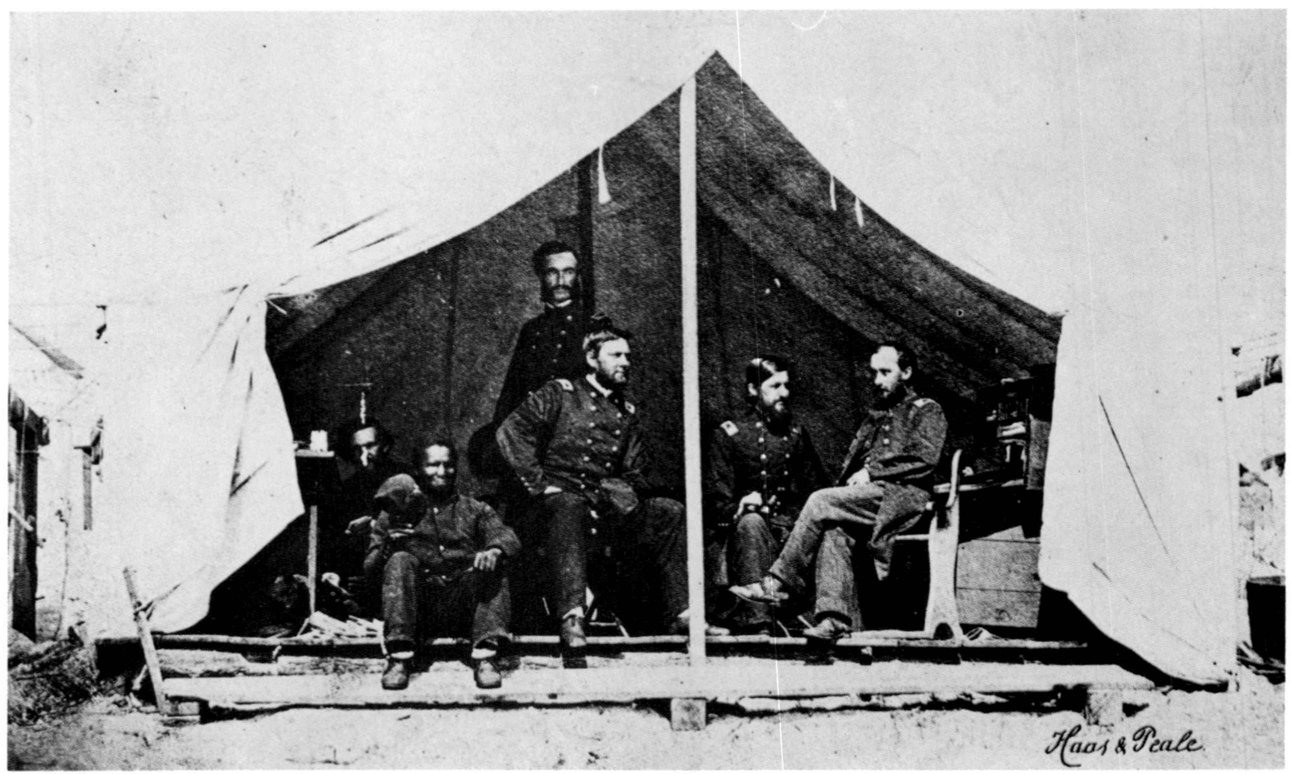

When not digging or firing, it was a siege of boredom for Gillmore's little army. These regimental officers had plenty of time to pose for Haas & Peale. (USAMHI)

Now and then, mostly for practice, Gillmore's field batteries drew up in formation, looking formidable, but utterly ineffectual against Sumter's walls or against Fort Wagner's earthworks and bombproofs. Battery B, 1st U.S. Artillery. (USAMHI)

The Beacon House on Morris Island was sufficiently ventilated that heat no longer appeared to be a problem. (USAMHI)

It could get awfully hot out there under the sun. (LC)

Haas & Peale.

But the heat and boredom got to a few, including this unfortunate fellow. He bears a sign proclaiming his offense: "THIEF. This Man, Benj. Ditcher, 55th Mass. Vol's, Stole Money From a Wounded FRIEND." Ditcher had his head shaved, his hands bound behind him, and was paraded through the camp by a guard carrying their rifles upside down and musicians playing the "Rogue's March." Ditcher, like the rest of the 55th Massachusetts, was a Negro, and his "wounded friend" was almost certainly injured in the skirmishing on Folly Island. (CHS)

An orderly delivers a message for the camera on Folly Island. The colonel receiving it is duly formal for the occasion, but the men in the neighboring tent seem unimpressed by the ceremony. (CHS)

Meanwhile the work of reducing Sumter went on, as did Haas & Peale's work of capturing it with their camera. Battery Kirby, with its two 8-inch seacoast mortars. (USAMHI)

One of the "splinter-proofs" to protect gunners from flying chunks of wood and debris as Confederate shells sporadically returned fire. (USAMHI)

In the seemingly endless siege work against Fort Wagner, Gillmore, ever the engineer, created miles of trenches and siege works, pushing parallels ever closer to Wagner. The workmen pushed this rolling sap ahead of them, dug behind it, and thus inched their way toward the fort. (SOUTH CAROLINA HISTORICAL SOCIETY)

Meanwhile, the tent city grew ever larger, and the buildup of supplies never stopped. Gillmore was intent upon victory. (LC)

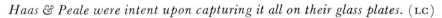

Haas & Peale were intent upon capturing it all on their glass plates. (LC)

And the irrepressible common soldiers on Morris Island were simply intent upon finding a shady spot wherever they could, even in the shadow of one of their wounded but still dangerous monsters. (USAMHI)

Into the Wilderness

ROBERT K. KRICK

Grant and Lee meet at last, and will not part

BRANDY STATION and Stevensburg and Culpeper had seen some bitter fighting before the war reached 1864. The locale seemed to attract cavalry forces and mounted charges. In the spring of 1864, however, the whole width and breadth of Culpeper County seemed to be carpeted with Northern canvas. The mighty Federal host was commanded by George G. Meade, but it was to be accompanied on its operations by the general-in-chief of all the Northern armies, U. S. Grant.

On May 4, Grant and Meade launched their long-suffering Army of the Potomac across the Rapidan River into dangerous country. Pontoon bridges carried seasoned veterans and frightened youngsters alike into the Wilderness of Spotsylvania. The river crossings at Germanna Ford and Ely's Ford were historic ones. Lafayette had been here two generations before; this same army had crossed these same fords to disaster just one year and five days earlier.

The Wilderness was a dank and unlovely piece of country, about 70 square miles in extent. Its tangled brush and confusing ravines had enfolded and bemused Joe Hooker's army during 1863's Chancellorsville Campaign. The 1864 edition of the same Federal force might be mired in the same morass, and the Confederate Army of Northern Virginia was just the agency to collaborate with the Wilderness in the undertaking.

R. E. Lee had reunited his army in the month before the Wilderness fighting opened. His I Corps had been on an ill-starred winter campaign in Tennessee, suffering through James Longstreet's failure as an independent strategist. General officers languishing in arrest and deteriorating morale in the ranks gave evidence of the change in the old reliable body. When Lee reviewed the returning corps near Gordonsville, the atmosphere was electric. A hard-nosed brigadier, not given to outbursts of emotion, wrote, "The General reins up his horse, & bares his good gray head, & looks at us & we shout & cry & wave our battle flags & look at him again. . . . The effect was that of a military sacrament."

Federal columns thrusting through the Wilderness on May 5 were threatened from the west by two separate Confederate corps moving on the Orange Turnpike and the Orange Plank Road. The battle was fought along those two corridors. Dense intervening Wilderness segregated the two fights into bitter enclaves, all but independent of each other. Richard S. Ewell's II Corps and the Union V Corps contested the Turnpike. Fighting raged with particular ferocity around a small clearing

The quiet general from the West, come east to face the undefeatable Lee. U. S. Grant was a lieutenant general, the only man of such rank in the Union Army, and now he commanded all of Lincoln's forces in the field. Grant, with his horse Cincinnati, in early June 1864. (NA)

known as Saunder's Field or Palmer's Field. The Turnpike bisected the field and a shallow wash ran perpendicular to the road. A Union battery in the clearing was repeatedly taken and retaken. Infantrymen from both armies sought shelter in the draw. Both sides entrenched with desperate enthusiasm.

Muzzle flashes in the woods ignited leaves, the fire spread to brush and trees, and soon the wounded were burning to death. The sound of cartridge boxes exploding could be heard over the crackling of flames. Federal wounded who could be reached were carried back to surgical stations beyond the Lacy house, "Ellwood," where Stonewall Jackson's arm had been buried twelve months earlier. There were also Federal hospitals farther east toward Wilderness Church and other landmarks from the Chancellorsville Campaign. Skeletons of the unburied dead from that earlier fight were macabre prophets, watching the wounded thousands streaming back.

The costly stalemate achieved during May 5 along the Turnpike was duplicated two miles to the south, along the Plank Road. George W. Getty's division of the U.S. VI Corps stood strong around the intersection of the Plank and Brock roads. The Confederate III Corps followed A. P. Hill up to the fringe of the key intersection and threatened to make it their own, thus isolating the sizable Northern force which had advanced farther south—and setting the stage for destroying the stranded Federals. But the balance of affairs swung away from A. P. Hill and by the end of the day his forces were in dire straits. Hancock's II Corps had pushed the Confederates to the point of breaking when darkness halted operations. One third of Lee's army had not yet reached the field—the I Corps—and its arrival during the night was the only way to forestall disaster.

Grant had spent the 5th near the intersection of the Turnpike with the road from Germanna Ford. He had directed most of the VI Corps under John Sedgwick to strengthen the right flank, above the Turnpike. The troops had moved obliquely into the fray, turning off the Germanna Road near Mrs. Spotswood's house and heading southwest on what was known as the Culpeper Mine Road.

Throughout the 6th of May, Ewell's Confederates and the troops of Sedgwick and Warren struggled inconclusively along the Turnpike. The fragmented gains and losses in the woods yielded a frightful casualty count but no real tactical advantages. John B. Gordon alertly discovered a golden opportunity to turn the Federal right and destroy it; the potential rewards were dazzling. Corps commander Ewell, of the striking personality and the fatal irresolution, equivocated. Not until R. E. Lee arrived in the area during the evening could Gordon get approval to pluck his prize. Gathering darkness constricted the opportunity, but Gordon had little trouble in catching several hundred prisoners—two Union brigadiers among them. The Georgian always believed, using some fragile but persuasive hypothesis, that the lost opportunity was among the greatest that ever slipped through Southern fingers.

Meanwhile, the separate battle along the Plank Road on May 6 had caromed from the brink of Confederate disaster to the brink of Northern disaster and then settled comfortably near a neutral,

He would station himself with the Army of the Potomac and send it into the Wilderness to find Lee and never let him go. Here Grant sits in June 1864, at Cold Harbor, after the Wilderness Campaign is over. Seated beside him is his chief of staff, Brigadier General John A. Rawlins. Standing is Major Theodore S. Bowers. (CHS)

All through that winter and early spring of 1864 the Army of the Potomac prepared itself for the drive into the Wilderness. Part of the army was stationed around Culpeper, Virginia, including the brigade of Brigadier General Alexander S. Webb, standing, hand on sword, in front of his tent. His brigade was almost wiped out by Pickett's Charge at Gettysburg, and in the coming campaign Webb will nearly lose his life. An A. J. Russell image. (USAMHI)

if bloody, equilibrium. Hancock threw his II Corps into a solid attack early in the morning, exploiting the success he had won the previous evening. Longstreet's corps was not in line, despite Lee's expectations. The Southerners were driven in disorder along the Plank Road all the way back to a small clearing where stood the house and orchard of a widow named Tapp. Lee's army faced disaster. Veteran units, overwhelmed, ran "like a flock of geese."

In this extremity, the first of Longstreet's arriving men filtered into the clearing. Lee's desperation showed through his usually calm mein as he tried to lead the reinforcements into action. They turned his horse back forcibly and promised to restore the situation. The episode was the first of four "Lee to the rear" incidents during a seven-day period. The Federal initiative was blunted, then turned back. Lee grasped the initiative for his own. A flanking movement down an unfinished railroad grade (the same that had figured prominently at Chancellorsville) rolled up the Federal lines "like a wet blanket," in the words of Hancock. At the height of the Confederate surge, Longstreet and General Micah Jenkins were shot down by the mistaken fire of advancing Confederates. In the aftermath, momentum dissipated and the Confederates were obliged to accept a result which forestalled Southern disaster but did not inflict a thorough defeat on the enemy. Longstreet's wounds were thought to be mortal but he recovered and returned to duty in October; Jenkins died during the afternoon.

Nearby, just north of Brandy Station, sat the VI Corps. Here Major General John Sedgwick made his headquarters in the home of Dr. Welford. Sedgwick himself stands third from the right. He will not survive the campaign. (WAR LIBRARY AND MUSEUM, MOLLUS-PENNSYLVANIA, PHILADELPHIA)

The Northern army had come across the Rapidan nearly 120,000 strong. Lee was able to counter with about 65,000 men of all arms. That lopsided arithmetic actually grossly understates the case, because the Southern barrel was scraped to its bottom and the Northern barrel was virtually without bottom. Two days of bloodshed in the Wilderness had cost Grant perhaps 18,000 readily replaceable pieces of his army. It had cost Lee less than half that many irreplaceable troops. (Numbers and losses verities—always subject to divergent interpretations—are especially elusive in the 1864 spring campaigns.) Precedent clearly showed Grant the route back across the Rapidan. But the general-in-chief had his eye set on some ghastly and inexorable logic based in the simplest forms of arithmetic—addition and subtraction. On the night of the 7th he prodded the Army of the Potomac into a lunge to the southeast, where there would be unquestioned opportunity to destroy more of the dwindling crop of Southern boys who stood between the North and victory.

Grant's move was toward Spotsylvania Court House, an unobtrusive country settlement composed of three churches and a hotel and a store and a few county buildings. Lee's men raced Grant's for the place, starting long before any other ranking Confederates had deduced what was afoot. Lee's prescience won the race for his side by a matter of seconds. The Federals slogged southeastward along the Brock Road. Southern cavalry resisted the advance from each hedgerow and wood line. Near Todd's Tavern there was a violent clash with Federal cavalry, which was otherwise notably ineffective during this move.

While tired Federal infantry fought and stumbled down the Brock Road, the Confederate I Corps marched most of the night along a parallel route farther west. Richard H. Anderson had had command of the corps since Longstreet's wounding, and he got a very early start. On the morning of May 8, advance elements of Anderson's command were within a mile of the key intersection, which was near a farm called Laurel Hill. Alarms

All around Brandy Station the tents of the waiting Federals sat through the winter. The men were anxious for another chance at "Bobby Lee." (P-M)

reached them, and they rushed forward just in time to hurl back the first Federal infantry to approach the intersection.

The Union troops were members of Warren's V Corps. The men had been fighting or marching, with little or no rest, for five days. As more of them came up, someone set the bands to playing as faint encouragement, and more assaults were attempted, with the same fatal results. A Confederate officer riding along the lines spied his little brother, an artillerist just through his first action, sheltered behind a dead horse. The boy jumped to his feet, flushed with his newfound valor, and called incongruously across the deadly field, "Bubba, Bubba, I wasn't scared a bit—not a bit!"

Federal reinforcements stumbled into line and Confederate reinforcements arrived opposite them. Both sides entrenched quickly and deeply. After darkness fell on May 8, the Southern line was stretched to the northeast in a great salient angle which came to be known as "The Mule Shoe" because of its shape. The next morning, as the lines were being consolidated, a Confederate sharpshooter firing from very long range killed John Sedgwick. The corps commander had been purposely standing under fire to encourage his men, saying, "They couldn't hit an elephant at this distance."

On May 10, brilliant young Emory Upton, of New York, led an attack against the Confederate salient's western shoulder. He had recognized the opportunity, sold the plan to his superiors, and executed the attack with skill. The absence of promised support kept the fruits of success beyond

Anxious, too, was the immediate commander of the Army of the Potomac, the only man in the army who had ever beaten Lee, Major General George Gordon Meade. Here he stands, fourth from the right, with some of his officers, among them Sedgwick—second from the right—and Brigadier General A. T. A. Torbert, far right, who commands a division of cavalry that will protect Meade's flank in the advance. (P-M)

reach, but when the Federals were driven back they took along a substantial number of prisoners.

Grant may have concluded that the time was ripe to take Lee head on; or perhaps he decided that that had always been the solution which earlier Federal leaders had missed; or perhaps his ghastly arithmetic suggested that any sort of fighting was going to do the job, and tactical niceties therefore verged on irrelevance. In any event, the successful frontal assault by Upton began a month of frontal assaults in which tens of thousands of Federals were shot with relative ease by sheltered Confederates.

Two days after Upton's temporary success, the Army of the Potomac went right over the top of the Confederates' Mule Shoe earthworks and raised havoc with Lee's entire position. An early morning assault by the Federal II Corps under Hancock shattered the nose of the salient and pushed into the heart of the Southern lines. Near the McCoull house the advance was blunted. Desperate counterattacks pushed the Federals back to the tip of the salient and then the fight deteriorated into a brutal brawl at arm's length for some 20 hours. Only earthworks separated the ragged lines as they fought in the rain and mud and blood. Quite early in the struggle a 20-inch-thick oak tree toppled to the ground, having been chewed off by the incessant streams of balls flying in such profusion that the hard wood was gnawed as thoroughly as though by beavers. When Confederate survivors stumbled back to a new line across the base of the

But there were some old faces in the army that would not be going, and one of them that Meade would not miss was Major General William H. French. Here he stands, fifth from the left, among officers of his III Corps. Meade blamed French for the failure to bag Lee the previous November, and shed no tears when the III was reorganized out of existence and French himself mustered out of active service. (USAMHI)

salient, their abandoned works had more than justified the *nom de guerre* "The Bloody Angle."

The logistics which controlled the will of generals had dictated a change of base to Grant. His lifeline was shifted from his right rear at Culpeper to his left rear by way of Fredericksburg to the Potomac River at Belle Plain landing. The success of the early morning attack on the salient on May 12 was traceable in part to a coincidence resulting from Grant's change of base. Lee received word of the activity in that direction and for once his uncanny perception of enemy intentions failed him. He feared a major enemy move to the southeast (which eventually came on May 21), and weakened his front line in preparation for a countermove of his own. That fringe benefit was unknown to Grant, but the logistical merits were large. The maritime might of the North steamed to Belle Plain and made it into an overnight city. Confederate prisoners and Federal wounded were funneled out through the landing; recruits and war material and horses passed them en route to the front.

The grisly night of May 12 also brought terrible news to Lee from Richmond. J. E. B. Stuart had been harrying Federal raiders, who were being led toward Richmond by Philip Sheridan. On May 11 a severe cavalry fight had taken place at Yellow Tavern, just north of the capital. Promising young North Carolina Brigadier James B. Gordon had been killed and Stuart himself had suffered a mortal wound. He died in Richmond during the evening of the 12th, while distraught friends and colleagues sang "Rock of Ages" at his request.

Back at Spotsylvania, Grant had Meade moving his army steadily around to its left flank. Warren's

V Corps, which had started the battle on the right, moved around to the far left and set up headquarters at the Francis Beverly house, not far from the Court House. Every day there was fighting of varying intensity; sometimes it was localized, sometimes it spread along the lines, but always there was fighting. On May 18, Grant ordered Meade to move against the strongly fortified Confederate main line. Defending artillery so thoroughly swept the attackers that many Confederate infantrymen hardly noticed the whole affair. Meade wrote disgustedly to his wife that finally "even Grant found it useless to knock our heads against a brick wall."

On May 19, Lee sent most of his II Corps, under Ewell, to swing up behind the abandoned Bloody Angle and probe the right rear of the new Federal alignment. The result was an intense struggle around the Harris farm. The Confederates played havoc with some green heavy-artillery regiments, which fought with admirable tenacity, although only recently converted to infantry service. In the confusion many Federal units fired on one another. A disgusted quartermaster watched "Kitching's brigade firing at the enemy; then Tyler's men fired into his; up came Birney's division and fired into Tyler's; while the artillery fired at the whole damned lot." In the final analysis, Ewell had more than he could handle and fell back in confusion under cover of some horse artillery which happened along. The newly blooded Federal heavy artillerists buried their own dead and the Confederate dead around the Harris house and the nearby home of Widow Alsop. Black troops of Ambrose Burnside's IX Corps played a small role in this affair; it was their first action with the Army of the Potomac.

When the armies moved away from Spotsyl-

Finally came May 4, 1864, the great day. Grant ordered the army to move, and the once-teeming winter camps were deserted. James Gardner caught this scene near Brandy Station shortly before the army moved out. (LC)

The first to cross was the V Corps, its wagon train seen here rolling over a bridge at Germanna Ford on the Rapidan. Timothy O'Sullivan photo. (USAMHI)

vania on May 21 they left behind the bloodiest ground in North America. The campaigns in the vicinity from 1862 to 1864 had resulted in more than 100,000 casualties. Grant's route took him past Massaponax Baptist Church in the eastern fringe of Spotsylvania County. A Federal surgeon riding past the church noticed the generals and their entourage seated in the yard of the church on pews. He also watched the ungainly snout of a camera poking out of an upstairs church window recording the high command at deliberations as the Army of the Potomac was being spurred southward on May 21, 1864. The new movement prompted another change of base by the Federals, this time to Port Royal on the Rappahannock River. Grant luxuriated in the flexibility which Union naval prowess gave him.

For two days the armies raced for an advantage, then for five days (May 23–27) they fought and maneuvered along the North Anna River. There were four main river crossing points from west to east: Jericho Mills, Quarles Mills, Ox Ford, and at the Chesterfield Bridge. The commanding heights of the north bank of the river overlooked the south bank and its river flats at all of these points except Ox Ford. Lee skillfully anchored his line at Ox Ford, where the terrain made it all but impossible for the Federals to force a crossing. He then fortified a strong line running away from the river in two lines, covering the absolutely vital rail facilities at Hanover Junction. The line formed an inverted "V," with its apex at Ox Ford.

The Army of the Potomac laid pontoons at the other three crossing points and pushed across in strength. The heaviest skirmishing was in the vicinity of Jericho Mills. Lee pulled his units back into the entrenched line and contemplated a superb opportunity to hurt Grant. The Confederate grip on

Timothy O'Sullivan recorded the ensuing crossings as the Army of the Potomac supplied the campaign that would drive Lee to cover. Soldiers of the VI Corps cross on pontoon bridges over the Rappahannock at Fredericksburg later in May. (LC)

Ox Ford meant that Lee could move his troops to either side of his line for an attack on a Federal fragment; Federals rallying to the point of attack from the other end of the line would be forced to trek in a huge half circle and cross the river twice. The opportunity was an exciting one, but the prospects for execution revealed the state of Lee's army. Not only was mighty Stonewall gone, but also A. P. Hill was not meeting Lee's needs, Ewell was freshly relieved of his command, and the army could not be put to the task with the verve that had made it famous.

Lee himself was suffering physically during the week and was unable to personally carry the command load at the corps level, although that was to be his lot for much of the remainder of his army's existence. Grant got away from North Anna unscathed. If he noticed the shadows that had been held from his path, and had some understanding of his good fortune, he must have seen reason for optimism; the Army of Northern Virginia had lost its power to assume the offensive, and the most egregious Federal blunders would yield no more than temporary embarrassment.

The next move to the southeast took the Army of the Potomac from the North Anna to the Pamunkey River and beyond to Totopotomoy Creek. The Union columns poured across the Pamunkey at and near Hanovertown. Grant moved his supply base again, down to the White House on the

Awaiting them all was the man who had been the nemesis of so many Federals before them, General Robert E. Lee. There is a deceptive peacefulness about his visage in this image by Richmond photographers Vannerson and Jones. He will be ready for Grant and Meade. (CHS)

He will meet them first here, along the Orange Turnpike, four miles west of the Wilderness Church. This is Palmer's Field, and just visible at the base of the trees in the background are the hasty entrenchments behind which Lee awaits Warren. Photo taken late in 1865 or early 1866. (USAMHI)

Pamunkey. The house and estate had been owned by General W. H. F. Lee before the war and had connections with Lee's Custis and Washington ancestors. An earlier Federal occupation, during the 1862 Richmond operations, had left the house in ashes. Now it was to serve as the port of entry for another onset.

During the last five days of May there was heavy localized fighting but no widespread action. Through it all, Lee maintained a tenuous grip on the irreplaceable Virginia Central Railroad, barely west of his positions. There was a sharp cavalry fight north of Totopotomoy Creek on the 29th at Haw's Shop and another south of the creek at Old Church the next day. Also on the 30th the Confederates sent John Pegram's excellent brigade forward in an attack near Bethesda Church. Division commander Stephen D. Ramseur was widely blamed for the disastrous result of this attack. James B. Terrill of the 13th Virginia was killed; the Confederate Congress confirmed his nomination as brigadier general the next day.

The last meeting of the armies north of the James came at Cold Harbor. During the last night of May both armies completed the gradual slide to the southeast which had been leading to a crossroads called Cold Harbor. A few days short of two years earlier, Lee had fought on this same ground his first major battle as commander of the Army of Northern Virginia, driving McClellan from his po-

Charging against these log breastworks, Warren is unsuccessful. His men are caught in a deadly crossfire. An early postwar image. (USAMHI)

sition in the Battle of Gaines' Mill. Fitzhugh Lee's cavalry attempted to hold the Cold Harbor crossroads for the Confederates on May 31 but Alfred Torbert's Federal troopers forced Lee away. William F. "Baldy" Smith's XVIII Corps was coming along to help, having been transferred to this front from the scene of the ineffectual operations being bungled by Ben Butler below the James.

The dispute between Fitz Lee and Torbert served as a foundation on which both armies eventually built a network of fortifications. A good opening was lost to the Confederates on the morning of June 1 as a result of some inexperienced leadership and some well-handled Federal Spencer carbines. Late on the 1st, a determined Union assault won some ground from Lee, but at heavy cost. Grant planned a massive attack for June 2 but the delayed arrival of Hancock's II Corps resulted in a postponement until the next morning. Opportunistic Southern initiatives on each flank captured some prisoners during the day; among the Confederate dead was competent, seasoned brigade commander George P. Doles, a thirty-four-year-old Georgian.

About 4:30 on the morning of June 3, Grant sent the Army of the Potomac forward in a massive frontal assault which has since come to symbolize the nadir of generalship. The II, VI, and XVIII Corps attacked in directions which left their flanks exposed to vicious enfilade fire as well as head-on punishment. Within a few minutes the attacks had been beaten down, although many of the Northern survivors stubbornly held their ground near the Confederate lines and began to protect themselves with earthworks. The flames and smoke from Southern weapons hid their enemies

One of the defenders is Brigadier General John Marshall Jones, who leads his brigade in defense of those breastworks. During one of Warren's desperate assaults, Jones sat on his horse gazing at the approaching enemy when a bullet ended his life. (VM)

from the stunned Federals hugging the ground. The roar, they were certain, exceeded the musketry of any other battlefield, even without the artillery thunder. More than 7,000 Union troops had been shot within a few minutes. Four days later Grant requested a truce to tend to the survivors; for ten days the armies lay within 100 yards of each other. The heat and stench and flies and sharpshooters vied for attention. Trench warfare was becoming a way of life. The disgruntled chief of staff of the Federal VI Corps declared that Cold Harbor "was the dreary, dismal, bloody, ineffective close of the . . . campaign . . . and corresponded in all its essential features with what had preceded it."

While the armies glowered across the lines around Cold Harbor, events elsewhere in the state affected them. Union General David Hunter's predations in the Shenandoah Valley demanded Lee's attention. On June 13, Jubal Early led the Confederate II Corps away from Richmond toward Lynchburg. Lee was also obliged to weaken his army by detaching Wade Hampton, with two divisions of cavalry, in order to contain a Federal cavalry force raiding under Philip Sheridan. Below the James, Union forces under Benjamin Butler posed a threat to Richmond and Petersburg and the crucial rail net around those cities. On June 9 a scratch force defended Petersburg by the barest margin against Federal cavalry under August V. Kautz.

The same day that Early marched away toward the Valley, Lee discovered that Grant was moving away from Cold Harbor. In the tangled countryside between the Chickahominy and the James, Lee lost track of his adversary and Grant took advantage of the terrain to outmaneuver the Confederate commander. By June 16 almost all of the Army of the Potomac was across the James River, having crossed on a pontoon bridge of great length and marvelous engineering. From the 15th through the 18th, Petersburg was held by P. G. T. Beauregard against increasingly heavy masses of attackers. Beauregard knew what was happening and pleaded for reinforcements from Lee, but Lee was slow to respond, in part because Beauregard was habitually importunate.

An almost unbelievable series of accidents and failures kept the overwhelming Federal force from taking Petersburg when it was ripe for the taking. Odds ranging up toward ten-to-one were frittered away. The frustrated commander of the Army of the Potomac finally issued peremptory orders for an assault by each corps, regardless of supports which just could not quite be coordinated. When it was made, the precious opportunity had slipped away, and veteran Confederates had arrived to man the earthworks and destroy the attackers. Eager but unseasoned heavy artillerists-turned-infantrymen (the same who had stood so firmly at the Harris farm a month before) continued the attacks. Veterans tried to stop them with "Lie down, you damn fools, you can't take them forts." The damn fools lost more men in one regiment that day than any other Union regiment lost in any battle through the entire war! Grant had suffered about 12,000 casualties while failing to get into Petersburg. It would cost many more, and almost a year of trying, before the town finally fell.

Behind these defenses, the Confederates could withstand everything Warren hurled at them. It was to be a foretaste of the bitter, often inconclusive fighting of the Wilderness. Taken within months of the end of the war. (USAMHI)

During that day's fight on May 5, Warren made his headquarters in the Lacy House, seen in the far distance in this view taken from the Wilderness Tavern. The battle line lay just another mile over the hill. (USAMHI)

Still farther behind the line, though still taking its name from this tangled mass of woods and thickets, stood the Wilderness Church, itself almost lost among the trees. (USAMHI)

Many died that first day, among them Brigadier General Alexander Hays, shown here at his headquarters near Brandy Station. He stands tenth from the right, hand on hip. (COURTESY OF LLOYD OSTENDORF)

Viewed from the Orange Turnpike, the Wilderness Church nestles at left in the trees, with the Hawkins farm on the right. This was some of the only cleared ground in the vicinity of the battlefield. (NA)

The rest looked like this, these grinning skulls now as much a part of the Wilderness as the leaves and underbrush. (USAMHI)

On their way to the battle line, Warren's men and the others to follow came down the Germanna Plank Road to Wilderness Tavern, then marched straight down the Orange Turnpike, shown here running off to the horizon. The tavern stands at left. (USAMHI)

Sedgwick followed Warren into the battle with the Confederate defenses, his leading division belonging to Major General Horatio G. Wright. Wright, standing in the center beneath the peak of his tent, displays the VI Corps banner behind him. He seems almost to be smiling, and others definitely are. When this photo was made in June 1864 at Cold Harbor, Confederate shell fire was occasionally coming their way, and while the camera was laboriously being adjusted, one wag in the scene commented that he could "Wish a shell would hit the machine." *The officers were still smiling when the exposure was made.* (USAMHI)

The 56th Massachusetts and the 36th Massachusetts were both repulsed in a bloody assault the afternoon of May 6. At war's end their regimental colors were little better than rags. (USAMHI)

And some of the regiments that fought here were little better. Company I of the 57th Massachusetts went into the fighting on May 6 numbering 86 men. Several weeks later, these nine men, commanded by Sergeant R. K. Williams at right, were all that was left. (USAMHI)

Commanding Meade's II Corps was Major General Winfield Scott Hancock, seen here with his generals and staff. Leaning in front of the tree is Brigadier General Francis Barlow, who began the war as a private. Just to the right of the tree stands Hancock, and next to him is Major General David B. Birney. As the fighting left the Wilderness and moved on to Spotsylvania, Birney and Barlow won glory by capturing over 3,000 Confederates. In the front row next to Birney is Brigadier General John Gibbon. (USAMHI)

Colonel Samuel S. Carroll led one of Gibbon's brigades in the Spotsylvania fighting until a wound put him out of action. He won a brigadier's star for his conduct, but spent months recuperating, as shown here. (P-M)

The terrain in the Spotsylvania fighting was not any better than the Wilderness, tangled woods filled with Confederate rifle pits and log breastworks. (USAMHI)

Some, like the brilliant Confederate Brigadier General John B. Gordon, continued to win laurels as the campaign progressed. (VM)

Some, like Brigadier General James S. Wadsworth, were left behind, dead in the Wilderness. A Brady & Company photo, probably made in 1862 when Wadsworth was military governor of the District of Columbia. (ROBERT J. YOUNGER)

There were others who would not see Spotsylvania either. Caught in the accidental fire of his own Confederates, the popular and talented young South Carolina Brigadier Micah Jenkins took a bullet in the brain on May 6. In his delirium he urged his men forward, forward. (CHS)

And shot with Jenkins, though only wounded, was the commander of Lee's I Corps, his old war horse, Lieutenant General James Longstreet, back in Virginia after his ill-fated Knoxville Campaign. The wound put him out of the war for months. Probably an early postwar portrait, taken in New Orleans. (WA)

This is the view that Jenkins and Longstreet were not there to see. Timothy O'Sullivan's image was taken near Spotsylvania Court House. In the foreground are baggage wagons attached to the headquarters of the V Corps, Army of the Potomac. (LC)

Spotsylvania Court House itself, like so many of the places visited by these warring armies, was a simple country village until war made its name terrible. (USAMHI)

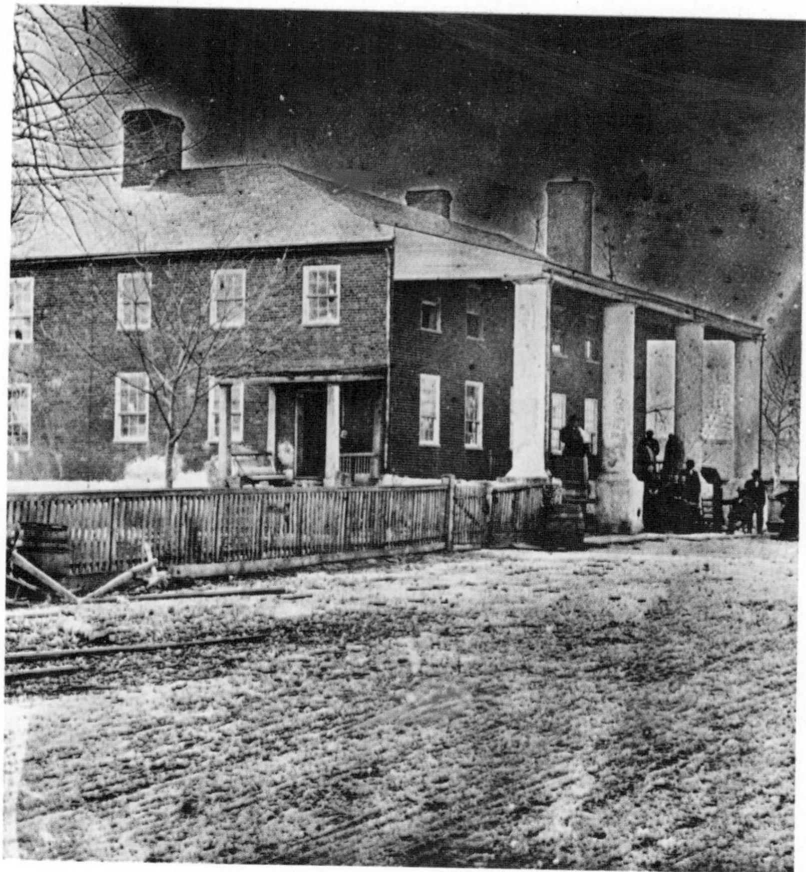

The Spotsylvania Hotel, near the Court House, in a late 1865 view. (USAMHI)

Opposite the hotel was so-called "Cash Corner." (USAMHI)

That same day, in the attempt to reach and hold Spotsylvania Court House before Lee could arrive, the Federals sent Brigadier General David McM. Gregg and his Second Cavalry Division on a reconnaissance that was stopped by the arrival of most of Lee's army. Gregg is seated at right. (USAMHI)

Some of the first fighting in the Spotsylvania operations took place here at Todd's Tavern at the junction of the Brock, Catharpin, and Piney Branch roads. Grant tried to use those roads to get around Lee but could not. (USAMHI)

The first Confederate to arrive on the scene at Spotsylvania was Major General Richard H. Anderson, now risen to replace the wounded Longstreet. Just in time he stopped the Federal drive for the Court House. (VM)

Leading one of Anderson's divisions was Major General Charles W. Field. After the war he took service in the army of the Khedive of Egypt. (USAMHI)

Fighting with him was Brigadier General Harry T. Hays, who received a desperate wound that left him convalescent for much of the rest of the war. (VM)

On May 9, Grant suffered a major loss when Major General John Sedgwick, commanding his VI Corps, was killed by a Confederate sharpshooter. "They couldn't hit an elephant at this distance," he calmly boasted just before the marksman's bullet brought him down. (USAMHI)

The next day, May 10, the desperate and bloody assaults that characterized the Spotsylvania fighting commenced. Warren's V Corps spearheaded much of it. His Second Division commander, Brigadier General Charles Griffin, is seen standing just right of the tent pole. There were few better soldiers in the army. (USAMHI)

Most brilliant of all was the attack led by Colonel Emory Upton, shown here wearing the brigadier's stars that his assault on "The Bloody Angle" won. He was just twenty-four. (NA)

It was some of the most desperate fighting anywhere in the war. Hardly a tree in the vicinity came through it without some memento such as this Confederate shell, found near the position of the 7th Rhode Island. (USAMHI)

Desperately, Confederates like this private, David Hicks of Virginia, sought to drive Upton back. (AMERICANA IMAGE GALLERY)

Two days later Grant ordered an even more massive attack where Upton's had almost succeeded. It was in an area called "The Mule Shoe," and here it was that Birney and Barlow overran the Confederates and captured several thousand. Reinforcements rushed to "The Mule Shoe," among them Brigadier General Abner Perrin. "I shall come out of this fight a live major general or a dead brigadier," he supposedly declared. He came out a dead brigadier. (P-M)

While the Spotsylvania fighting continued on into the middle of May, Grant constantly built up his supplies for the overland campaign through his supply base at Belle Plain, on the Potomac. Once it had belonged to the Confederates, and their earthworks could still be seen on the hill above the landing. (WRHS)

But in May 1864 it belonged to the Union, and it teemed with men and wagons. A Brady & Company image taken probably on May 16, 1864. (USAMHI)

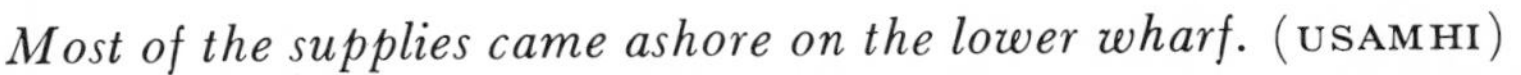
Most of the supplies came ashore on the lower wharf. (USAMHI)

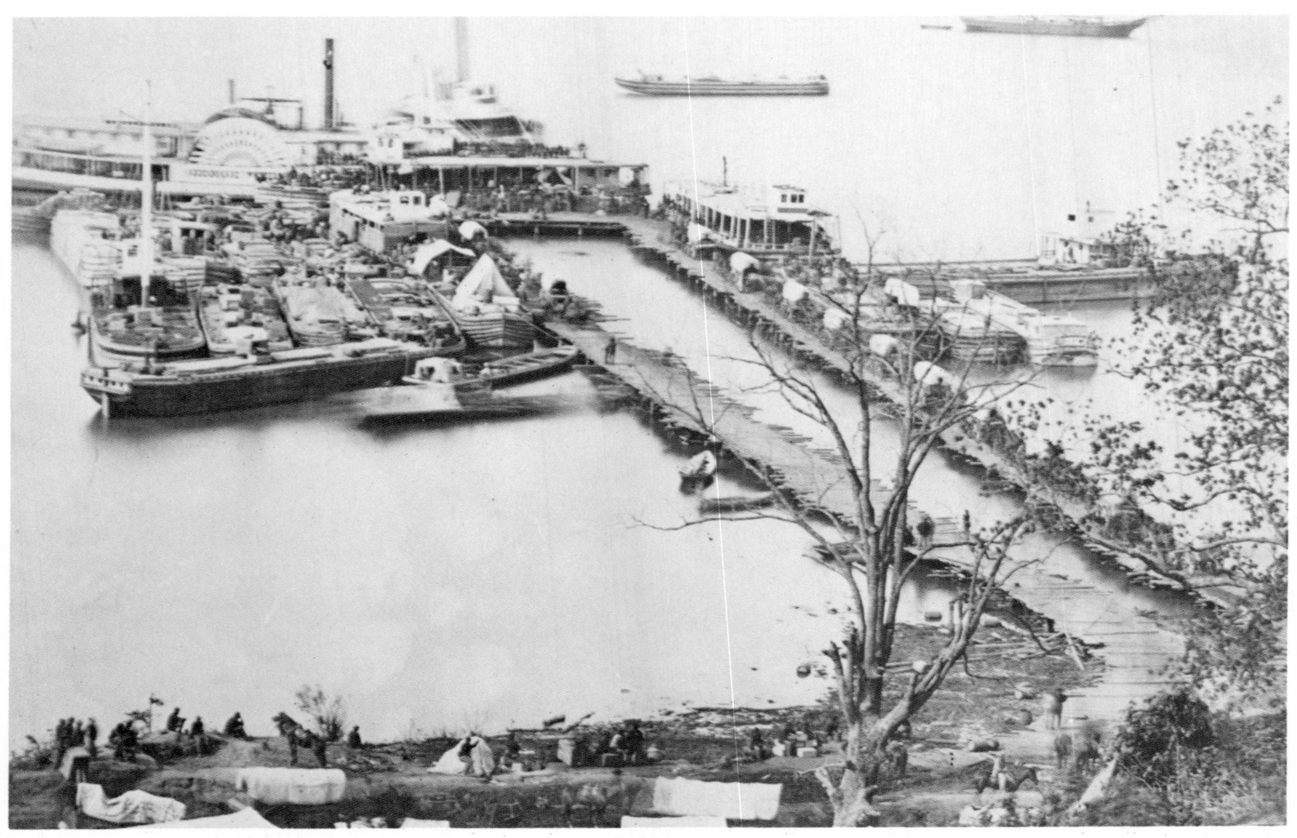

It saw the constant comings and goings of supply steamers as the wagons lined up on the wharf to take on their burdens. (USAMHI)

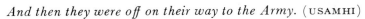

And then they were off on their way to the Army. (USAMHI)

Brigadier General James J. Abercrombie, seated at right, had just taken command at Belle Plain on May 12 and was still new to it when this and other Belle Plain images were taken. He was one of the oldest officers on active service, born in 1798. He will later be relieved of command at Grant's next supply base when he appears to be "bewildered and lost." (KA)

A. J. Russell's view of the upper wharf at Belle Plain, just the day after engineers built it. Already a barge awaits unloading. (LC)

There was more than supply to contend with. For one thing, Grant was taking thousands of prisoners in the Spotsylvania fighting. Here a host of them wait at Belle Plain for transportation to prison camps in the North. (WRHS)

In the days ahead, Grant would take even more Confederates, many of them lean and tattered. (RINHART GALLERIES, INC.)

Then there were the wounded, like these stretched on the Marye House lawn in Fredericksburg. (USAMHI)

There would be more wounded and dead to come. One of the severest blows to Lee came at Yellow Tavern on May 11, when his beloved—if erratic—cavalry chief, Jeb Stuart, was mortally wounded. He was, perhaps, the last of the cavaliers. (VM)

While Stuart was dying, another bold cavalryman, Brigadier General James B. Gordon, took his own mortal wound. Slowly, Grant was bleeding Lee to death. Portrait by Vannerson and Jones of Richmond. (VM)

Many were already dead. Here at the Francis Beverly house mounds of earth may testify to the field burials. (WRHS)

The dead seemed uncountable. A Confederate who fell in the attack of May 19, when Lee tried vainly to probe Grant's right flank. (USAMHI)

Another dead Southerner, with nothing before him now but burial, and probably in an unidentified grave. (USAMHI)

O'Sullivan captured the scenes of burial with his camera in May, after the fighting near the Alsop house. As the dead man clutches at the air in rigor, at least one of the burial detail appears to be wearing a mask. The stench would be terrible if the men were not interred quickly. (LC)

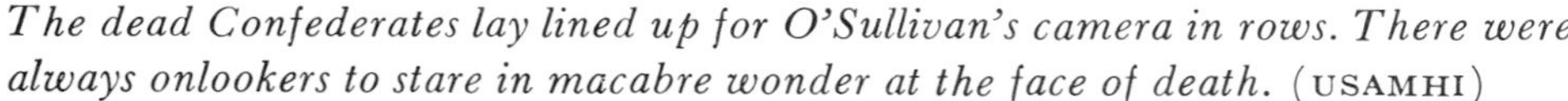

The dead Confederates lay lined up for O'Sullivan's camera in rows. There were always onlookers to stare in macabre wonder at the face of death. (USAMHI)

Back in Fredericksburg, artists photographed the interment of Federal dead. At least they would get caskets—rude though they were—and headboards. When there was more time later, they could be removed to permanent plots. A lens from Russell's equipment lies in the foreground. (USAMHI)

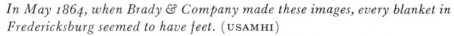

In May 1864, when Brady & Company made these images, every blanket in Fredericksburg seemed to have feet. (USAMHI)

Meanwhile, the campaign wore on, as Grant continued to try to get around Lee's flank. As the armies marched, Grant made his temporary headquarters on May 21 at Massaponax Church. (USAMHI)

Here he had aides pull pews out of the church so he could hold an open-air council of war. Happily, a photographer positioned his camera in one of the church's windows and recorded what followed. Grant sits on the pew at upper left, directly in front of the two trees. His cigar is in his mouth. Just left of him is probably his aide and brother-in-law, Colonel Frederick Dent. To the right of Grant sit Charles A. Dana, Assistant Secretary of War, and Chief of Staff Rawlins. General Meade sits at the upper end of the pew at far left. Next to him is an aide, and then sits Lieutenant Colonel Adam Badeau, Grant's military secretary, and then probably Grant's aide, Lieutenant Colonel Horace Porter. The man standing inside the circle of pews at right appears to be reading something aloud, to which Grant is listening. The blur in the background is caused by a constant flow of supply wagons moving to keep pace with the army. (USAMHI)

Grant has moved now and is leaning over the pew at left talking with Meade as they both look at a map. (USAMHI)

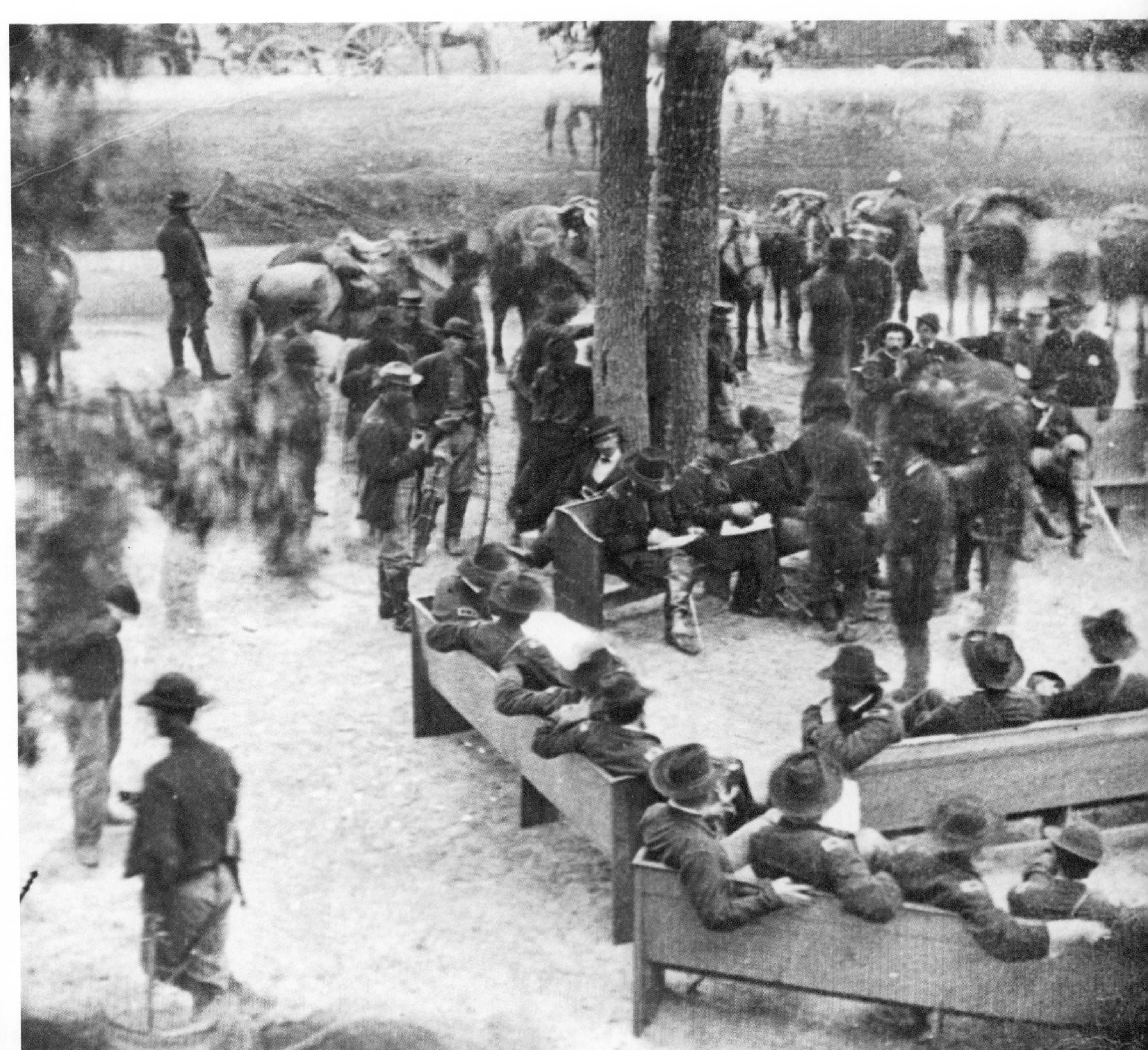

And now Grant is seated once more, writing out an order that will keep his army constantly on the move against Lee. (USAMHI)

Now the Federal commander changed his supply base from Belle Plain to Port Royal on the Rappahannock River. As his army advanced, Grant was able to make his supply bases advance with him, continuing the endless flow of succor to the marching Federals. (USAMHI)

To help protect his Rappahannock River supply base, Grant also enjoyed the cooperation of the Navy. Here the USS Yankee *poses on the river on May 19.* (USAMHI)

By May 23, Grant was on the North Anna River, 20 miles south of Spotsylvania, and Lee was waiting on the other side. That day Warren's V Corps began crossing here at Jericho Mill. This is what they saw ahead of them. (USAMHI)

There was only a shallow ford at first, but Warren quickly threw a pontoon bridge over to facilitate the passage of his wagons and artillery. (USAMHI)

The men who drove away the Confederate pickets at the ford were men like this Pennsylvania "bucktail," Private Samuel Royer of Company C, 149th Pennsylvania. Every man in the regiment wore a bucktail in his cap. Royer barely lived out the war, dying June 19, 1865, from the effects of a war wound. (TPO)

Warren's V Corps ammunition train crosses the bridge the day after Jericho Mill was taken. (USAMHI)

And here the 50th New York Engineers work at cutting a wagon road out of the tangled underbrush to make way for Warren's wagons. Every arm of the Army worked in coordination toward the common goal. (USAMHI)

The IX Corps crossed downstream at Quarles Mills, first attacking and overrunning Confederate works at the top of the hill. Then came another bridge, and thousands more Yankees were one river deeper into Virginia. (USAMHI)

Meanwhile, on May 23, as Warren crossed at Jericho, Hancock and his II Corps attacked the redoubt shown on the horizon that guarded the Chesterfield Bridge over the North Anna. They took the redoubt and swept over the bridge. O'Sullivan made this image only a few days later. (USAMHI)

And he took his camera inside the redoubt to capture the view of Yankee cavalry crossing over the bridge toward Hancock's camps in the distance. (LC)

The Federals soon settled into abandoned enemy works like this, where they could protect their important crossings over the North Anna. (USAMHI)

Yet another destroyed bridge, this one on the North Anna. (USAMHI)

All along the North Anna pontoon bridges sprang up to maintain the flow of foot and wagon traffic that sustained Grant's advance. This one was built by II Corps engineers, downstream from Chesterfield Bridge. (USAMHI)

But when Lee confronted Grant on the North Anna, the Federals simply pulled back and moved southeast once more, then crossed once again, this time over the Pamunkey River at Hanovertown Ferry. Lee was ready for him once more. (USAMHI)

Meanwhile, Grant once again shifted his supply base, this time from Port Royal on the Rappahannock to White House Landing on the Pamunkey, 15 miles downriver from Hanovertown Ferry. The first troops to arrive found only "inadequate means of landing." Yet by the time this image was made in June, White House was a busily functioning port. (WRHS)

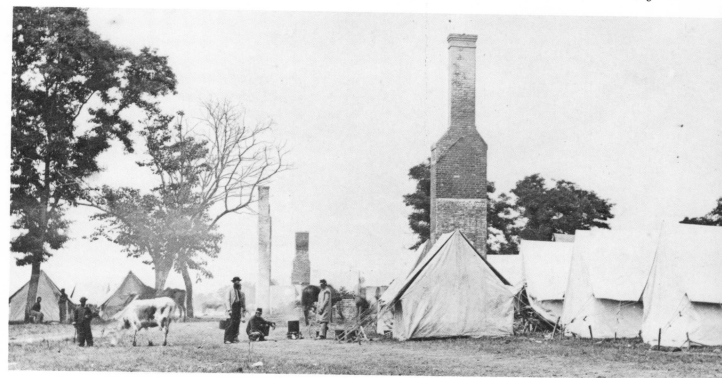

The landing took its name from the White House, which by May 1864 was nothing but lonely chimneys. The man in the felt hat with the beard may be David B. Woodbury, Brady's photographer. (KA)

Here it was that General Abercrombie became bewildered and had to be removed. For his soldiers, however, it was just one more supply base to keep Grant moving. (USAMHI)

And Grant never stopped moving. Here at Old Church, on May 30, Federals skirmished with Lee as Grant's cavalry protected his left flank in the advance. Here a cavalry detail stops outside the Old Church Hotel on June 4. (USAMHI)

That same day, at Bethesda Church, Grant and Lee began the fighting that would culminate a few days after in the Battle of Cold Harbor. Colonel James B. Terrill was killed leading one of Lee's regiments near Bethesda. He died without knowing that his promotion to brigadier would be official the next day. Ironically, too, his brother William had been a general in the Union Army, and he, too, fell in battle. (USAMHI)

On June 2 the fighting around Bethesda claimed another promising young leader, Brigadier General George P. Doles of Georgia. (MC)

Men like these officers of Doles' 4th Georgia had to look to a new commander. They found him in . . . (COURTESY OF STEVE MULLINAX)

. . . Colonel Philip Cook of the 4th Georgia. Months later he became a brigadier general, as pictured here. (USAMHI)

By June 2, Grant was nearing Cold Harbor. He pushed aside cavalry protection commanded by Robert E. Lee's nephew, General Fitzhugh Lee. (USAMHI)

Soon the Federals were advancing toward the swampy woodlands like this that bordered the Chickahominy River. Lee was waiting for them. (CHS)

And that led, on June 3, to the dreadful battle of Cold Harbor. Photographer J. Reekie's April 1865 image of part of the Confederate works that stopped Grant's disastrous attacks. (CHS)

Major General William F. Smith with his XVIII Corps had recently arrived, via White House Landing, in time to take part in the attack. His corps, like the others engaged, was dreadfully battered, and he never forgave Meade for sending him into battle at Cold Harbor. (USAMHI)

Brigadier General Goode Bryan missed the fight by just a few hours, his failing health forcing him to turn over his brigade to a senior colonel. A few months later he would have to resign his commission. (USAMHI)

But Confederates like Brigadier General Evander McI. Law were in perfect health and anxious to deliver death to Grant's attacking Federals. Law himself was wounded in repulsing the enemy's charges. (USAMHI)

The men in those assaults were soldiers like these zouaves of the 114th Pennsylvania, here captured by O'Sullivan's camera. They were part of the headquarters guard of the Army of the Potomac, however, and spent more time at parade than in real fighting. (TPO)

Not so the 8th Michigan. With drummers like Robert H. Hendershot of Company B, these Wolverines were in the thick of the bloody fight. (TPO)

What stopped them were Confederate divisions led by men like Major General Henry Heth, said to be the only general that Lee addressed by his given name. (NA)

Brigadier General Joseph Finegan of Florida had just arrived from his home state with a brigade in time to help stem Grant's assault. Few Floridians got the chance to serve with the fabled Army of Northern Virginia. (WRHS)

One of the hundreds who fell in attacking works held by the Confederates was Colonel Peter A. Porter of the 8th New York Heavy Artillery. He died on the field that June 3, killed fighting troops led by his own cousin and childhood playmate General John C. Breckinridge. (USAMHI)

His foolhardy attack at Cold Harbor failed, Grant sent his cavalry on a raid into the heart of Virginia to distract Lee. Confederate cavalry followed, excepting the division of Lee's son, Brigadier General William H. F. Lee. One of "Rooney" Lee's troopers was this man of the 10th Virginia Cavalry, Private Benjamin Franklin Lincoln. His second cousin Abraham was President of the United States. (COURTESY OF DALE SNAIR)

Undeterred, Grant would continue looking for a way to trap Lee and end the war in Virginia. It would not come for another year, but he would never stop trying. Grant stands here at his headquarters at Cold Harbor in early June surrounded by his staff. Colonel Rawlins sits at far left. Brigadier General John G. Barnard, chief engineer of the Union armies at center, hands in lap, and standing just to the right of him is Grant's old friend and military secretary, Lieutenant Colonel Ely S. Parker, a full-blooded Seneca Indian. Parker will be with Grant nine months from now at Appomattox to see the end and to transcribe the terms of surrender. But for both of them, that was still far in the unseen future. (USAMHI)

The Atlanta Campaign

RICHARD M. McMURRY

"Hell has broke loose in Georgia," and Sherman makes it so

IT WAS A LONG WAY from the Wilderness to where the western armies of the Union stood poised along the Tennessee and Mississippi rivers preparing for the summer's campaign into the Confederacy's industrial and agricultural heartland in Georgia and Alabama. Three years of warfare had set the stage for the struggle that, more than any other, would determine the outcome of the war.

The Federals who were to assail the Southern heartland were led by Major General William T. Sherman, a forty-four-year-old, red-headed, red-whiskered, hot-tempered native of Ohio. Sherman commanded the Military Division of the Mississippi, embracing all Northern forces between the Appalachian Mountains and the Mississippi River. For the 1864 campaign he assembled three armies. The Army of the Cumberland (60,000 men) was led by Major General George H. Thomas, a Virginian who had remained loyal to the Union. Major General James B. McPherson, a handsome young Ohioan, led the Army of the Tennessee (25,000 men). The 15,000-man Army of the Ohio was commanded by Major General John M. Schofield, a native of New York.

The Confederate heartland was defended by General Joseph E. Johnston's Army of Tennessee, based at Dalton, Georgia, 30 miles below Chattanooga. Johnston was a Virginian, in his late fifties, whose Civil War career was marred by a bitter personal feud with Confederate President Jefferson Davis. By late 1863, Johnston believed that his greatest enemy was the President; Davis was convinced that Johnston could not be trusted with an army. Pride prevented Johnston from resigning; public pressure forced Davis to keep the popular general in command. Johnston's army numbered about 55,000 and was organized into two infantry corps and a cavalry corps. Lieutenant General William J. Hardee, a grumpy Georgian, commanded one infantry corps; Lieutenant General John Bell Hood, a young Kentuckian turned Texan, led the other. The cavalry was under Major General Joseph Wheeler, a young irresponsible Georgian.

During the winter Johnston and the Confederate authorities debated strategy for 1864. The government wanted to drive the Federals from Tennessee. Johnston, convinced that his army was too weak to advance, preferred to select a strong position, fight a defensive battle, and, if successful, move forward against a defeated enemy. This difference could not be resolved, and the Confederates began the campaign with no clear plan.

The Federals, by contrast, had unified their command under Lieutenant General Ulysses S. Grant, who wanted to use the North's full power by having all Union armies advance simultaneously. While he attacked Lee in Virginia, Grant planned for Sherman to move against Johnston while another force captured Mobile and invaded Alabama, thus extending Federal control to a line running along the Chattahoochee River and on to Montgomery and Mobile. Owing to political factors, the campaign against Mobile was abandoned, and Sherman's drive into Georgia became the Union's major 1864 offensive in the West.

Sherman's forces were based in Chattanooga—a city that had been captured by the Federals in late 1863 and the uppermost point on the Tennessee River from which a railroad ran into the heart of the Confederacy. That railroad, the Western & Atlantic, led southeast some 120 miles to Atlanta. Geography and the railroad meant that the campaign would take place in Georgia.

Atlanta, meeting place of four railroads, site of major industrial establishments, hospitals, government and military offices, and the key to control of the West, had come into being as a railroad terminus in the early 1840s. Other railroads were built to link up with the original line, and the city grew to a population of 10,000 in 1860. The influx of refugees, military personnel, and government employees doubled that figure by 1864.

The Federals had many advantages in the campaign. Most important, Sherman and Grant trusted each other and worked together with the support of their government in pursuit of their objective. Johnston's differences with Davis made it impossible for the Confederates to cooperate or even to communicate. Also, Sherman was a more thorough, better-organized, more resourceful, and more flexible leader than Johnston, and he commanded Federal forces in Kentucky, Tennessee, Georgia, Alabama, and Mississippi. There was no overall Confederate commander in the West. Sherman could strike into Alabama against the railroads that supplied Johnston's army, while Johnston could do no more than urge local commanders in Alabama to act. Sherman had, in Thomas and McPherson, chief subordinates of high caliber; Johnston's chief lieutenants, like Johnston himself, were at best mediocre generals. The inability of the Southerners to agree upon a plan, and Johnston's reluctance to take risks and assume responsibility lest he be criticized by Davis, meant that the Federals would have the initiative and determine the character and tempo of the campaign. Finally, Sherman's forces outnumbered Johnston's about 1.5 to 1 when the campaign opened. Although there was no difference in the quality of men in the opposing armies, Sherman's greater strength gave him another advantage. Circumstances so favored the Federals that only leadership of the highest quality could give the Southerners even a hope of victory.

Rocky Face Ridge, a steep height west of Dalton, runs from north to south. Johnston put his army on that ridge and across Crow Valley, north of Dalton. He believed that Sherman would attack

Come spring of 1864, it was time for hell to break loose in Georgia. The man to unleash it knew a lot about making war hell, Major General William Tecumseh Sherman. (USAMHI)

Through that winter of 1863–64, while waiting for the next campaign, the men of Sherman's armies waited at places like Wauhatchie Bridge, guarding his supply lines as he built up his readiness to strike. (USAMHI)

this strong position and was confident that the Confederates could repulse any assault.

Sherman, too alert to fall into such a trap, planned to demonstrate against Johnston's position and swing McPherson's army around to the southwest to the railroad that supplied the Confederates at Dalton. Once the Western & Atlantic was broken, Johnston would have to retreat. Originally Sherman planned to move McPherson toward Rome, Georgia, 35 miles southwest of Dalton, to threaten Johnston's railroad. Because McPherson's army did not attain its expected strength, Sherman decided to send him only to Snake Creek Gap, an opening through Rocky Face Ridge about 12 miles below Dalton. A few miles east of the gap was Resaca, where the railroad crossed the Oostenaula River.

Sherman's plan worked almost perfectly. Johnston, confident in his Dalton fortifications, was deceived by the demonstrations that Thomas and Schofield staged there in early May. The area to the Confederate left was ignored, and when McPherson reached Snake Creek Gap on May 8 he found it unguarded.

On May 9, McPherson cautiously pushed toward the railroad. Surprised to find numerous Confederates in the area, he drew back to the gap. Johnston had stationed a small force at Resaca to guard the bridge, and by the 9th those men had been joined by advance elements of a 15,000-man force from Mississippi and Alabama that the government had ordered to reinforce Johnston. This force, a third infantry corps, was commanded by Lieutenant General Leonidas Polk, the corpulent Episcopal Bishop of Louisiana who had left military service in 1827. He had resumed his career in 1861 to aid the Confederacy.

Although McPherson had not achieved all for which Sherman had hoped, he had given the Federals a great strategic advantage, and Sherman fol-

The XV Corps camped around Scottsboro, Alabama, and here its commander, Major General John A. Palmer, made his headquarters. (USAMHI)

lowed up on his opportunity by shifting Thomas and Schofield to Snake Creek Gap. By nightfall on May 12 only a small detachment of Federals remained in the Dalton area.

Johnston, who had the shorter distance to cover and the use of the railroad, did not abandon Dalton until the night of May 12–13. The Confederates deployed in the rough terrain north and west of Resaca, holding a line that began at the Oostenaula and curved around to rest its right on the Conasauga River. Hood's corps held the right of this line; Hardee's the center; Polk's the left.

On the 13th, Sherman moved against Resaca, his force fanning out, to form a line paralleling that of the Confederates. The first day of the Battle of Resaca was spent in skirmishing. On the 14th, Sherman struck the right center of Johnston's line but was hurled back with heavy loss. Hood lashed out at Sherman's extreme left, and only reinforcements prevented a Confederate victory. Other local attacks took place on the 15th, but Sherman, realizing that such fighting would accomplish little, sent a detachment down the Oostenaula to Lay's Ferry, where it crossed the river and threatened Johnston's railroad. During the night of May 15–16 the Confederate leader crossed the river and marched southward, seeking terrain for the defensive battle he wanted to fight.

The opening days of the campaign set the pattern for what followed. Sherman had demonstrated that he could plan complicated operations and the logistical details necessary to support them. When it proved impossible to execute his original plans, he had quickly adapted to new situations. He had held the initiative, and he had used his superior numbers to pin down and outflank the Rebels. He

Major General George H. Thomas, the man who had become the "Rock of Chickamauga" back in September 1863, now led the Army of the Cumberland, and here on May 5, 1864, at Ringgold, Georgia, he made his headquarters, readying for the campaign that would shatter the lower South. (USAMHI)

had not, however, pushed aggressively after the Confederates. Johnston had remained passive and twice was maneuvered out of his chosen position. He had neglected Snake Creek Gap and had not defended the south bank of the Oostenaula. In less than two weeks he had abandoned the region north of the Oostenaula (including Rome, an important industrial town) and fallen back into a more open area where Sherman's superior numbers would give the Federals an even greater advantage.

Over the next several days Johnston moved south toward the Etowah River. On May 19 he made an unsuccessful effort to concentrate against a detached part of Sherman's force near Cassville, and that evening he was forced to retreat across the Etowah when his position at Cassville proved vulnerable to artillery. The Rebels took up a strong position about Allatoona Pass. Sherman, after securing his hold north of the river, allowed his men a few days' rest.

On May 23, Sherman crossed the Etowah in open country west of Allatoona. His objective was the small town of Dallas, 14 miles south of the river, from which he could move east to the railroad or southeast toward the Chattahoochee River. "The Etowah," Sherman wrote, "is the Rubicon of Georgia. We are now all in motion like a vast hive of bees and expect to swarm along the Chattahoochee in a few days."

As Sherman's armies closed on Dallas on May 25, they found Confederates posted at New Hope Church, northeast of the town. Overruling his subordinates who believed a strong Rebel force to be in their front, Sherman ordered an attack. The resulting battle of New Hope Church was a victory for Hood's Confederates, who repulsed the Northerners with ease. Two days later another Union attack was defeated at Pickett's Mill, northeast of New Hope Church.

Both sides concentrated along the Dallas-New Hope Church-Pickett's Mill line, and for over a week deadly skirmish warfare went on in the heavy woods. The soldiers were made even more uncomfortable by the torrential rains that began on May 25 and continued with but few letups for a month.

Unable to defeat Johnston and experiencing difficulty supplying his men over muddy roads, Sherman began to work his way east, shifting troops from his right to his left. By early June the Northerners had regained the railroad near Acworth. Sherman had again outmaneuvered Johnston and bypassed the Allatoona hills.

By June 10, Sherman had received reinforcements, repaired his railroad, rested his men, and was ready to advance. Johnston, meanwhile, had occupied the hills north of Marietta. Over the next several days Sherman's forces pushed Johnston back to a line running along Kennesaw Mountain and off to the south. On June 14, Polk was killed by Federal artillery fire. Major General William W. Loring took temporary command of his corps.

When the Federals encountered the new Rebel position, Sherman began extending to the southwest to outflank it. Rain and mud slowed movements and hampered efforts to supply units distant from the railroad, but the Federal right slowly stretched southward. Johnston extended his left in an effort to hold his line. By June 22 the armies were strung out along a line that began north of

And here on May 5 or 6 sat several of Thomas' generals, with the opening of the campaign less than 48 hours in the future. Seated at far left is Brigadier General Jefferson C. Davis, and next to him, with legs crossed, is Brigadier General John M. Brannan, Thomas' chief of artillery. The man writing at the table is Brigadier General Richard W. Johnson. Seated next to him, hat in lap, is Brigadier General John H. King, and Brigadier General William D. Whipple, army chief of staff. Each will see his share of fighting in the days ahead, and Johnson will be severely wounded. (USAMHI)

Ringgold seemed a peaceful enough place in this image, believed to have been taken in 1865 by George N. Barnard. (WRHS)

Marietta, swung to the west and then south to a point several miles southwest of the town near Olley's Creek. Skirmishing, artillery fire, and sometimes large-scale assaults raged along this line.

In late June, when the rains ceased, Sherman changed his tactics. Believing that Johnston's long line would be weak, the Northern leader determined to assault. He planned to attack at three places—the southwestern end of Kennesaw Mountain, Cheatham's Hill west of Marietta, and along Olley's Creek. If the Federals could break through to the railroad, a large part of Johnston's army might be cut off and destroyed.

Sherman attacked on the morning of June 27. After heavy artillery fire, Northern infantry gallantly rushed against the fortifications on Kennesaw and at Cheatham's Hill. Although some Yankees reached the Confederate lines, the Southerners were able to repulse the attacks, inflicting heavy loss on the assaulting forces. Only along Olley's Creek, where Schofield's men managed to gain a position on the south bank, could Sherman claim success.

Schofield's advance gave Sherman a position from which to slice eastward to the railroad or south to the Chattahoochee. A few days after the failure of his attack Sherman began to shift troops to his right, forcing Johnston to choose between giving up the Kennesaw line or being cut off from Atlanta.

Johnston, expecting such a maneuver and believing that he could stretch his army no farther, had begun a new line at Smyrna, four miles below Marietta. On the night of July 2–3 he moved to the Smyrna line. Advancing Federals confronted Johnston's new position late on the afternoon of July 3. After a day of skirmishing, Sherman's right threatened Johnston's communications with Atlanta, and during the night of July 4–5 the Southerners fell back to the north bank of the

Not so Buzzard Roost, Georgia. Here on May 8–9, Sherman first met and began to press the Confederate defenses. As Barnard's photo shows so well, even where no major battle was fought, still the passing of the armies left a considerable mess in its wake. (USAMHI)

Chattahoochee where they occupied a heavily fortified position.

Realizing that the Rebel line was too strong to be attacked, Sherman sent his cavalry to capture Roswell, 16 miles upriver, and planned to attempt a crossing above Johnston's fortifications. On July 8, while Johnston was distracted by demonstrations downstream, Schofield's men crossed the river, using pontoon boats and the ruins of a dam. By nightfall the Yankees were securely dug in on the south bank. Johnston, during the night of July 9–10, crossed the Chattahoochee and went into position along Peachtree Creek, a few miles from Atlanta. For a week Sherman rested his men and planned his next move.

Johnston had not kept the government informed of the progress of the campaign, and his long retreat had displeased Confederate officials. The authorities were especially worried because it would be possible for the Federals to use the Chattahoochee as a moat while they wrecked Alabama's virtually undefended industrial area. Sherman's presence on the Chattahoochee, even if he advanced no farther into Georgia, would assure Federal success in the campaign and cripple the Confederacy's ability to wage war. If Johnston abandoned Atlanta, the blow to the Confederacy would be devastating. Criticism of Johnston mounted, and Davis, as early as July 12, began to consider replacing him with a commander who could be counted on to fight for Atlanta. On the 17th the President, with great reluctance, named Hood to command the Army.

Most historians have been critical of Davis, but their criticism stems more from a knowledge of what happened after Johnston was removed than

It was Major General William B. Bate who held those Confederate works against Sherman's first tentative stabs. He could not hold for long before the Yankee horde. (USAMHI)

from an evaluation of the decision itself. Davis faced two different but related questions in July 1864. First, he had to decide if Johnston should be relieved from command. All evidence available to the President indicated that Johnston had mismanaged the campaign and that he would make no real effort to hold Atlanta. Johnston seemed to have no appreciation of the city's logistical, economic, political, or psychological importance. If the Confederacy was to survive, Atlanta must be held and Sherman pushed away from the Southern heartland. Nothing indicated that Johnston had the will, ability, or even intention of trying to do so.

If Johnston were removed, who should replace him? Time dictated that a new commander come from the army at Atlanta. There were only two realistic choices: Hardee and Hood (the III Corps commander, Lieutenant General Alexander P. Stewart, had but recently been named as the permanent replacement for Polk). Hardee, like Johnston, was on bad personal terms with important government officials, had declined to take permanent command of the Army in December 1863, and, it was reported to Davis, had supported Johnston's policy of falling back into Georgia. These factors made Hood the choice by default.

Other factors were also involved. Hood was a bold officer who had led many successful attacks on the enemy. He seems to have worked to undermine Johnston by informing Davis' military adviser, General Braxton Bragg, that Johnston had missed many chances to strike a blow against Sherman. Hook's crippled condition—he had lost a leg and the use of an arm in earlier battles—might have caused Davis some hesitation, but, wounds and all, Hood was the best, indeed the only, alternative to Johnston in mid-July 1864.

WHEN HOOD ASSUMED COMMAND on the morning of July 18, he faced a desperate situation. Sherman was north and east of Atlanta. Thomas' army, with its right on the Chattahoochee, was a hinge on which Schofield and McPherson were swinging to the east to reach the Georgia Railroad, Hood's direct link to the Carolinas and Virginia.

As Thomas' men came down into the valley of Peachtree Creek north of Atlanta, a gap opened in the Federal line. Hood saw a chance to attack the isolated Federal right, and he planned to concentrate the corps of Hardee and Stewart to assail Thomas while his old corps, under Major General Benjamin F. Cheatham, and the cavalry defended Atlanta against Schofield and McPherson. Hood worked through the night of July 19–20 to position his army for this battle.

On the 20th, Hood found the Federals east of Atlanta advancing more rapidly than he had anticipated, and he had to strengthen his eastern flank. The confusion caused by this redeployment delayed the attack. When Hardee and Stewart advanced, they found that Thomas' men had built fortifications. Thus what Hood had intended as a quick blow against an unprepared force became an assault on a strong position. The Confederates, fighting bravely, were repulsed in the Battle of Peachtree Creek.

Sherman drove for Resaca, Georgia, a tiny hamlet that held the key to the Confederate rear. This image shows Rebel earthworks in the right distance. (USAMHI)

On July 21, Hood's attention was drawn to the east side of the city. McPherson had advanced along the Georgia Railroad through Decatur to the outskirts of Atlanta. Hood decided to send Hardee's corps south and around to the east to roll up the left of the Federal line and drive it back onto the center and right. That night Hardee's men set off on their march. The roads were narrow and crowded, and the march was slow. Not until early afternoon was Hardee ready to attack. Meanwhile, the advance of the Northern armies had contracted the Federal lines and crowded part of McPherson's army out of place. McPherson ordered these displaced men to his extreme left. Thus, by accident, reinforcements were sent to the point where the attack fell.

Hardee's men struck a line of battle rather than an undefended flank. The resulting Battle of Atlanta raged through the afternoon of July 22, as Hardee's troops, joined by units from the Atlanta defenses, assaulted the Union position. In bitter fighting the Southerners temporarily overran part of the Yankee position, captured several guns and hundreds of prisoners, and killed McPherson. The Confederates, however, were unable to break the Northern line and at night drew back, leaving the Yankees in the position they had held when the battle opened.

By July 26, Sherman had decided upon his next effort. He would extend his army to the west and south of Atlanta to cut Hood's remaining railroads. The Atlanta & West Point Railroad and the Macon & Western ran southwest to East Point, where they forked, the Atlanta & West Point going southwest and the Macon & Western into central Georgia. If the Federals broke those lines, Hood could not hold Atlanta.

Major General Oliver Otis Howard, a native of Maine, had been selected to replace McPherson, and Sherman transferred Howard's Army of the Tennessee from the Federal left to the right. By the afternoon of July 27, Howard's men were west of Atlanta, pushing southward against slight opposition.

With seasoned veterans like the 33d New Jersey, Sherman fought the Battle for Resaca on May 14–15. (TPO)

Hood, learning of Sherman's movement, sent his old corps, now led by Lieutenant General Stephen D. Lee, supported by Stewart's corps, west from Atlanta on July 28. Hood hoped that Lee would block the Federals, and then, on the following day, Hood would move around their right to attack the rear of the position they had taken confronting Lee.

Lee, finding the Yankees near Ezra Church, attempted to drive them away. He launched a series of sharp, but uncoordinated, assaults on the Northerners, who had hastily built works from logs and church benches. Stewart, coming to Lee's support, joined the attacks. The resulting battle lasted through the afternoon and ended with the Northerners secure in their new position. Hood abandoned his plans for flank attack on July 29.

In his first ten days of command, Hood had thrice lashed out at the Federals. Although none of the battles had fulfilled Hood's expectations, he had demonstrated that he would strike whenever he thought it advantageous to do so. Sherman's movements became more cautious, and as July ended, many Confederates took hope in the belief that Hood's hard fighting had at last stopped the enemy, who seemed always to outflank the Southerners.

THERE WAS NO LARGE-SCALE FIGHTING in the Atlanta area for a month after Ezra Church. Sherman cautiously extended to the southwest, and Hood constructed a parallel line of works covering the railroad. Federal artillery damaged Atlanta but could not drive out the Rebel troops. Both sides resorted to the use of cavalry. Sherman launched several mounted raids against the railroads below Atlanta, hoping to cut Hood's supply line. Although the Federal horsemen inflicted some damage, they were unable to break the rail lines beyond repair.

Hood, on August 10, launched a counterraid, sending Wheeler, with about 4,500 men, to cut the

Over rugged, fence-strewn ground like this the armies struggled. (USAMHI)

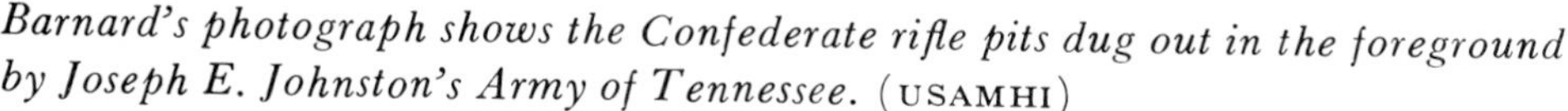
Barnard's photograph shows the Confederate rifle pits dug out in the foreground by Joseph E. Johnston's Army of Tennessee. (USAMHI)

Brigadier General Thomas Sweeney, a troublesome Irishman from County Cork, commanded a division of the XVI Corps in the fight at Resaca. A career fighter, he lost his arm at Churubusco in the Mexican War, and a few years hence will lead an "army" of Fenians in an abortive invasion of Canada. (USAMHI)

railroad that supplied Sherman. Although Wheeler interrupted operations on the Western & Atlantic, the line was too well protected for the Rebel horsemen to break it thoroughly. Instead of returning to Hood, Wheeler began a raid into East Tennessee, a foolish venture that damaged Hood at a crucial time in the campaign.

In late August, with Wheeler out of the picture, Sherman again attempted to oust Hood from Atlanta. Realizing that only infantry could wreck the Rebels' railroads, the Federal commander, on August 25, began his movement. He sent part of the Army of the Cumberland to hold the Chattahoochee bridges and the railroad while the remainder of his force marched far to the south and west. On August 28, Howard's Army of the Tennessee reached the Atlanta & West Point Railroad at Fairburn, 13 miles southwest of East Point. All that afternoon and through the 29th, Sherman's men so thoroughly destroyed the railroad that only the Macon & Western could supply the Rebels at Atlanta.

Meanwhile, many Confederates had interpreted Sherman's disappearance as a retreat brought on by Wheeler's raid. For a few days optimism reigned among the Southerners. "The scales have turned in favor of the South," wrote an Arkansian, "and the Abolitionists are moving to the rear."

When the Rebels learned of Sherman's presence on the West Point Railroad, they realized that his next objective would be the Macon & Western. Hood, however, without cavalry to ascertain the enemy's strength and intentions, seems to have believed that the force below Atlanta was only a raiding party. He did not realize the magnitude of the disaster moving toward the Macon & Western when, on August 30, he ordered Hardee to take two corps (Hardee's own and Lee's) to Jonesboro (14 miles southeast of East Point) to protect the railroad.

On August 30 the Northerners crossed the Flint River and entrenched on the eastern bank. During the night Hardee moved to Jonesboro, where, on the morning of August 31, the Confederates deployed west of the town. That afternoon Hardee assaulted the Federals. The attack was fierce but uncoordinated, and it failed. With more Yankees closing on the town, Hardee drew back and deployed to make a last defense of the railroad. Hood, still not realizing what was happening, concluded that Sherman was going to attack Atlanta from the south. He ordered Hardee to return Lee's corps to Atlanta, leaving only one corps to face the main Union force at Jonesboro.

On September 1 the Northerners fell upon Hardee. Late in the afternoon the Confederate line gave way, and Hardee retreated to the south. Sherman's hold on Hood's last railroad was unbreakable. The Battle of Jonesboro sealed the fate of Atlanta. With the railroad gone, Hood had to give up the city. During the night of September 1–2 the Southerners destroyed what they could not carry away and marched via a circuitous route to join Hardee.

The campaign that began in the north Georgia mountains four months earlier was over. The war would last another nine months, but the capture of Atlanta was a tangible victory demonstrating that the Federals could reach the heart of the South. Hood would go north that fall to meet overwhelming defeat at Nashville in December, while Sherman, leaving Atlanta a burned wreck, marched across Georgia to the sea.

Helping defend the little railroad town was Confederate Brigadier General William F. Tucker. He survived a desperate wound here that put him out of the war for good, but in 1881 an assassin's bullet cut him down. (VM)

Despite every effort to hold the position, the Confederates had to pull out of Resaca, leaving the village and their defenses to Sherman's victorious Federals. It would be repeated many times in this campaign. (USAMHI)

Brigadier General Randall L. Gibson covered the Southern retreat from Resaca. (LSU)

Behind them the Confederates left the battlefield to the victors, and their hastily buried dead to the soil. Rude boards mark the resting spots of those who died in the fight. A Barnard image. (WRHS)

On the armies went, through Kingston. Here for two days they fought before moving on. Barnard followed them in 1865 with his camera. (USAMHI)

Brigadier General Jacob D. Cox led a division of the XXIII Corps in that fighting. He ordered one of his brigades to find and destroy the . . . (USAMHI)

. . . . Mark Cooper Iron Works, outside Cartersville. The factory had supplied arms to the Confederacy, but after Cox's raid it was left a ruin. A postwar image. (GEORGIA DEPARTMENT OF ARCHIVES AND HISTORY)

Finally, Sherman pushed Johnston back across the Etowah River here at Etowah Bridge. Barnard's image shows the fortifications erected by the Confederates to guard the bridge, as well as the beginning of structural supports being erected to keep the Western & Atlantic Railroad crossing operable. (LC)

Already, off in the distance down the Western & Atlantic line, Barnard's camera looks toward the next goal, Allatoona Pass. (USAMHI)

Allatoona itself, nestled in the pass, would not see a battle. (USAMHI)

Rather than face fortifications like the earthwork atop the ridge at left, Sherman moved around Johnston and forced the Confederates to pull out of Allatoona. Yet finally the armies would meet in deadly battle at . . . (USAMHI)

. . . New Hope Church. Here for nearly two weeks in late May and early June 1864 the armies glowered at each other from positions like these Confederate works. Barnard captured much of it in the summer of 1865. (LC)

Amid all the trees and brush and entanglements, it was like fighting in a briar patch. (USAMHI)

Rebels like Uriah Crawford of the 54th Virginia, one of very few Old Dominion units with Johnston's army, were heartily glad to move away from New Hope Church. Alas, for Crawford, he would be captured just two weeks later. (COURTESY OF DELBERT CRAWFORD)

Johnston pulled back to a line along Pine Mountain on June 4, and here skirmishing continued for several days. (LC)

A casualty of that skirmishing was Lieutenant General Leonidas Polk. On June 14 a Federal cannon ball struck him in the chest and he died instantly. He had been an Episcopal bishop, and then a corps commander for the Confederacy. In this remarkable unpublished, and badly faded, portrait he stands wearing the loose pleated uniform blouse that was popular with many generals in the Army of Tennessee. (MC)

It was Brigadier General Absalom Baird's division of the XIV Corps that was skirmishing at Pine Mountain that day. He appears here in 1865, at war's end, wearing mourning crepe for the murdered Lincoln. (KA)

Pine Mountain was only a stop, however, before a bigger and more deadly fight at Kennesaw Mountain. Here, as Barnard's image shows, the armies turned farmers' fences and fields into places of battle. (USAMHI)

It was the greatest fighting yet in the campaign, and the men of the 125th Ohio led the skirmishers in Sherman's attack. The losses were dreadful. This regiment alone suffered 43 casualties just acting as skirmishers. (USAMHI)

There were casualties on both sides, though. Brigadier General Lucius E. Polk, nephew of the slain Leonidas, was put out of the war by a desperate wound at Kennesaw. (USAMHI)

Yet it was Sherman who suffered the most. Placed behind works like these shown in Barnard's image, the Confederates delivered deadly fire into the attacking Federals. Sherman had to admit defeat. (WRHS)

So did his chief of artillery, Brigadier General William F. Barry. "The nature of military operations in a country like ours is peculiar," he claimed, and unfavorable to artillery. The dense cover forced the guns to work out in the open, exposed, but still they did good work. It cost them. Three division chiefs of artillery were killed in the fighting. (COURTESY OF EUGENE WOODDELL)

The view from behind Johnston's rifle pits on Kennesaw tells the whole story of the dreadful ground over which Sherman had to attack. The broken and battered trees tell the story of the fight's ferocity. (USAMHI)

For fiery Brigadier General Francis M. Cockrell of Missouri, Kennesaw was a tough fight in which his men faced the Federals for an hour within thirty paces of each other. His skirmishers could hear the Yankees, hiding behind rocks, giving the order to "fix bayonets" for the charge. Some of Cockrell's men fired more than sixty times. (GOELET-BUNCOMBE COLLECTION, SOUTHERN HISTORICAL COLLECTION)

Despite the victory at Kennesaw, Johnston had to fall back once more as the enemy threatened to get around his flank. Now the Confederates withdrew to the Chattahoochee River, getting ever closer to Atlanta. When Johnston destroyed the bridges in his path, Sherman at once started rebuilding them with lightning speed. (USAMHI)

After the fight at Kennesaw, most of the combat for several days was on the fringes of the armies, at places like Vining's Station. There, on July 4, Brigadier General Alfred J. Vaughan, Jr., had his leg blown off by a Federal shell. He appears here months later, near the end of the war, with the crutch that was his companion for the rest of his life. (HP)

Finally, Richmond would stand no more of Johnston's retreats. By July 17, Sherman had pushed to within a few miles of Atlanta. Johnston was replaced by an audacious, sad-eyed fighter from Kentucky, General John Bell Hood. He would do no better than Johnston, and at greater cost. (MC)

This portrait is believed to be of Hood's chief of staff, Brigadier General Francis A. Shoup, a native of Indiana. He would have to cope with all the paper work of running an army, for Hood had no patience for it. (ERNEST HAYWOOD COLLECTION, SHC)

Just three days after taking command, Hood attacked Thomas at Peachtree Creek, proving himself once more to be a vicious fighter, if an unwise one. It was Thomas who emerged the victor, with Atlanta now threatened with encirclement. Barnard's photo shows the graves of those who died on the field. (USAMHI)

Brigadier General James Cantey was absent from his brigade with ill health, but his men led the Confederate attack that for a time stunned Thomas at Peachtree Creek. (CHS)

While the armies began the final battle for Atlanta on July 22, Brigadier General George Stoneman, seated at right, led his cavalry corps on a raid that hoped to capture the notorious prison at Andersonville and free its inmates. Instead, five days later, Stoneman was himself captured. (MICHAEL HAMMERSON)

It was Confederate cavalry led by able officers like Brigadier General William H. Jackson that disrupted Stoneman's plans. (NA)

Meanwhile, men were dying for Atlanta. In the first day of fighting, Major General James B. McPherson became the only Union Army commander of the war to die in battle. His men saw him ride off to a threatened point during a Confederate attack. A few minutes later his riderless horse returned. (USAMHI)

He fell and died here, among the cannon balls and the macabre, grinning skull of a dead horse. Sherman particularly mourned the loss of one of the most beloved young generals in the service. (GDAH)

At McPherson's death, command of his army went for a time to one of the most able civilians-turned-soldier of the war, Major General John A. Logan of Illinois. The only trouble was, he was not West Point trained. (USAMHI)

Sherman consulted with Major General George H. Thomas, commanding the Army of the Cumberland, and between them they agreed that permanent command of McPherson's army should go to a professional. Thus . . . (COURTESY OF WANDA WRIGHT)

. . . Major General Oliver O. Howard took over from Logan. (LC)

That incensed Howard's senior officer, Major General Joseph Hooker, the "Fighting Joe" who lost a major battle at Chancellorsville the year before. Unwilling to serve under his inferior in seniority, Hooker asked to be relieved. For him it was the end of the war. (USAMHI)

With Hooker's departure, command of his XX Corps went for a time to Brigadier General Alpheus S. Williams, a grizzled old fighter and veteran of the battles in Virginia, shown here with his daughter. Thus did the death of McPherson shift commands throughout his army for a time. (USAMHI)

Meanwhile, for several days after the battle of July 22 the armies watched each other across the lines. Barnard was able to get his camera into some of the abandoned defenses in the summer of 1865. (USAMHI)

He and his instrument could survey some of the scenes of the bloody day's fight. (LC)

Then came the rugged July 28 battle at Ezra Church, Hood's last hope to keep from being driven back into the city. Brigadier General D. H. Reynolds led two Confederate brigades in Hood's attack, intended to keep Sherman from encircling him. A bold officer, born in Ohio, Reynolds fought for five hours in heavy fire before being called back. He suffered 40 percent losses. (MC)

The defenses were well prepared. All around Atlanta ran ditches and rifle pits, with fences, sharpened stakes in the ground . . . (USAMHI)

. . . fortified hilltops . . . (USAMHI)

. . . and makeshift obstructions everywhere. (RJY)

Sherman's attackers would have to march across hell to get to the city this way. (USAMHI)

East of the city the Confederates even piled brush on the slopes leading up to their rifle pits. (WRHS)

After the fall of Atlanta, Barnard turned his camera toward the successive waves of vicious obstructions near the Chattanooga railroad line. (GDAH)

Wherever the camera looked, the environs of Atlanta bristled with trenches and rifle pits and stakes in the ground. (GDAH)

It had been the luckless task of Brigadier General Marcus J. Wright to command the District of Atlanta for a time, but before the Federals closed in finally he was sent off to Macon in the center of the state. Before long, the front might be there as well. (M. J. WRIGHT COLLECTION, SHC)

Meanwhile, the Confederates who stayed behind sat in their defenses—like this one—and glowered at the enemy. (GDAH)

It was all they could do, while Sherman slowly encircled them. (USAMHI)

Just two days before the Ezra Church fight, Brigadier General John M. Corse, seated second from the right, took command of the Second Division of the XVI Corps. His division led the way in the flanking movement by which Sherman hoped at last to cut Hood off from retreat. Seated with Corse are the other officers of his division, Brigadier General Richard Rowett, at left, McPherson's old adjutant, General William T. Clark next, and at far right Brigadier General E. W. Rice. This image, made in May 1865, shows all of them at higher grades than they were during the Atlanta Campaign. (USAMHI)

This was the prize they sought. Atlanta in 1864. A Barnard image. (LC)

In the center of the city, not far from the Western & Atlantic depot, stood the Trout House, one of Atlanta's better-known hotels. (LC)

Symbolic of Atlanta, however, was the "car shed" of the Western & Atlantic depot. It was through this depot that Hood's lifeline ran, for Atlanta was the rail communication center of the deep South. (LC)

Barnard did some of the best work of his career once Sherman took Atlanta. This scene, not far from the depot, is one of his most brilliant. (LC)

The Potter house showed to Barnard's camera some of the terrible effects of Federal fire during the bombardment of Hood's defenses. (LC)

The poor Potters' backyard became a major position in the defensive perimeter around the city. It could almost be a scene from the 1914–18 war in Europe. (LC)

When finally Sherman took Atlanta in September, he found there more and more evidences of the defensive strength of the place. It was no wonder that he wisely chose to drive Hood out by encircling him rather than attacking. Kennesaw Mountain had been a costly lesson, but well learned. (LC)

Here, in a Confederate fort on Peachtree Street, Barnard's camera looks south toward the city, over the barrel of cannon No. 211, manufactured in 1863. (LC)

Where once hundreds of Rebels stood ready to fight, now a lone sentry sits atop the earthworks looking off toward his old lines. (LC)

The thought of having to charge across that no-man's-land of entanglements, under unrestricted fire from the enemy, sobered even the most hardened of Sherman's men. They were delighted that he used strategy instead of force. (LC)

By the end of August, Sherman was ready. Brigadier General Thomas E. G. Ransom temporarily led the XVI Corps as the Federals sealed off Hood's last rail link at Jonesboro. (CHICAGO PUBLIC LIBRARY)

Brigadier General Jefferson C. Davis, seated at left, led his corps in the heaviest of the fighting at Jonesboro, yet was so impressed with the valor of the Kentucky Confederate troops opposing him that he personally looked to the welfare of those he captured. He sits in his tent here with Lieutenant Colonel A. C. McClurg. (LC)

Lieutenant General William J. Hardee commanded Hood's unsuccessful attack at Jonesboro. He had to drive Sherman back, or else Atlanta would have to be evacuated. (CHS)

It was bitterly hot fighting. Some Confederate brigades ceased to exist after Jonesboro. Brigadier General Zachariah C. Deas led a brigade in the front line of the initially successful attack. (LC)

Brigadier General George Maney commanded a division in the battle but managed to make someone in the army high command angry, for he was relieved of his command within minutes of the end of the battle. (MC)

For Brigadier General Daniel C. Govan of Arkansas, Jonesboro was his last battle for quite a while. Captured, he would not return to the service for several months. (USAMHI)

Even with their victory at Jonesboro, the Federals suffered their share as well. Private Henry Cordes of the 18th United States Infantry, seated at right, was part of the 65 percent losses suffered by his regiment. Poor Cordes took a gunshot wound in the left arm and had his limb amputated on the field. (TPO)

The 9th Indiana took part in the chase after Hood's evacuating army. On September 2 they caught up with him near Lovejoy's Station, but the Confederates successfully withdrew deeper into Georgia. It was effectively the end of the Atlanta Campaign. (NA)

Now Sherman could survey what he had conquered, assisted by Barnard's ubiquitous camera. Here on the Georgia Central tracks they found the remains of Hood's ordnance train, destroyed to prevent capture. It was a scene of perfect desolation. (KA)

In the city they found more cars and buildings like the Lard Oil Factory destroyed by Hood's retreating Confederates. (GDAH)

But most of the city proper survived both the fighting and the withdrawal, and in time the grounds around city hall sprouted Yankee winter quarters. (RJY)

Here was the encampment of the 2d Massachusetts. (USAMHI)

And here was the conqueror, William T. Sherman, astride his charger in the works he fought so long to take. "Atlanta is ours, and fairly won," he wired to Washington. (USAMHI)

Here, probably in the position of Battery K, 5th U.S. Artillery, in Fort No. 7, Sherman and his staff and generals could pose proudly. They are, from left to right: Major L. M. Dayton, aide; Lieutenant Colonel E. D. Kittoe, medical director; Colonel A. Beckwith, commissary; Colonel Orlando M. Poe, chief engineer; Brigadier General William F. Barry, chief of artillery; Colonel W. Warner; Colonel T. G. Baylor, chief of ordnance; Sherman; Captain G. W. Nichols; Colonel C. Ewing, inspector general; an unidentified major; and Captain J. E. Marshall. (USAMHI)

Now the once-Confederate works became revitalized forts in the Federal defensive line around Atlanta. Once Confederate Fort No. 7, this is now Yankee Fort No. 7 and looks off toward No. 8. (GDAH)

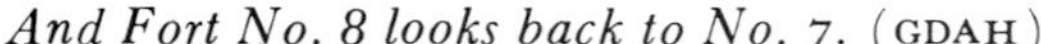

And Fort No. 8 looks back to No. 7. (GDAH)

Once the building in the background was Hood's headquarters. Now it looks quietly onto Fort No. 10, with guns removed and work parties with shovels enhancing its strength. (USAMHI)

And more work for the men laboring in Fort No. 12, part of a largely new line of defenses. (GDAH)

Far more sophisticated than the Confederate lines around the city, the Federal defensive perimeter would never be tested but stood as a monument to Colonel Poe's capability and the soldiers' hard work. (USAMHI)

Fort No. 19, with Atlanta in the background, protected the Georgia Central line, precautions against a Confederate counteroffensive that never came. (USAMHI)

Before too long it came time for Sherman to leave the city, bound for the sea on his march through Georgia. He could leave nothing useful behind, should the enemy strike for Atlanta. And so the work of destroying began. Here soldiers heat railroad rails before bending them out of shape. Some called the final product "Sherman's hairpins." (LC)

With the ruins of the car shed in the right background, more Yankees lift track from the ties. (USAMHI)

Rails heat over fires and boiler parts and other locomotive pieces await their own fate as Sherman destroyed Atlanta as a rail center. (LC)

Barnard caught the scene as the roundhouse was reduced to rubble. (LC)

Sherman's wagons prepare for the march toward Savannah while the car shed and track beside it live out their last hours before destruction. With one campaign successfully done, the man who made war hell was off for another one. (CHS)

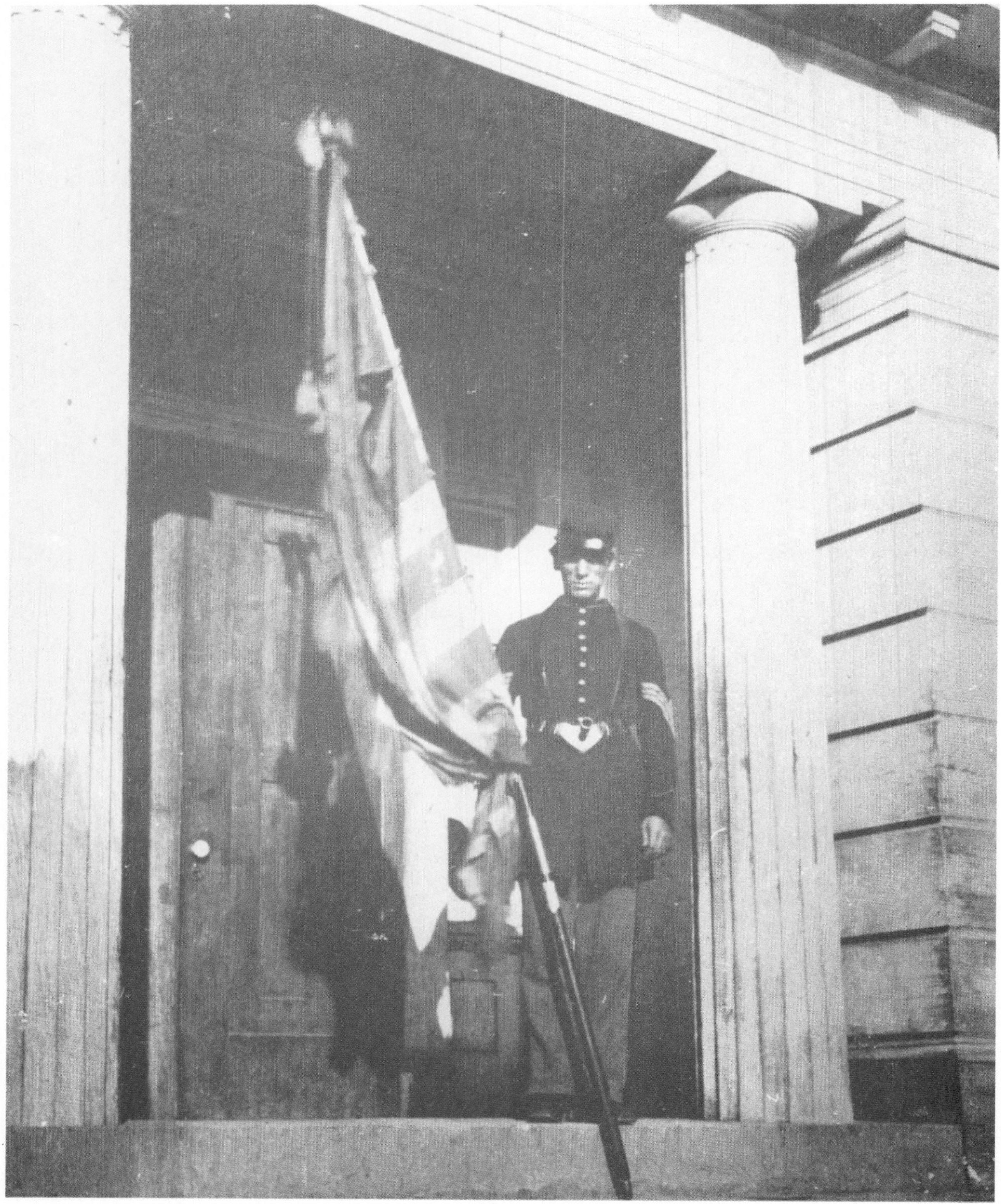

Behind him he left a conquered Atlanta, and at the city's court house, the flag of the old Union flew once more. Color Sergeant Johnson, of the 2d Massachusetts, stands with his banner on the court house steps in September 1864. (MICHAEL J. HAMMERSON)

Back to the Valley

EVERARD H. SMITH

Some of the faces are new, but the sound of battle is the same in the Shenandoah

IN 1864 THE SHENANDOAH VALLEY of Virginia again became the scene of major military action, while the Wilderness and Georgia echoed from the guns. Once more, reprising the now-familiar theme, a Rebel army muscled confidently into western Maryland and southern Pennsylvania, spreading havoc as it went. Momentarily—as cannon rumbled at Fort Stevens, near Washington, D.C.—it appeared that the very course of the war might be suddenly reversed, and no less an observer than the London *Times* was moved to conclude, "The Confederacy as an enemy is more formidable than ever."

Yet 1864 was not 1862, and the Confederate successes of midsummer proved only transitory. Northern superiority in numbers and resources, combined with a destructive new philosophy of warfare, soon broke the Southern hold on the Valley, and in the process reduced much of that beautiful vale to a smoldering ruin. The Shenandoah became, in fact, a microcosm of the final summer of the Civil War: here, as elsewhere, by the end of the year the Confederacy tottered on the verge of final defeat.

Matters began in April when Major General Franz Sigel, the local Union commander, persuaded Ulysses S. Grant to add a diversionary Valley offensive to his plans for the Old Dominion. A small, wizened German expatriate, Sigel was an officer passionately devoted to the Northern cause but regarded by his men as something of an albatross because of his political connections and foreign background. His strategy, however, was sound: a two-pronged attack on the town of Staunton, with one column, directed by himself, to advance from Harpers Ferry and the other to be led by Brigadier General George Crook from West Virginia.

Unhappily for Sigel, his opponents treated him as the greater threat, and on May 15 they concentrated most of their available forces against him at the Battle of New Market. The Southern ranks included the cadets of the Virginia Military Institute, whose youngest member was barely fifteen. The Rebels also had a superior leader, the charismatic Major General John C. Breckinridge, former U.S. Vice President and veteran corps commander—"that soldierly man," as one of his subordinates remembered him, "mounted magnificently . . . and riding like a Cid." Sigel was driven from the field in rout, provoking Chief of Staff Henry W. Halleck to comment sarcastically, "He will do nothing but run. He never did anything else."

Under heavy political pressure from Washing-

The pivotal spot for all operations in the Shenandoah Valley was Harpers Ferry, northern gateway. Here the Shenandoah flowed into the Potomac, and here, too, the Baltimore & Ohio crossed on its way west. The Harpers Ferry Arsenal and Armory, now mere shells of gutted buildings, stand across the river. (USAMHI)

ton, Grant quickly replaced Sigel with a new commander, Major General David Hunter. The little German had been no paragon, but his replacement was worse. Sixty-one years old, stocky, with thinning black hair and long Hungarian mustaches, Hunter was an intensely bigoted man whose mind had been dominated by abolitionism. He harbored vindictive feelings toward all Southerners, and his brief stay in the Valley unleashed many passions which had previously been suppressed.

Hunter's swift resumption of the offensive caught Valley defenders by surprise, and the early stages of his campaign were marked by considerable success. A small Rebel army under Brigadier General William E. "Grumble" Jones entrenched at Piedmont in a last-ditch effort to save Staunton, but was soundly defeated on June 5. Next day the Union Army entered the town, and shortly afterward it was joined by General Crook, completing the Federal juncture.

Now Hunter had to plan the next phase of the advance, and he guessed disastrously. Ignoring Grant's sensible suggestion to transport his united army east of the Blue Ridge, then follow the railroad south from Charlottesville to Lynchburg, he elected instead to take the army all the way up the Valley to Buchanan before curling in on Lynchburg from the west. As far as it went, the plan of attack was a good one, enabling him to destroy another important railroad, the Virginia & Tennessee. But it also lengthened his march and gave his opponents adequate time to reinforce the town.

As he progressed, it became increasingly evident that Hunter intended to scourge the Valley with fire as well as the sword. In alleged retaliation for harassment by Rebel partisans such as Lieutenant Colonel John S. Mosby, the homes of numerous Southern sympathizers were put to the torch. Some suspected, however, that the general enjoyed his self-proclaimed role as basilisk. "Frequently, when

Troop trains bringing men from the west passed through Harpers Ferry regularly when the Union controlled the town. These are probably Ohioans, resting on flatcars before continuing their journey, while a train laden with supplies approaches from the left. (SPECIAL COLLECTIONS, U.S. MILITARY ACADEMY LIBRARY)

we passed near houses, women would come running out, begging for protection," noted General Crook. "His invariable answer would be, 'Go away! Go away, or I will burn your house!' " Ultimately such acts of retribution had little impact on the guerrillas, but they set in motion a cycle of violence which gradually escalated as the campaign progressed, affecting both Yankees and Confederates and culminating in the devastation which left much of the lower Valley a scorched plain.

By June 12, Hunter's slow but insistent advance had become so alarming that the Confederate high command could no longer ignore it. To Robert E. Lee, whose continuing defense of Richmond rested largely on his ability to maintain the railroad network around it, Lynchburg was a transportation

The Massanutten Mountain broods over the Valley itself, the object of Stonewall Jackson's first great campaigns, and now, in 1864, the scene of yet more bitter fighting. This image was probably made shortly after the war, and shows part of the village of Strasburg. (USAMHI)

hub as vital as Petersburg. Only by detaching part of his own command could he deal with the threat. Hence that evening the II Corps of the Army of Northern Virginia, Lieutenant General Jubal A. Early commanding, departed Richmond for the Valley. Making a virtue of necessity, Lee instructed Early to dispose of Hunter first, then either return to Richmond or effect a Maryland invasion of his own.

Lee could scarcely have chosen a more able, or controversial, lieutenant to execute his orders. "Old Jube," a Valley native, was forty-seven, grizzled, and stoop-shouldered. Afield he affected the dingiest of uniforms, which he covered with an enormous linen duster and surmounted with a white slouch hat and incongruous ostrich plume—withal, as one reporter carefully observed, "a person who would be singled out in a crowd." A man of firm opinions, he inspired similar judgments among his associates, who praised his audacity but criticized his sarcasm and abrasiveness.

A forced march brought the II Corps to Lynchburg just as Hunter's vanguard arrived from the opposite direction. Demoralized by the unexpected turn of events, and unable to retreat back north without being cut off, Hunter immediately withdrew into West Virginia. In so doing he saved his army but took it out of the war for the next three weeks, leaving the Shenandoah completely unprotected.

Since Stonewall's campaign, there had been only one real battle in the Shenandoah, here at Winchester on June 14–15, 1863. This faded image is believed to have been taken in the so-called Milroy's Fort soon after the fight, and perhaps shows some of the 23 cannon captured from the routed Federal General Robert Milroy's army. (WINCHESTER-FREDERICK COUNTY HISTORICAL SOCIETY)

Of this strategic opportunity Old Jube promptly took full advantage. His army surged down the Valley in a series of marches which invoked the spirit of Stonewall Jackson's old "foot cavalry." After fording the Potomac on July 6, the gray columns circled eastward along a trajectory that directly threatened both Baltimore and Washington, D.C.

This sudden reversal of Federal fortunes precipitated a crisis in the Union chain of command which came appallingly close to costing the United States its capital. Isolated at Petersburg, Grant had no solution to the situation other than the suggestion that his chief of staff should handle the matter. Henry W. Halleck, who was at heart little more than a petulant Washington bureaucrat, and

For months thereafter, the Valley was rather quiet, but affairs in southwest Virginia soon threatened. The Confederate commander, Major General Samuel Jones, was not up to the difficult command, and, in February 1864, Richmond replaced him with . . . (VM)

. . . Major General John C. Breckinridge. The youngest Vice President in American history, he had run against Lincoln for the presidency in 1860. Now he was a Confederate officer, charged not only with defending southwest Virginia but also the Valley if it were invaded. (VM)

had besides a fine track record for avoiding responsibility, declined action unless his superior initiated it. So nothing was done. Meantime, subordinates pleaded for instructions, refugees thronged the roads leading east and south, and Early calmly occupied Frederick, Maryland, on July 9, exacting a "contribution" of $200,000 from the unhappy town fathers.

Fortunately for the North, one officer possessed sufficient courage to act in the absence of orders. From Baltimore the Rebel invasion had been watched with mounting concern by Major General Lew Wallace, an Ohio political general with the sad eyes of a basset hound and a romantically literary turn of mind. Gathering a greatly outnumbered force at the Monocacy River, Wallace contested Early's passage on the 9th. The forlorn hope ended in defeat, but it delayed the Southern advance for a crucial 12 hours. While the battle was in progress, Grant emerged from his lethargy long enough to dispatch portions of the VI and XIX Corps from Petersburg to Washington. Had Wallace not made his stubborn stand, the commanding general later conceded, Early "might have entered the capital before the arrival of the reinforcements I had sent."

Such an upset was just beyond the pugnacious Rebel leader's grasp, though the might-have-beens remained to haunt Southern apologists thenceforth. The Confederate army reached Washington's northern defense perimeter two days after the Battle of Monocacy. But Early, intimidated by the formidable earthworks he faced, confined his activities to a show of strength, and within hours Grant's veterans had arrived to ensure the safety of the

In May threats came from all over. Union Brigadier General George Crook swooped into southwest Virginia from West Virginia and met part of Breckinridge's command at Cloyd's Mountain. (WRHS)

Breckinridge was not at the battle. Instead, commanding the small Confederate army there was Brigadier General Albert Jenkins. In the battle on May 9, 1864, he lost the fight, his arm, and, within a few days, his life. (NA)

city. The following afternoon Abraham Lincoln visited Fort Stevens, where, to the consternation of Major General Horatio G. Wright, commanding the VI Corps, he casually climbed to the parapet to view the battlefield. Only feet from the President an army doctor collapsed, wounded by a sniper. Swallowing his diffidence, Wright firmly ordered his Commander-in-Chief off the wall (aided, it is alleged, by the youthful Captain Oliver Wendell Holmes, Jr., who shouted unthinkingly at the tall figure, "Get down, you fool!").

The raid on Washington proved the Confederate high-water mark of the summer. When word arrived that Hunter was finally struggling out of the West Virginia wilderness, Early slipped away from the capital unimpeded and regained the sheltering Blue Ridge walls. Still the Confederates were not quite ready to surrender their hard-won initiative. An abortive effort by Hunter to secure the lower Valley ended in near disaster on July 24 when the Rebels pounced on Crook's command at Kernstown. Then, six days later, Early determined to strike back at those who had brought devastation to western Virginia and, in the process, to teach the North a lesson which it would not soon forget.

On the morning of July 30 two mounted brigades under Brigadier General John McCausland entered Chambersburg, Pennsylvania, bearing with them a demand similar to that visited upon Frederick earlier in the month: pay a ransom of $500,000 in currency ($100,000 in specie) or face destruction. Unwilling to believe the threat, the townspeople declined to raise the money—whereupon McCausland ordered the entire town fired.

Meanwhile, Breckinridge watched another Federal thrust, south into the Valley. His eyes were the partisan rangers and cavalry scouting all through the Shenandoah, among the most effective being the command of Lieutenant Colonel John Singleton Mosby, the "Gray Ghost of the Confederacy." He appears here near war's end as a full colonel. (VM)

The Yankee army he watched was commanded by Major General Franz Sigel, a man of no military ability but potent political influence. His soldiers proudly declared, being largely Germans themselves, that they "fights mit Sigel." (USAMHI)

Sigel's army was filled with men no more able than himself, men like Brigadier General Jeremiah Sullivan, commanding his infantry. Toward the end of the war he would be relieved of command because no superior wanted him. (USAMHI)

Four hundred buildings, more than half of them homes, were destroyed. As the conflagration raged, some troopers engaged in drunken pillage while others helped residents save their possessions. "The burning of Chambersburg was generally condemned by our regiment *at first,*" admitted a cavalryman, "but when reason had time to regain her seat I believe that they all thought as I thought at first: that it was justice, and justice tempered with mercy. . . . Now everyone knows that the conciliatory policy has failed—utterly failed—and we are driven *nolens volens* to the opposite mode of procedure."

Clearly, attitudes were hardening on both sides, and this fact was apparent in the momentous change in Union leadership which Grant announced two days after the Chambersburg raid. To Major General Philip H. Sheridan, the new commander, went orders "to put himself south of the enemy and follow him to the death." Presaging future events, the general-in-chief also outlined a specific objective for the campaign: "Such as cannot be consumed, destroy," a sentiment expressed with equal cogency in Sheridan's oft-quoted remark that a crow flying over the Valley would have to carry its own rations.

Yet they led good troops, veteran regiments like the 34th Massachusetts, shown here in 1862 outside Alexandria, Virginia. (USAMHI)

"Restless, full of the combative quality, not politic in language, somewhat reticent, half stubborn and fond of hazard enterprises . . . he was the embodiment of heroism, dash, and impulse." Thus Grant described Phil Sheridan, the five-foot-five, black-haired, bullet-headed son of Irish immigrants from County Caven. Despite tactical abilities that were never more than modest, Sheridan had won prominence as one of the hardest-fighting generals in the Army of the Potomac. For his forthcoming operations he possessed an army that eventually included seven infantry and three cavalry divisions, plus substantial artillery. His opponent's command mustered no more than five divisions of infantry and two of cavalry, in addition to one brigade of artillery. In terms of manpower the Northern superiority was even more pronounced, probably on the order of two-to-one.

Reflecting his superiors' concern that further Confederate successes would endanger Lincoln in the fall elections, Sheridan proceeded cautiously at first. However, when he finally moved on September 19 against the Southern position at Winchester, just west of Opequon Creek, his juggernaut rolled forward with irresistible momentum. Combined infantry and cavalry assaults smashed the Confederate left flank; Early was sent, in Sheridan's own expressive phrase, "whirling through Winchester." Battered but still defiant, the gray forces entrenched 20 miles farther south at Fisher's Hill, near Strasburg. Here, three days later, Sheridan attacked again, once more outflanking the Confederate left.

Grant now counseled his subordinate, as he had Hunter, to occupy the Valley as far south as Staunton and then move eastward toward Charlottesville. But Sheridan resisted, citing logistical difficulties and the dangers of partisan bedevilment. Instead he argued that the ravaging of the lower

Rushing to meet and stop Sigel, Breckinridge enlisted the aid of the Corps of Cadets of Lexington's Virginia Military Institute. Lieutenant Colonel Scott Ship led the boys, some no more than fourteen, in the battle that followed. (NEW MARKET BATTLEFIELD PARK)

Cadet William Nelson, at nineteen, was among the oldest in the corps who fought at New Market. (VM)

Shenandoah should remain his primary goal. Accordingly, he sent out raiding parties to destroy as much of the recent harvest as possible. The rest of the army began digging in at Cedar Creek for an indefinite stay. To clear up the details of his strategy, the War Department ordered him to Washington for a brief conference on October 16. For the summons which took him from the front at this critical moment, Sheridan was of course not to blame. Nevertheless, his defensive arrangements at Cedar Creek were open to criticism, for he left his army indifferently posted, its left flank resting unsupported above a defile at the foot of Massanutten Mountain.

Out of the foggy dawn on October 19 rose the spine-chilling wail of the "Rebel Yell" as Old Jube struck the Federal left end-on with the full strength of four divisions. Totally surprised, the Union Army reeled backward along the Valley turnpike for four miles. Sheridan, who learned of the attack just as he was returning from Winchester, spurred furiously toward the battlefield, 14 miles away. En route he passed thousands of fleeing soldiers who turned with a cheer to follow him as he shouted, "About-face, boys! We're going back to our camps! We're going to lick them out of their boots!" In a

A distinguished yet little known Confederate officer who led one of Breckinridge's brigades at New Market was Brigadier General Gabriel C. Wharton, himself a VMI graduate. (LC)

There were distinguished men in Sigel's army, and Captain Henry A. DuPont of Delaware was one of them. Though he did not arrive on the field in time for the battle, he did save the rout of Sigel's army from becoming a complete disaster. Years later he would sponsor legislation to rebuild VMI after the ravages of the war. (ELEUTHERIAN MILLS HISTORICAL LIBRARY)

famous poem published shortly after the battle, T. Buchanan Read exaggerated by half the distance Sheridan's ride covered (and with it the endurance of his charger, Rienzi), but accurately depicted its psychological impact:

He dashed down the line, 'mid a storm of huzzas,
And the wave of retreat checked its course there,
  because
The sight of the master compelled it to pause.
With foam and with dust the black charger
  was gray;
By the flash of his eye, and his red nostril's play,
He seemed to the whole great army to say:
"I have brought you Sheridan all the way
  From Winchester down to save the day."

By way of anticlimax, when Sheridan arrived he discovered that General Wright had already stabilized the front. Whether Early himself neglected to press the attack, or whether his men simply stopped to plunder the enemy's camps, the impetus of the Southern offensive gradually slowed. The inevitable Northern counterattack precipitated a rout unprecedented even by Valley standards. With dogged tenacity, Early once again assembled his forces farther south, but the final Confederate bid for mastery in the Shenandoah had failed.

Affairs well in hand, Sheridan's men resumed the task of despoliation, their success illustrated by the grim record of the property which they seized or destroyed: 1,200 barns; 71 flour mills; 8 sawmills; 7 furnaces; 4 tanneries; 3 saltpeter works; 1 woolen mill; 1 powder mill; 1 railroad depot; 1,165 pounds of cotton yarn; 974 miles of rail; 15,000 swine; 12,000 sheep; 10,918 cattle; 3,772 horses; 545 mules; 250 calves; 435,802 bushels of wheat; 77,176 bushels of corn; 20,397 tons of hay; 500 tons of fodder; 450 tons of straw; 12,000 pounds of bacon; 10,000 pounds of tobacco; and 874 barrels of flour. These depredations did not affect the upper Valley, where Early still lurked. Even so, between Staunton and the Potomac they were thorough indeed. Thousands of refugees moved north, and a full year after the war a British traveler found the region standing as desolate as a moor.

While the plundering was under way, Rebel guerrillas continued to plague the invaders, at one point even spiriting General Crook off into captivity. For a while it appeared that the North had a solution to this problem too. Six of Mosby's men were hanged at Front Royal by Brigadier General George A. Custer, a brash young cavalry commander already displaying signs of the faulty judgment which would cost him his life on the Little Big Horn. But anyone could play this game, and after Mosby retaliated in kind both sides mercifully halted the executions. A final stage in the escalation of violence was thereby avoided—yet here in Virginia, as well as elsewhere in the South, rapid progress had been made toward the dreadful 20th century concept of total war.

Sheridan's operations concluded in February 1865, when he overwhelmed the last remnants of Confederate strength at Waynesboro and then rejoined Grant at Petersburg. To contemporaries his campaign was one of the signal accomplishments of the Civil War, and it figured prominently in postbellum song and story. It is true that, in the harsh light of historical retrospection, his exploits fall short of epic proportions. Less than half the Valley suffered from his scorched-earth tactics. Moreover, by nullifying Grant's repeated orders to resume the offensive east of the Blue Ridge, he may well have lost a golden opportunity to end the war six months before Appomattox. All this being said, however, the incompleteness of his victory probably did not matter. To his credit, he achieved more than any Union leader before him, for he demolished an important symbol of Southern invincibility. In so doing, he also removed one of the few remaining props upon which rested the fate of the Confederate nation.

Immediately after the Confederate victory at New Market, Richmond sent Colonel Edwin G. Lee, shown here as a brigadier later in the war, to assume command at Staunton and recruit more troops for the defense of the Valley. It was obvious that the Yankees would come again. (CHS)

In fact, they came within two weeks, led now by a general just as incompetent as Sigel, Major General David Hunter. His destruction of private property, including VMI, would make his name reviled in Virginia. (WRHS)

His adjutant, Colonel David Hunter Strother, was much better liked, and better known by his pen name "Porte Crayon." He drew sketches of army life that were widely published in the North. (USAMHI)

To stop Hunter, Richmond assigned one of Lee's premier fighters, Lieutenant General Jubal A. Early of the II Corps. Cranky, cantankerous, a confirmed bachelor who offended many, still he was more than Hunter's match. (VM)

Hunter was turned back, and with him his chief of cavalry, Major General Julius Stahel, a Hungarian who won the Medal of Honor for his bravery in the Battle of Piedmont in June. (USAMHI)

Less distinguished was the service of Colonel August Moor of the 28th Ohio. Within weeks of Piedmont, he would be out of the service. (USAMHI)

When Early came to the Valley, he brought with him several officers of high merit. He would need them, for barely had he driven Hunter out before he launched his July raid on Washington itself. Confederate cavalry led by Brigadier General Robert Ransom was the vanguard. (USAMHI)

Serving with the Confederate infantry in the raid, and at the Battle of Monocacy, Maryland, which delayed Early, was perhaps the biggest general of the war, Brigadier William R. Peck of Tennessee. He stood six feet six inches tall and won commendation for his bravery in the battle. (USAMHI)

The real hero of Monocacy, however, was a Yankee, Major General Lew Wallace. With inferior numbers, still he managed to stall Early long enough for vital reinforcements to reach Washington and prevent its capture. Years after the war he would write his great book, Ben Hur. (USAMHI)

Early got as close as Fort Stevens, only a few miles outside the capital. On this ground he fought his hesitating battle that ended the raid. Had he pushed, he might still have broken through despite . . . (MHS)

. . . last-minute reinforcements from Grant's army at Petersburg, among them Brigadier General Frank Wheaton and his division of the VI Corps. Ironically, Wheaton's wife was the daughter of the Confederacy's highest ranking general, Samuel Cooper. (P-M)

This house near Fort Stevens shows the effects of Early's artillery fire during the fighting. (USAMHI)

It was as close as the ravages of war came to the District of Columbia, and quite close enough for President Lincoln, who was in Fort Stevens during part of the firing. (USAMHI)

For a few hours Confederates even occupied the home of Breckinridge's cousin and old friend, Montgomery Blair, at Silver Spring, Maryland. Breckinridge saved the house from looting. (USAMHI)

Nevertheless, later on Confederate stragglers would vandalize the home of Blair, Lincoln's postmaster general. (USAMHI)

Early, too, took losses, among them the personable young Brigadier General Robert D. Lilley. Back in Virginia, near Winchester, he was so severely wounded that he lost his right arm. Here his empty sleeve is pinned to his blouse. (USAMHI)

Early did not forget the depredations of Hunter in the Valley. In retaliation, he sent Brigadier General John McCausland to demand a payment of half a million dollars from Chambersburg, Pennsylvania. When the town could not produce it, McCausland gave . . . (COURTESY OF ALEXANDER MCCAUSLAND)

. . . Brigadier General Bradley T. Johnson orders to burn the town. (USAMHI)

Johnson applied the torch, and Chambersburg burned. Local photographers, the Zacharias brothers, recorded the aftermath. (MHS)

All that was left of the Bank of Chambersburg. (MHS)

The skeleton of the Franklin County court house. Chambersburg would eventually receive compensation from Washington for its loss—in the 1970s! (MHS)

But in 1864 there was nothing to assuage the loss. Yankees called it barbarism. Confederates called it revenge. (COURTESY OF MAURICE MAROTTE)

Early's successes in the Shenandoah forced Washington to stop sending political hacks to oppose him. Instead, Grant sent one of his most trusted lieutenants, the ruthless Major General Philip H. Sheridan, small, combative, merciless. He stands at front, fifth from the left, among his staff in 1864. (USAMHI)

Through August and into September, Early and Sheridan feinted at each other. Then on September 19 the Federals attacked, pushing across Opequon Creek and moving toward Winchester. A postwar view of the creek. (USAMHI)

With Early falling back before them, Sheridan's divisions drove toward the Valley pike, shown here looking south toward Winchester. (USAMHI)

In bitter fighting, one of the best young officers of the Confederate Army, Brigadier General Robert E. Rodes, was killed in action, his division being taken by another promising young officer . . . (USAMHI)

. . . Brigadier General John Pegram. (COURTESY OF W. HAYS PARKS)

Yankees, too, started to fall. Brigadier General David A. Russell, who had helped save Washington in July, fell leading a brigade when a shell fragment pierced his heart. He stands at left, with Generals T. H. Neill in the center, and John H. Martindale at right. (USAMHI)

Before long the Confederates were pushed back into Winchester itself, desperately holding out against Sheridan's attacks. An 1885 view, with Milroy's Fort visible on the crest in the distance. (USAMHI)

Brigadier General R. D. Johnston led his brigade with particular bravery in trying to stem the Yankee tide, but Sheridan was too powerful, and Early too scattered. (VM)

From this spot in Milroy's Fort civilians looked out and watched the battle for Winchester as it raged off in the distance. (USAMHI)

Brigadier General James McIntosh and his cavalry brigade had helped open the battle. For four hours that morning he held a position against Early's infantry. In the end his battling cost McIntosh a severe wound and a leg. (USAMHI)

For Colonel James Mulligan, it cost more than that. Wounded while leading his brigade, he was captured by the Confederates and died a few days later. (NA)

Around the already ruined Hackwood house the contending armies raged as Sheridan pressed ever closer to Winchester. (USAMHI)

Here, late in the afternoon, elements of Sheridan's XIX Corps poised before the final attack that drove Early out of Winchester. A postwar image. (USAMHI)

What put Early's army to flight out of Winchester was the final attack of the day, led by Brigadier General Wesley Merritt. An unpublished image believed to be of the youthful and talented cavalry officer. (COURTESY OF THOMAS SWEENEY)

Colonel Rutherford B. Hayes won a reputation for himself at Fisher's Hill, and after the war his record helped win him a term in the White House. (P-M)

The armies met next at Fisher's Hill on September 22. Southwest of Strasburg, Fisher's Hill proved to be another Confederate stampede, as Sheridan's attack drove Early from his position on the crest in the center background. Many a Confederate was buried in the little cemetery at left. An 1885 view. (USAMHI)

Viewed from the crest of Fisher's Hill, the Federal positions are off in the distance. By getting around his flank, Sheridan forced Early to retreat and almost cut off escape but for the stubborn rearguard stand of Confederate cavalrymen . . . (USAMHI)

. . . Brigadier General W. C. Wickham, who outwitted Sheridan's pursuers and saved Early from possible disaster. (VM)

Old Jubal smarted under his twin defeats, and through September and into October he planned a counterattack. At Cedar Creek on October 19, 1864, he made it. Spearheading the attack was a bold march around Sheridan's flank led by Major General John B. Gordon, one of the fightingest generals in the Confederate Army. (NA)

Along with Gordon's flank march, Kershaw's brigade crossed Cedar Creek here to assist in the flank attack. It achieved complete surprise and threatened to put the Yankees to rout. A postwar image. (USAMHI)

This hill is where the Federals' unsuspecting left was placed when Early struck. The bluecoats could not stand in the face of a lightning attack. (USAMHI)

Brigadier General Daniel D. Bidwell fell with a mortal wound while trying to resist Early's assault. (USAMHI)

Confederates like Brigadier General Cullen Battle paid a price for their surprise, however. Leading a brigade in Gordon's attack, Battle took a wound that put him out of the war for good. (USAMHI)

Only the heroic efforts of men like Brigadier General Lewis A. Grant managed to build a line where the retreating Federals could hold long enough for reinforcements to come and resist Early's drive. (P-M)

Brigadier General Alfred T. A. Torbert's cavalry division also stood in the face of the advancing Confederates, buying enough time for Sheridan to rush to the battlefield and start sending more regiments. A native of Delaware, Torbert actually held a commission in the Confederate Army briefly at war's outset but was at the same time raising the 1st New Jersey. (USAMHI)

Sheridan was some distance behind the lines when Early struck. Feverishly, he rode his charger forward to take command and rally his army. This postwar image of his horse was made in Leavenworth, Kansas, by photographer E. E. Henry. (USAMHI)

Here, on the Valley turnpike, Sheridan rejoined his army and began salvaging victory from imminent defeat. (USAMHI)

Once more the Federals advanced, across ground like this where they had been placed that morning, unsuspecting the storm that Early would unleash. (USAMHI)

By that afternoon it was Early who was hard-pressed. Here sat his left flank when the revitalized XIX Corps and VI Corps struck in an unstoppable attack that drove the Southerners from the field. Early had his third consecutive defeat. (USAMHI)

Sheridan made his headquarters at Belle Grove mansion, seen here in the distance, a magnificent country house built by the Fairfax family. Here after the battle mortally wounded Confederate Brigadier Stephen D. Ramseur was brought to die. Old friends like Custer and Merritt surrounded him at his deathbed. (USAMHI)

And that was virtually the end of the Valley Campaign. Through the fall and on into the winter of 1865 the armies glowered at each other, but Early could no longer risk meeting his foe. New officers came to him, men like Colonel Thomas T. Munford, who would command his remnant of cavalry, but they were too few to save the Shenandoah. (VM)

Early himself was relieved in March 1865 and replaced by Major General Lunsford L. Lomax, in command of the Valley District. By then it was a command without an army. (USAMHI)

Through that winter the Federals, too, played a game of watch and wait. For them and for the Valley, the war was almost over. Here, just outside Winchester, the camera captures the headquarters of Colonel Alexander Pennington's cavalry brigade on February 23, 1865. (USAMHI)

And here in Winchester a jaunty Brigadier General George A. Custer sits at the head of the steps, surrounded by his wife and friends. The boy general had distinguished himself in the campaign. (AMERICANA IMAGE GALLERY)

They had all distinguished themselves, and with Early dispatched, Sheridan and his generals could be off for the east of the Blue Ridge, back to Grant, and the last irresistible surge at Lee. Sitting on the ground are Brigadier General James H. Wilson, at left, Torbert in the center, and Sheridan at right. Seated behind them are Brigadier General Thomas Davies at left, Brigadier General David M. Gregg in profile, and Merritt at far right. They were a constellation of stars. (KA)

A Campaign That Failed

LUDWELL H. JOHNSON III

Cotton and politics and the Red River make strange war in Louisiana

THE RED RIVER EXPEDITION, like the Shenandoah campaign part of the Union's nationwide advance, was perhaps as strange and complicated an episode as the Civil War has to offer. It originated in a combination of motives that included a missionary-imperialist impulse to promote a New England settlement of Texas, fears of French influence in Mexico, President Lincoln's determination to establish a Unionist state government in Louisiana, the machinations of unscrupulous cotton speculators and textile mill interests, the U.S. Navy's thirst for prize money, and the strategic vagaries of Chief of Staff Major General Henry W. Halleck.

The Union plan of campaign called for a powerful column based in New Orleans to advance to the Red River from the south, another force to come down the Mississippi from Vicksburg, a third to march southwestward from Little Rock, and the Mississippi Squadron to accompany the main force up the Red River. The objective was to capture Shreveport, headquarters of the Confederate Trans-Mississippi Department, and from there to invade Texas. The campaign was to begin in March 1864, when the Federals needed every available man for the decisive campaigns east of the Mississippi. It was set in motion against the wishes of U. S. Grant, who succeeded Halleck as chief of staff soon after the expedition began. It continued without benefit of an overall commander, met with severe reverses, almost saw the Mississippi Squadron lost or sunk, tied up thousands of troops that otherwise would have been employed with Sherman in Georgia and in an attack on Mobile, and ended in total failure.

Commanding the column coming up from New Orleans was Nathaniel P. Banks, a Massachusetts politician with no prewar military experience who had been repeatedly beaten by Stonewall Jackson in Virginia. Late in 1862, Banks replaced Benjamin F. Butler as commander of the Department of the Gulf, where his principal task was the political reorganization of Louisiana. The Vicksburg column, detached from W. T. Sherman's army, had for its leader the hard-bitten A. J. Smith, who came under Banks' orders when he reached the Red River. Naval forces consisted of the Mississippi Squadron, 23 vessels, mostly ironclads. The admiral of this armada was David Dixon Porter, courageous, vainglorious, and money-hungry, whose sailors were skilled in "capturing" cotton as a prize of war. Frederick Steele led the troops who were to come down from Little Rock. Preoccupied by the task of Republicanizing Arkansas and acutely aware of the logistical pitfalls of a march

When an invasion of the Red River was proposed, many, including the man who would lead it, were not enthusiastic. But chief of staff Major General Henry W. Halleck managed to force it to be undertaken. (USAMHI)

through south-central Arkansas, Steele would have preferred to make a mere demonstration, but Grant ordered him to move on Shreveport in cooperation with Banks.

Confederate forces were under the general direction of E. Kirby Smith, commander of the Trans-Mississippi Department. Sterling Price, silver-maned former governor of Missouri, led the cavalry contesting Steele's advance. Bearing the brunt of the Federal invasion up the Red was Richard Taylor, son of the late Zachary Taylor and brother to Jefferson Davis' first wife. Highly educated and widely read, Taylor was a very capable amateur soldier who had won his spurs with Jackson in the Shenandoah Valley. He was supremely confident, pugnacious, a leader of men, and an imaginative strategist.

Both Smith and Taylor found it hard to believe reports of an impending offensive against Shreveport. Surely, said Smith, the enemy could not be so "infatuated" as to divert troops from the central South, where the war would be decided. All doubts were laid to rest when Porter's squadron and A. J. Smith's 11,000 veterans appeared at the mouth of the Red River on March 11. The Federal troops marched inland and overwhelmed the little garrison at Fort De Russy. Porter then carried part of Smith's command to Alexandria, which was occupied on the 15th. When Banks' men reached the town ten days later, Federal forces totaled 30,000 troops, while on the river there were 60 vessels, including transports. To confront this host Taylor had 7,000 men. His only course was to fall back, collect reinforcements, and hope for an opportunity to strike the enemy in detail.

At Alexandria, while Banks was holding elections for the "restored" government of Louisiana, Porter's men rounded up wagons and teams and ranged the countryside collecting cotton. They stenciled "CSA" on the bales to convince the prize court it was Confederate-owned cotton, and under that "USN." One envious army officer told Porter the initials stood for "Cotton Stealing Association of the United States Navy." Porter also had less congenial work to attend to at Alexandria. The river had failed to rise at the usual season, a fact that would give the Navy much grief before the campaign was over, but 13 gunboats and 30 transports managed to scrape into the upper Red, including the huge ironclad *Eastport*.

When Banks pushed out from Alexandria, Taylor fell back before him. Union infantry entered Natchitoches on April 1, having marched 80 miles in four days. A few miles farther, at Grand Ecore, the main road to Shreveport turned away from the river and, for Banks, away from the shelter of Porter's big guns. On April 6, without waiting to look for a river road, which did exist, Banks plunged

The man who would actually command the expedition was Major General Nathaniel P. Banks of Massachusetts, seated at center among his staff. A man of no military experience, and even less ability, he was a political powerhouse, and that got him command. Halleck complained that it was "but little better than murder" to put men like Banks in the field. (MHS)

into the forbidding pine woods. Porter continued up the narrow, winding river the next day. Taylor withdrew as far as Mansfield, about 40 miles from Shreveport; there he made a stand, deployed his little army, and waited for Banks. Smoldering with anger because reinforcements were so few in number and so long in reaching him, bitterly resenting the gossipers at departmental headquarters who blamed him for the failure to stop the invaders, Taylor was in a dangerous frame of mind.

The Federals tramped through Pleasant Hill and on toward Mansfield. First came the cavalry, then the cavalry's large wagon train, then the infantry. At noon on April 8 the troopers emerged into a clearing, on the far side of which they could see the Rebel skirmish line. Infantry filed into line but did not attack. By four o'clock Taylor's small store of patience was exhausted, and he came down on the enemy with crushing force. Outflanked, the Federals fell back, stiffened as reinforcements arrived, then broke and ran for the rear. When they found the narrow road blocked by the cavalry train, panic spread through the ranks. At last, two miles from the battlefield, a fresh Union division checked the pursuers well after night had fallen. In the darkness, cries of the wounded mingled with joyous shouts as the Confederates plundered the captured wagons. Banks

To back Banks in the Red River Campaign, Washington assembled a mighty ironclad fleet, including 13 ironclads and several more gunboats. A part of that fleet poses here on the Red in May 1864. (USAMHI)

fought most of the battle with about 7,000 men, as compared to Taylor's 8,800. Banks lost 2,235 men, of whom two thirds were captured. Taylor lost 1,000 killed and wounded; there was no report of anyone missing. He captured 20 pieces of artillery and 156 wagons, valuable booty for the lean gray army.

Banks retreated to Pleasant Hill, where he took up a defensive position, strengthened by A. J. Smith's command. Taylor followed, having been reinforced by two small divisions under Thomas J. Churchill. These troops had recently arrived from Arkansas in response to orders from Kirby Smith, who had correctly decided to concentrate against Banks first.

Taylor had followed Stonewall Jackson to some purpose and did not intend to make a simple frontal attack at Pleasant Hill. His plan called for Churchill to envelop the Union left while the rest of the infantry attacked in front. Cavalry would move around the enemy's right flank. If successful, Taylor would cut off all of Banks' avenues of retreat. Churchill's weary soldiers, who had marched 45 miles during the last day and a half, advanced with spirit at three in the afternoon, drove the Federals back, reached the road to Natchitoches, and seemed to have the battle well in hand. However, the Federal left was not where it seemed to be. Churchill had in fact crossed his right in front of A. J. Smith, who attacked at just the right moment. Although it resisted stubbornly, the Confederate right gave way in disorder. Darkness ended the fighting; Taylor had been sharply repulsed.

Banks rode up to Smith. "God bless you, General," he exclaimed, "you have saved the army." Later, without consulting Smith, Banks decided to retreat; soon after midnight the army started down the road to Grand Ecore. At Pleasant Hill each side had had approximately 12,000 men engaged. Banks lost 1,400 casualties, Taylor more than 1,600. The "Fighting Politician" had been lucky. With another general there would have been no need to retreat, but probably most of Banks' officers would have agreed with William B. Frank-

Commanding the naval end of the operation was Admiral David D. Porter, flamboyant, scheming, and anxious to confiscate the abundant cotton on the Red River for the prize money. (USAMHI)

lin, commander of the XIX Corps: "From what I had seen of General Banks' ability to command in the field, I was certain that an operation depending on plenty of troops, rather than skill in handling them, was the only one which would have probability of success in his hands."

One arm of the pincers movement on Shreveport was broken when Banks retreated from Pleasant Hill. The other, Steele's army, was advancing on the Confederate stronghold from the northeast; by the time Taylor attacked Banks, the campaign in Arkansas was two weeks old. For the Federals it was a dismal ordeal from start to finish. Steele set out from Little Rock with 6,800 effectives on March 23. A cooperating column of 3,600 men joined him at Elkins' Ferry on April 9, but brought no supplies. The roads were wretched, food and forage scarce, and Price's cavalry swarmed about the column. "Our supplies were nearly exhausted and so was the country," said Steele. "We were obliged to forage from 5 to 15 miles on either side of the road to keep our stock alive." Therefore, on April 12, Steele abruptly changed his direction from southwest to east and made for the town of Camden. There he hoped to accumulate supplies and eventually to resume the offensive.

Ironically, just as Steele was turning back, Kirby Smith decided to strip Taylor of most of his infantry and take them to Arkansas, even though he had learned that Steele was heading for Camden and posed no immediate threat to Shreveport. Taylor argued to no avail for a concentration against Banks and Porter; Kirby Smith was obdurate. He marched off, leaving the fuming Taylor with his cavalry and one small division of infantry. Without doubt this was a strategic mistake of the first magnitude, one that not only affected operations on the Red River, but conceivably had an important bearing on the major campaigns east of the Mississippi.

Kirby Smith left for Arkansas on April 16, the same day that the rear of Steele's column entered Camden. There the beleaguered Federals began their search for food. The capture of a Confederate steamer loaded with corn eased the pinch somewhat, as did the arrival of a wagon train from Pine Bluff with ten days' half-rations. But these successes were more than offset by the loss of a wagon train in a bloody little affair at Poison Spring that cost the Federals almost a third of the escort, and of another in a bigger fight at Marks' Mills, where 1,300 of 1,600 men were lost. The capture of these trains precipitated a crisis: Steele no longer had the means to feed his men and animals. There was only one possible decision: on April 25 Steele ordered an immediate retreat to Little Rock.

With the infantry from Taylor's army now at hand, Kirby Smith took up the pursuit. This was his second serious mistake. The proper course would have been to return swiftly to Louisiana and join Taylor in attacking the Federals before they could extricate themselves from the Red River country. Instead he kept on after Steele, both ar-

Porter himself made the famous Black Hawk *his flagship. She sits here at anchor in the Mississippi with a small steam tug at her bow.* (GLADSTONE COLLECTION)

mies contending with rain and mud, bridging rivers, struggling against hunger and exhaustion. On April 30 he overtook Steele at Jenkins' Ferry, a crossing of the Saline. Fighting across flooded bottom lands, knee-deep in water, assaulting log breastworks, the Confederates made little headway. All during the battle Steele labored to get his trains and artillery across the river. By early afternoon the bloodied Confederates had given up the attack, and the Federals staggered the last miles into Little Rock in peace. The Arkansas phase of the campaign was over.

Back on the Red, Banks had entrenched at Grand Ecore, presenting the strange spectacle of 25,000 men hemmed in by 5,000. Meanwhile, Porter's flotilla had proceeded up the river, headed for Shreveport. When Porter learned of the army's retreat, he managed to turn his vessels around in the narrow, shallow channel and begin the difficult trip downstream. Grinding along the bottom, sticking on submerged stumps, colliding with one another, braving Confederate musketry and artillery fire, they at last reached Grand Ecore safely. This trip, however, was only a foretaste of troubles yet to come.

Banks dismissed his chief of staff and two cavalry generals, scapegoats for his failure, called up reinforcements, and even thought of resuming the offensive. The thought passed quickly; on April 19 he began the retreat to Alexandria. His route took him down a long island formed by the Cane and Red rivers, and Taylor attempted to encircle the enemy as they prepared to leave the island at Monett's Ferry. Had the infantry Kirby Smith

Brigadier General A. J. Smith, shown here as a colonel in late 1861, was ordered to cooperate with Banks. He was not very popular with his men, some of whom hissed him when he rode past. And later in the campaign he would suggest arresting Banks for incompetence. (LC)

marched off to Arkansas still been with Taylor, his plan might well have succeeded; now the odds were too heavy. Pushing the Confederates aside after brisk fighting, Banks' men reached Alexandria on the 25th. They had left behind them a smoking wasteland. "The track of the spoiler," said one observer, "was one scene of desolation. . . . A painful melancholy, a death-like silence, broods over the land, and desolation reigns supreme." A. J. Smith's men, not long back from Sherman's devastating Meridian expedition, were the stars of the drama. "The people now will be terribly scourged," promised one of Smith's generals, and scourged they were.

As the navy paralleled the army's withdrawal, Porter was having more trouble. The ponderous *Eastport,* sunk below Grand Ecore by a torpedo and laboriously refloated, proved to be a dangerous encumbrance to the vessels assigned to shepherd her downstream. After grounding repeatedly, *Eastport* finally stuck fast, and Porter had to blow her up. The other boats, including Porter's flagship *Cricket,* had to run an artillery gauntlet five miles above the mouth of Cane River. Two transports were total losses, *Cricket* received 38 hits and, like *Juliet* and *Fort Hindman,* suffered heavy casualties. To make matters worse, when Porter reached Alexandria, he found that the river had fallen, trapping above the falls the backbone of the Mississippi Squadron: *Lexington, Fort Hindman, Osage, Neosho, Mound City, Louisville, Pittsburg, Chillicothe, Carondelet,* and *Ozark.* Should the army continue its retreat, they, like *Eastport,* would have to be destroyed.

On April 21 the War Department heard that the army, badly damaged, had retreated to Grand Ecore. Grant, who had intended to use Banks' force in a campaign against Mobile, gave up all idea of using those troops east of the Mississippi that spring. Banks would be lucky, it seemed, not to lose the army and the fleet. Something had to be done to secure better leadership. Remove Banks, Grant told Halleck, but Lincoln demurred. "General Banks," Halleck told Grant, "is a personal friend of the President, and has strong political supporters in and out of Congress." Lincoln would remove him only if Grant insisted upon it as a military necessity. Ultimately, too late to affect the campaign, a middle way was found: Banks' Department of the Gulf was absorbed in the newly created Military Division of West Mississippi under the command of Edward R. S. Canby. Although nominally retaining his position, Banks would never again take the field.

Ignorant of his impending demotion, Banks was fortifying Alexandria lest his 31,000 men be overwhelmed by Taylor's 6,000. It was an unhappy time for the man whose soldiers derisively called him "Napoleon P. Banks," or sometimes just "Mr.

Quickly the armies gathered, and the fleet assembled. The USS Ouachita *had formerly been a Confederate warship, the* Louisville, *before her capture in 1863. Now she was preparing to steam up the Red.* (MHS)

Banks." He could not stay where he was indefinitely, and he could not retreat without abandoning the navy, which was unthinkable. The way out of this dilemma came from an engineer on Franklin's staff, Lieutenant Colonel Joseph Bailey of Wisconsin. Experienced in the logging country, Bailey proposed to build a temporary dam to raise the water level on the falls. Porter was skeptical, but was in no position to reject any scheme, no matter how improbable. Banks made available the necessary manpower and gave much personal attention to the project. Work began late in April.

Porter and Banks were not the only people unhappy with the campaign so far. Cotton speculators who had trailed along with the expedition expecting a rich haul saw their dreams go up in smoke, or else into the holds of the gunboats. Part of the cotton which had been hauled into Alexandria was seized for use in building the dam, including some owned by one of Lincoln's old friends who had appeared on the Red with the President's permission to go through the lines and buy cotton from the Confederates. "I wish you would take somebody else's cotton than mine," he protested, "that is very fine cotton!"

The Confederates blockading the river below the town inflicted serious losses on Union shipping. On May 4, *City Belle,* with the 120th Ohio on board, was captured, and on the 5th a transport loaded with the 56th Ohio was lost, as were two gunboats, *Covington* and *Signal.* But Taylor's small force was unable to do the one thing that would have meant disaster for the enemy: stop construction of Colonel Bailey's dam.

Another captured Confederate gunboat was the General Price. *Now she was in the Yankee service, though the commander of the gunboat* Conestoga, *lying astern of her in this January 20, 1864, image by Baton Rouge artist A. D. Lytle, might well have wondered whose side the* General Price *was really on. Seven weeks after this photo of the two was made . . .* (COURTESY OF ROBERT G. HARRIS)

At the site of this formidable undertaking, the river was 758 feet wide, the water four to six feet deep, and the current a full ten miles an hour. By building from both banks simultaneously and by using every conceivable material, by May 8 Bailey had succeeded in creating a significant rise in the water level. The gunboats would have been able to come down then, but for reasons still unknown Porter had issued no orders to lighten ship by removing guns, ammunition, and stores, to say nothing of the "prize" cotton with which the vessels were gorged. Finally, at the urging of the dam builders, the navy came awake. On the 9th, four gunboats shot the roaring gap in the dam. The others were lightened, and by May 13 all were safe in easy water below the falls. "I have had a hard and anxious time of it," Porter wrote his mother.

Now the army was free to leave Alexandria. Soldiers spread out through the town, smearing wooden buildings with turpentine and camphine and setting scores of fires. A. J. Smith rode amid the flaming buildings exclaiming, "Hurrah, boys, this looks like war!" Some of Banks' staff and headquarters guard tried unsuccessfully to put out the fires. By noon on the 13th the town had been leveled. The burning continued all along the army's line of retreat. On the 16th, Taylor made one last effort to block the invaders, but after holding them back for several hours near Mansura he had to give way before odds of three to one, although he still harried the column's flanks and rear. But Banks marched on, and by May 20 his men had put the Atchafalaya between themselves and the persistent Confederates. The campaign was over.

. . . with Lieutenant I. F. Richardson in command, seated at right . . . (COURTESY OF ROBERT G. HARRIS)

. . . the General Price *collided with the* Conestoga *while both were on their way to the Red River. The* Conestoga *sank, ending a distinguished river career.* (NA)

Also along for the campaign was the hospital ship Red Rover. *She, too, had been a Confederate vessel, a barracks ship until captured and converted into the Navy's first commissioned medical ship.* (NHC)

Half of Porter's fleet, it seemed, had changed sides during the war. The Eastport *began its war career as a Confederate warship, an unfinished ironclad completed and put into service by the Yankees. On April 15, 1864, she would strike an underwater mine or "torpedo," and a few days later, crippled, she was sunk to avoid capture.* (USAMHI)

This McPherson & Oliver photograph shows Banks' goal, Alexandria, Louisiana, on the Red River. Federals took it unopposed on March 15 as Porter's fleet steamed up to the wharves. (USAMHI)

The Confederate commander of the Trans-Mississippi Department, General E. Kirby Smith, shown here in an early war photo, was ill prepared or equipped to resist a major invasion. (USAMHI)

His army commander at Alexandria, Lieutenant General Richard Taylor, was the son of President Zachary Taylor and an officer of unusual ability. He also knew he could not resist Banks at Alexandria, so he evacuated. (CHS)

Within a few days Banks had his army at Alexandria, and as ready to march on as he would ever be. With him was the 19th Kentucky, its headquarters photographed here by Lytle at Baton Rouge a few weeks before. (KA)

With him, too, were men of the 47th Illinois, led by these officers. (COURTESY OF WILLIAM ANDERSON)

With Banks' army there were a mixed bag of officers, including even a professional adventurer, Colonel C. Carroll Tevis, commanding the 3d Maryland Cavalry. His first name was really Washington, but names never were a point of accuracy with him. In the 1850s he served in the Turkish Army under the name Nessim Bey. When made a major in 1854 he changed his appellation to Bim-bachi, and with his next promotion became Quaimaquam! (P-M)

When finally the armies met for the first time, it was at Mansfield, or Sabine Cross Roads, on April 8. Brigadier General J. Patrick Major and his cavalry brigade held the left of the Confederate line. Going into battle, he shouted at his troopers to give the enemy "hell." (GOELET-BUNCOMBE COLLECTION, SHC)

Leading one of the two Southern infantry divisions was Major General John G. Walker, whose Texans outflanked the Federals and drove them back. (LSU)

The next day another battle was fought at Pleasant Hill, and this time Taylor was repulsed. Brigadier General Thomas J. Churchill of Kentucky opened Taylor's attack, but Banks stood his ground. (LC)

Commanding Banks' cavalry in the campaign was Brigadier General Albert L. Lee of Kansas. He had no more military experience than Banks, but better sense. Still, Banks would relieve him of command at the end of the expedition. (USAMHI)

There was another aspect to the Red River Campaign that proved to be ill-fated. Major General Frederick Steele was to move from his headquarters in Little Rock, Arkansas, with a column to support Banks. Steele took his time. Brigadier General Eugene A. Carr, standing at right, commanded his cavalry. Steele stands at left, with giant James Baker of the 13th Iowa between them. (RP)

Brigadier General John M. Thayer led one of Steele's two infantry divisions, little suspecting that their expedition would never reach Banks and would almost end in disaster. (USAMHI)

At Little Rock, Arkansas, Steele marshaled his forces and supplied his army from these warehouses. The men in the ranks supplied themselves from saloons like the one at left, the Star Saloon & Coffee Stand. (NA)

By the time Steele reached Camden, Arkansas, Banks was in retreat, and Steele was on his own. At Poison Spring, Brigadier General John S. Marmaduke of Missouri struck a supply train and captured or destroyed over 200 supply-laden wagons. (WA)

Major Thomas P. Ochiltree of Texas was one of the staff officers in the Confederate Army led personally by Kirby Smith to strike at Steele in Camden. Steele would hurry back to Little Rock instead. (NA)

Meanwhile, Taylor's depleted army kept Banks at bay at Grand Ecore. Major General John A. Wharton commanded about 2,500 cavalry, nearly half of the "army" with which he held Banks' 25,000 in check. A most able officer, Wharton would be killed only days before war's end when he quarreled with an officer, slapped his face, and was shot in return. This is an unpublished portrait. (VM)

When Banks finally retreated from Grand Ecore, Wharton pursued him, and Brigadier General Hamilton P. Bee was supposed to use his cavalry to cut off the enemy retreat. At Monett's Ferry, however, Bee was driven off and Banks managed to escape back to Alexandria. (TU)

But Alexandria did not mean automatic safety. Though the wharf shown here gives no indication of it, the river's rapids near the city were so low that only four to five inches of water stood in places. The fleet was trapped. (USAMHI)

All these steamers and transports, not to mention the ironclads, might fall into enemy hands or have to be destroyed. (USAMHI)

So heavy was the fire that the Fort Hindman *waited an extra day to brave the Confederate fire. A shot struck her steering and she drifted down the river out of control, luckily passing the enemy cannon to safety.* (USAMHI)

The unusual ironclad monitor Osage, *mounting its turret forward and its stern wheel protected by the iron hump at the rear, appears here on the Red River. She got back to Alexandria without difficulty under the capable leadership of her commander . . .* (NHC)

And the unusual little monitor Ozark *had been in service just two months when she joined Porter's fleet. She, too, seemed to be trapped by the low water.* (USAMHI)

The "tinclad" No. 19, the St. Clair, *steamed up from Baton Rouge to help support the fleet while it lay trapped at Alexandria.* (LSU)

But it took the ingenuity of Colonel Joseph Bailey, an engineer, to save the fleet of 33 vessels. He proposed damming the river to raise the water level. He was made a brigadier, as he appears here, for his feat. He saved the fleet. (USAMHI)

Photographers McPherson and Oliver captured the scene as Bailey's dam approached completion. It left just room enough between its wings for the ships to pass through. (USAMHI)

Bailey occupied 3,000 men in building the makeshift dam. Many thought it would not work. (USAMHI)

But Porter would be ever after grateful. "Words are inadequate to express the admiration I feel," said the admiral. "This is without doubt the best engineering feat ever performed." (USAMHI)

Thereafter, it was a race to escape the harassing Confederates. The Covington, *shown here off Memphis in 1863, was attacked even before the fleet left Alexandria, disabled, and captured.* (NHC)

Captured with her was the Signal, *shown here just a few days before assisting with Bailey's dam. The two warships were some compensation to the Confederates for the failure to bag Banks and his army.* (USAMHI)

As for Admiral Porter, he could regard their loss as a small price to pay for saving his fleet, and for saving him any further adventures with Banks. The general would be relieved from field command, and Porter could return to the Black Hawk, *shown here in September 1864, to plan his next voyage.* (USAMHI)

The Forgotten War: The West

MAURICE MELTON

From the Mississippi to the Golden Gate,
the Civil War is everywhere

THE RED RIVER CAMPAIGN was only part of the war in the vast "West." When the issues of the mid-1800s boiled into war, the United States was but half settled. Beyond the Mississippi the West was a mosaic of contrasts—plains, deserts, mountains, seacoasts, bustling cities, wide open spaces, and desolate waste. There were states, territories, and open and unclassified lands. Some areas were settled and relatively civilized, enjoying the traditional social structures of the eastern states. They took the North–South schism seriously, and in some places warfare erupted in intensely personal, no-quarter contests. Other areas were basic American frontier: Indians, outlaws, widely scattered white settlements, and little or no practical government. Wild and raw, the frontier demanded so much for simple survival that the war in the East often went almost unnoticed.

Missouri had been in the thick of the growing sectional split for decades. The act that opened the way to her statehood, the Compromise of 1820, was an effort to balance the opposing forces 40 years before the war. And the partisans who made Kansas bleed in the '50s begot the bushwhackers and Jayhawkers who burned and murdered across the length and breadth of Missouri during four years of official war.

Missouri's early settlers were Southerners. But commerce linked her economy to the North. Her elected officials in 1861 were predominately secessionist, and intended ultimately to ally Missouri with the Confederacy. They nearly succeeded in 1861 when defeat at Wilson's Creek drove Federals out of much of the state.

The Federals returned under Major General Samuel Curtis, who regrouped his forces and drove the Confederates out of Springfield. He followed them into northern Arkansas, where Major General Earl Van Dorn had marshaled a large Confederate force.

Curtis defeated Van Dorn at Elk Horn Tavern. Major General Ben McCulloch was killed and Major General Sterling Price wounded, and Missouri appeared safely in the grasp of the Union. The Federals even held northern Arkansas, from which they could threaten Little Rock, and parts of Louisiana and Texas beyond.

But the border defenses were porous, and control of Missouri was tenuous at best. Price and other Missouri Rebels regularly led military expeditions into Missouri, and fighting raged all over the state from war's outbreak until war's end.

Worse than the regular army campaigns and cavalry jaunts were the bushwhacking raids of the

The confused and troubled nature of the war west of the Mississippi went back long before the Red River Campaign. Texas suffered as much as any state or territory. Her governor in 1861 was the old hero Sam Houston. He opposed secession and resigned when a convention voted the Lone Star State out of the Union. (NA)

Only seven brave men in that convention stood with Houston and voted against secession. Proud of their stand, they posed for the camera soon afterward, even as Texas readied to join the Confederacy. (AUSTIN-TRAVIS COUNTY COLLECTION, AUSTIN PUBLIC LIBRARY C03277)

guerrillas. For despite Missouri's 40 years of statehood, her place on the edge of the frontier lent a savage madness to her war. Four years of border warfare in Kansas had fostered hatreds that festered and lingered. By the time the East followed Kansas and Missouri into war, there was a hardened cadre of Kansas militants ready to strike back at Missouri, and Missourians in general had gained a national reputation—unwarranted—as radical slavers, secessionists, and border ruffians.

The most notorious of the Kansans was Senator James H. Lane of Lawrence. Lane demanded extreme retribution against secessionists and slaveholders, and his Jayhawkers robbed and murdered with near impunity in Missouri, turning multitudes of Unionist and neutral Missourians toward the Confederate camp. Lane's raid on Osceola, his plundering and burning of the town, and the execution of nine of Osceola's citizens was a typical example of warfare on the border.

The savagery of the civilian conflict brutalized the entire Missouri occupation. The leading guerrilla bands, under William Clarke Quantrill, "Bloody Bill" Anderson, George Todd, and William Gregg, were farm boys mostly, children of families harassed, intimidated, robbed, burned out, or murdered by Federal soldiers or Kansas volunteers. They quickly evolved into the prototype of the hard-riding outlaw bands of the postwar West. The guerrillas used the firepower of their many revolvers, their mobility, and their local support to outmatch detachments of Union troops. Often they dressed in blue uniforms and hailed Federal columns as comrades before opening fire. Theirs was a ruthless, brutal war of extermination.

Major General Henry W. Halleck swelled the ranks of the guerrilla bands with a declaration of no neutrality. Those who were not for the Union, he decreed, would be considered against it. Then, in response to the no-quarter tactics of the guer-

Texans began to flock to the secession banners, and regiments were raised to be sent to Virginia in 1861. These are men of the 1st Texas, taken at or near Camp Quantico, Virginia. (AUSTIN-TRAVIS COUNTY COLLECTION, PICA03674)

rillas, he decreed that any civilian caught in arms could be tried and executed on the spot. Executions soon were extended to regular Confederate soldiers captured in Missouri and, occasionally, to townspeople chosen at random in reply to the murder of some local Union man.

The execution of soldiers and civilians, the abridgment of basic civil rights by the military, punitive taxation of towns in areas of heavy guerrilla activity, and finally a state-wide draft of all able-bodied men to help fight the guerrillas, all broadened the bushwhackers' base of support. In 1863 the Federals began attacking this base, imprisoning or exiling the friends and families who provided the guerrillas weapons, information, shelter, and sustenance. In August a group of women—including Bill Anderson's sisters and Cole Younger's cousin—were imprisoned in a dilapidated three-story brick building in Kansas City. Within a few days the building collapsed, killing four women and injuring others. The tragedy touched off an uproar in the South and the Midwest, newspapers accusing Federal authorities of undermining the prison.

Quantrill used the bitter emotions of the moment to pull several guerrilla bands together for their greatest effort, a massed raid on Senator Lane's home, Lawrence, Kansas. Within six days of the Kansas City tragedy, Quantrill had nearly 500 raiders at the outskirts of Lawrence. They struck the unsuspecting town at dawn, rampaging

In the early days of 1861, the threat and influence of the war to come stretched even out to California. There Colonel Albert Sidney Johnston was commander of the Department of the Pacific. When Texas seceded, he resigned and came east, to die a year later at Shiloh. (NA)

through the streets, dragging men from their beds, killing them in their own hallways and yards. Stores and homes were looted and burned, and the guerrillas killed every male they could find who looked big enough to carry a gun. Senator Lane, home on vacation, hid behind a log in back of his house and escaped.

Brigadier General Thomas Ewing's response to the Lawrence raid was drastic. His Order No. 11 virtually stripped the population from a four-county area near the Kansas border, requiring everyone residing more than a mile outside a major town to move from the region. Whether Confederate, Union, or neutral in sympathies, people were forced to abandon their homes, possessions, and livelihoods. The order drew harsh criticism, the press both North and South filled with tales of families brutally uprooted and forced, helpless, into the unknown.

Order No. 11 failed to defuse the guerrilla war, however. In fact, within a few months Quantrill's group destroyed a sizable Federal garrison at Baxter Springs, Kansas, then caught and slaughtered the escort party of Major General James G. Blunt, commander of the District of the Frontier.

Campaigns, raids, and guerrilla actions ranked Missouri third (behind Virginia and Tennessee) in the number of engagements fought during the conflict. The state was the dominant area in the frontier theater of war, and training ground not only for the James and Younger gangs, but for Union scout "Wild Bill" Hickok (who occasionally rode as a spy in Sterling Price's ranks), and for a 7th Kansas recruit named William F. Cody.

In New Mexico Territory, Colonel—later Major General—E. R. S. Canby commanded, and here blunted one of the earliest Confederate campaigns of the war when Sibley tried to invade New Mexico. Canby, after a distinguished career, would be killed by Indians in 1873. (P-M)

UNLIKE MISSOURI, the Territory of Minnesota opened its western lands to white settlement only in the decade before the war. In two 1850s treaties the Federal government forced the Santee Sioux to relinquish nine tenths of their Minnesota lands. In return, they were left a ten-mile-wide strip of reservation, an opportunity to learn the white man's ways of farming, housing, and dress, and cash annuities for 50 years.

Chief Little Crow, courtly, gentlemanly, and a consummate politician, had signed the 1850s treaties. He led a quiet cultural revolution that saw substantial brick homes and tilled fields developed on the reservation. But 1861 brought a bad crop year; 1862 was another. The cash subsidies should have seen the Indians through in comfort, but payments were delayed. Hunger became a fact of life for the Sioux, banned now from hunting on lands that had supported them for generations. For a year and more, poverty deepened and discontent

Fort Union, New Mexico Territory, was headquarters in 1862 for . . . (NA)

grew. Indian traders stocked food the Indians could subsist on, but because government subsidies were always late, the Indians could do limited business, and only on credit. Sioux who had learned to cipher kept track of their accounts, and found their figures consistently at variance with those kept by the traders. They were not surprised—just angry—when the government refused to accept their figures, paying their annuities directly to the trading posts to settle accounts on the traders' books.

In late August 1862, Little Crow met with Indian agent Thomas Galbraith to complain of the traders' embezzlement, the government's tardy payments, and his people's hunger. When Galbraith relayed these complaints to Indian trader Andrew Myrick, the storekeeper replied, "If they're hungry, let them eat grass and their own dung." The reply spread rapidly through the Sioux reservation and, two days later, four young braves killed four white men and two women.

Little Crow, struggling to make the best for his people in a desperate situation, saw his tribe's doom in the braves' act. For retribution, he knew, would be visited on all Indians. There was no beating the whites in a war: there were far too many and they were too well armed. But there would be no escaping the white man's wrath. In a late-night council, Little Crow outlined for his chiefs the consequences. "You will die like rabbits when the hungry wolves hunt them," he said. Then he added, sadly, "But Little Crow is not a coward. He will die with you."

The next morning Little Crow's braves launched

. . . Colonel Gabriel R. Paul, who helped support the repulse of Sibley. A year later, now a general at Gettysburg, he lost his sight when a bullet struck his eyes. (USAMHI)

the Sioux Indian War. First they struck the nearby trading post, then surrounding white settlements. Andrew Myrick, the contemptuous white trader, was left stretched dead outside his store, his mouth stuffed full of grass.

Troops at nearby Fort Ridgely heard the firing. They sent out a rescue expedition, but Little Crow was ready. He ambushed the column, killing 23 troopers, and soon attacked the fort itself. For two days the whites beat back Indian assaults. Heavy rains broke early in the battle, pouring so much water that fire arrows died in the shingles and logs of the stockade fort.

Frustrated, the Sioux withdrew and turned on the town of New Ulm, where fierce fighting raged from house to house. But again armed and aroused whites held off the Sioux.

At St. Paul, Colonel Henry Hastings Sibley gathered the 6th Minnesota Volunteers, 1,400 strong, and brought them west to fight. Sibley maneuvered through skirmishes and ambushes for a month before finally luring the Sioux into a pitched battle, breaking the back of organized Indian resistance in Minnesota. The Sioux scattered, some north to Canada, some west into Dakota. Some stayed, hoping for an arrangement that would allow them to continue existence on their own lands.

Aware from the outset that they could not win, the Sioux had taken a large number of prisoners to barter for terms. Sibley agreed to a truce to talk about prisoner exchange. Using the talks as a diversion, he surrounded the Indian camp, took back the white prisoners, and forced the Indians to capitulate. Over 300 warriors were imprisoned at Fort Snelling, where 36 were convicted and hanged for war crimes. The rest of the tribe was transported to a barren reservation in Dakota Territory, where nearly a quarter of them died the first winter.

The Sioux continued a desultory war in the Dakotas, occasionally raiding back into western Minnesota. In the summer of 1863, Major General John Pope, banished from the white man's war after Second Manassas, was sent north to resolve the Indian problem. He organized a two-pronged expedition and sent it deep into Dakota Territory, Sibley leading one column, Brigadier General Alfred Sully the other. Sibley fought three pitched battles in late July, and Sully destroyed a large Sioux village in August, driving the Indians across the Missouri River. Sporadic incidents continued, however, and another campaign was mounted in the summer of 1864, pushing the Indians into Montana Territory. This was the last major Indian campaign of the war years, but far from the last gasp of the Sioux. They would continue fighting in the northwestern territories for more than a decade.

MANY WESTERN SETTLERS were from the South, and their raucous vocal support of the Confederacy raised fears of dark conspiracies, armed Southern uprisings, and conquest by a great Rebel army from

New Mexico Territory, which included modern Arizona, was tenuously held by a string of frontier forts, like Fort Craig shown here in 1865. (NA)

Texas. With the Federal government's preoccupation with the crisis in the East, and a spirit of Southern nationalism apparent in Colorado, Nevada, New Mexico, and California, reasonable men thought they could see the prospect of an American West annexed to the new Confederacy.

The Lincoln administration paid considerable attention to Nevada, for her mines were turning out millions of dollars in gold and silver for the U.S. war effort. Nevada gained territorial status in 1861 and achieved statehood in 1864, just in time to cast Republican votes in the national election.

California was vital to the U.S. war effort, too. Her mining industry, with ten years maturity, was an El Dorado to the Treasury Department. Californians feared for their gold shipments, for Southerners were highly visible around the state's towns and mining camps. They were organizing companies and drilling in the spring of 1861, and some were, as feared, interested in disrupting the state's flow of gold. A delegation approached the commander of the Department of the Pacific, Colonel Albert Sidney Johnston, to enlist his aid in an attack on the gold shipments. But Johnston, still commissioned in the U.S. Army, refused to hear them. He soon resigned, and began a trek east to join the Confederate Army.

Most California secessionists (both Southern-born and California-born) had no intention of joining California to Sidney Johnston's Southern Confederacy. They envisioned, instead, an independent Pacific Republic. California's isolation had fostered the notion of a destiny of her own, and the idea of a Pacific Republic had long been popular. The chaos in the East gave its proponents the opportunity to open a strong campaign for California's independence, and it gained quick popularity in the press. Republicans and Union

And like Fort Marcy, at Santa Fe, headquarters of the department. (LC)

It was the goal of Confederate Brigadier General Henry H. Sibley's abortive campaign in the spring of 1862. It was rumored that Sibley was more devoted to alcohol than his duty. (VM)

Democrats combined to fight the movement in the State Assembly, and the firing on Fort Sumter swung opinion heavily in favor of the Union and California's continued place in it.

California was seriously threatened, however, by the early Confederate acquisition of the lower half of New Mexico Territory, which stretched from California to Confederate Texas. New Mexico was naturally divided, a gulf of desert splitting the region into two habitable sections, north and south. The north, with the territorial capital at Santa Fe, was tied to Missouri, where her trails ran. Supplies, news, and settlers all came through Missouri, and that state's decision would determine whether northern New Mexico Territory went Confederate or stayed Union. The southern half was linked in the same way to Texas.

An enmity between the two had already developed, the south feeling that the north dominated territorial government and ignored the south, even to the point of keeping all the troops in the north, exposing southern New Mexicans to death at the hands of the Apache or robbery and murder by marauding outlaws. So headstrong were the southerners that they had already broken with New Mexico and established their own Territory of Arizona, without a hint of official sanction, well before South Carolina seceded. Then, with new national boundaries drawn and a war having broken out, Arizona leaders met at La Mesilla, an Overland Mail stop above El Paso, and voted to ally their new Arizona Territory with the Confederacy. On the western border, near California, the 68 voting citizens of Tucson passed their own ordinance of secession and elected a delegate to the Confederate Congress.

Union influence crumbled rapidly in both territories. Most of the army officers in the West were Southern, and had resigned. The flow of resigned officers moving east from California, traveling from post to post across New Mexico, made it appear that the majority of the U.S. Army's officer corps was resigning and going south. The loss of military leadership compounded the effects of the daily difficulties under which the western soldier labored—few horses, a chronic shortage of supplies, and pay as much as half a year in arrears.

Brigadier General E. V. Sumner, Sidney Johnston's replacement, established control over California by disarming and disbanding the state's lingering secessionist groups. Then he sent an expedition to garrison Fort Yuma, on the Colorado River crossing from Tucson. In Nevada and Colorado the operating governments held firm against the early clamor of Southern secessionists. And in northern New Mexico, Colonel E. R. S. Canby, an obscure subordinate on the Indian frontier, banded together the demoralized, leaderless troopers scattered across the territory and began organizing a territorial defense.

Canby had no time to lose, for his brother-in-law and former superior, Brigadier General Henry Hopkins Sibley, had gone south and was gathering a small army in Texas to move into northern New Mexico. At the beginning of 1862, Sibley brought his troops north through the Rio Grande Valley, the only invasion route that could sustain a large body of troops. Canby and Sibley clashed at Val Verde, just outside Canby's base at Fort Craig. Unable to destroy Canby or take the fort, Sibley left

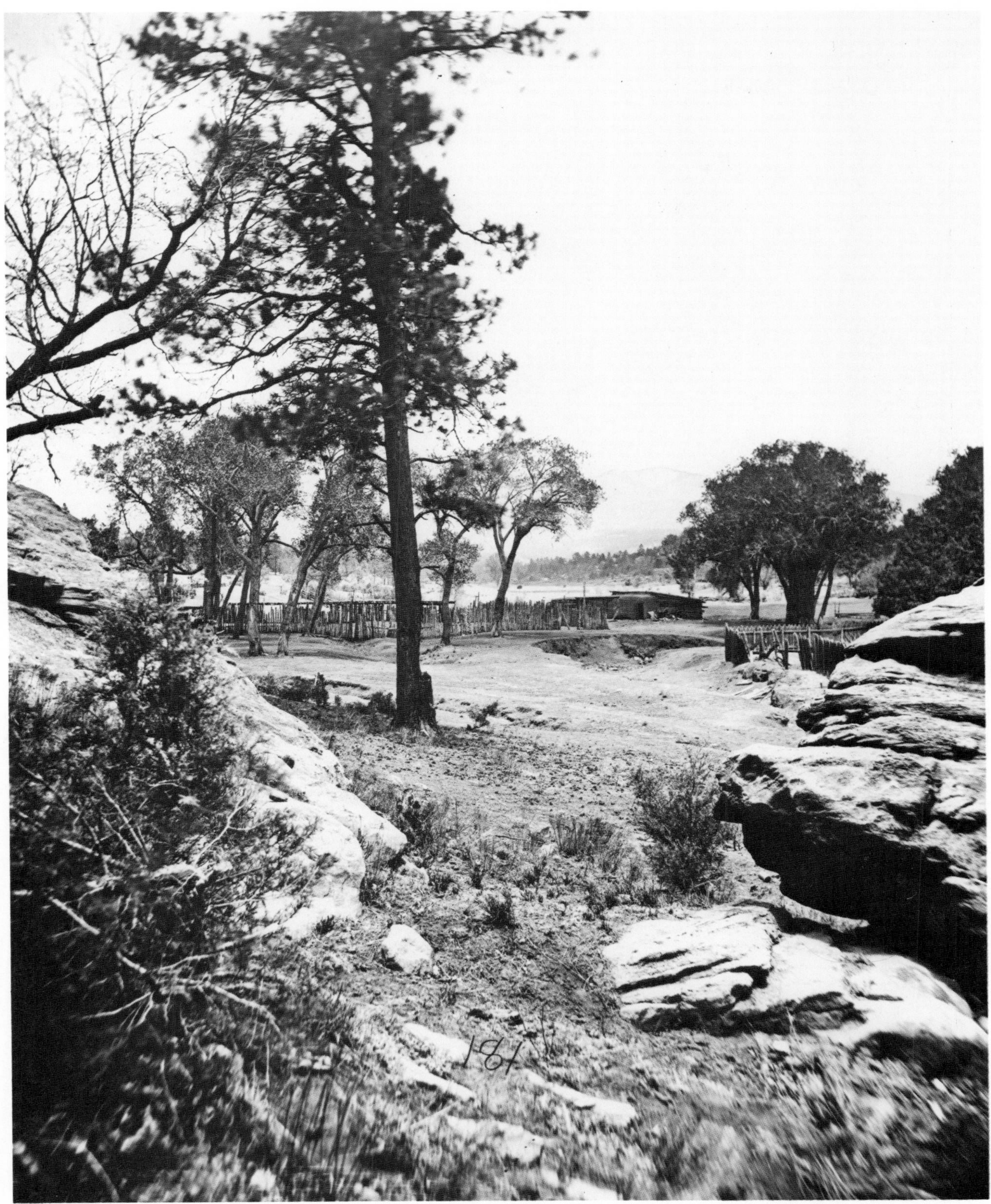

The invasion stopped here, at Glorieta, near Santa Fe, shown here in a June 1880 image. On March 28, Sibley won a tactical victory here while, in his rear . . . (COURTESY OF MUSEUM OF NEW MEXICO)

. . . Major John M. Chivington struck and destroyed the Confederate supply train. That ended Sibley's campaign and made a name for Chivington, who later achieved notoriety of another kind by massacring 500 Cheyennes and Arapahoes at Sand Creek, Colorado, in 1864. (COLORADO HISTORICAL SOCIETY)

the Federal force intact in his rear and marched on to Albuquerque. All along the route the Texans pillaged, alienating Southerners who might have welcomed them as liberators and countrymen.

The plundering occurred primarily because of the Confederates' short supplies. Sibley had gathered few rations in west Texas, and his men were hungry. Yet at Albuquerque, Sibley ordered the burning of accumulated Federal stores and foodstuffs, and fed his men nothing.

From Albuquerque, Sibley sent Major C. S. Pyron with a column to occupy Santa Fe, where officers again directed the burning of captured stores while troops stood by suffering in hunger.

The territorial governor fled Santa Fe for Fort Union, northeast on the Denver road. The fort was the strongest military post in the territory. Sibley had commanded it once and felt confident of taking it, solidifying Confederate control of New Mexico and Arizona. But Fort Union had been moved and rebuilt since Sibley's day and newly garrisoned by the 1st Colorado Regiment, commanded by Colonel John Slough.

Colonel Canby ordered Slough to hold Fort Union. Instead, the Colorado regiment took the road to Santa Fe in hopes of surprising the Rebels. Pyron left Santa Fe with intentions of occupying Fort Union, and the two collided in Glorieta Pass.

Slough's lead elements were commanded by the Reverend John Chivington, who had taken a major's commission in the 1st Colorado. Chivington bested Pyron in the initial fighting, and both sides fell back at nightfall and sent for reinforcements. Slough took a day and a night to reach the battlefield with the rest of his force, and the Confederates waited. Finally, after the entire Federal force had reached the field, Pyron attacked. While Slough and Pyron battled in the pass, Chivington led a raiding party behind the Confederates. In a daylong fight Pyron gained dominance on the battlefield, but Chivington's raid to the rear destroyed the Confederates' wagon train. The Rebels thought they had been struck by Canby's army from Fort Craig, abandoned Glorieta, and fell back to Santa Fe.

Canby ordered Slough to break off further action and wait, for Canby soon had his own force in motion and hoped to crush Sibley in a pincer.

Slough resigned in protest at Canby's orders. Chivington assumed his command, and Sibley, caught between the Federal soldiers to the rear and Chivington's Colorado volunteers ahead, committed his army to a pell-mell retreat through the desert. Hungry and short of ammunition, the army degenerated into a leaderless drove struggling for survival. Canby might have captured the lot, but had barely enough rations for his own men and none to feed prisoners. Some few Texans did surrender. Some made for California, many of these falling victim to the Apache. Most found their way back to Texas, happy to have survived the desert and the Indians.

The occupation of New Mexico and Arizona was done and Sibley's army had evaporated, leaving Texas' western border open and undefended. The loss of Missouri and northern Arkansas raised rumors of invasion from the north, and the fall of New Orleans nearly sealed off the state from the

Even after Sibley withdrew, New Mexico was still full of colorful characters, none more so than Major W. F. M. Arny, Indian agent for the territory. His Indian finery is in marked contrast to the typical army camp scene in the painted background. (M. J. WRIGHT COLLECTION, SHC)

east. The Mexican border was open, however, and a major trade route developed from San Antonio to Brownsville, then across the river to Matamoros. The Mexican town boomed as a free port, Texas cotton flowing out, war goods for the Confederacy coming in.

IN MARCH OF 1863, Lieutenant General Edmund Kirby Smith assumed command of the Confederacy's Trans-Mississippi, officially composed of Texas, Louisiana, Arkansas, Missouri, and the Indian Territory. The area clung to the east by a slender corridor open across the Mississippi from Vicksburg to Port Hudson. In July these two bastions fell and Kirby Smith's new command was completely cut off.

The general had inherited a department disorganized, dispirited, desperately short on manpower, and virtually leaderless. In an effort to turn the area around and make it productive, self-reliant, and defensible, he called a governors' conference at Marshall, Texas. There, the chief executives of the Trans-Mississippi's states grudgingly relinquished to the military many of their rights, duties, and powers in hopes of seeing the area run with some efficiency. The general now had a domain that would come to be known as "Kirbysmithdom."

The next spring the Trans-Mississippi came under attack. Major General Nathaniel Banks invaded, with support from David Porter's fleet, while Major General Frederick Steele pushed south from Little Rock to join forces. But Banks met defeat at the hands of Richard Taylor, Steele was beaten back to Little Rock, and Porter nearly lost his fleet to low water in the Red River. The Trans-Mississippi, it seemed, had established some defense. But in November the Federals moved again and captured Brownsville, cutting the vital trade route to Matamoros.

Meanwhile, the Indians had re-established control on the western border. Texas frontier troops were absorbed into the Confederate Army and moved east, and from early on, the far West was virtually defenseless. Kiowa and Comanche rampaged in west Texas and the Apache terrorized New Mexico. By the time Brownsville fell they had pushed white settlement out of west Texas and were threatening the middle of the state.

When reaction came it was brutal, in the nature of the untamed West. Texas volunteers caught and slaughtered a tribe of peaceful Kickapoo migrating to Mexico. Ironically, the Indians were fleeing the incessant warfare of the Indian Territory, where factions fought over internal disagreements within the Creek, Cherokee, and Chickasaw tribes. At Sand Creek, Chivington's Colorado volunteers attacked and destroyed a village of Arapaho and Cheyenne, killing men, women, and children. The slaughter was so indiscriminate and savage, even by frontier standards, that it resulted in Chivington's court-martial and blackened the name of his command.

Back in east Texas, Colonel John Ford raised a small army, retook Brownsville, and reopened

Brigadier General James H. Carleton led his colorful "California Column" east from the Golden State to relieve New Mexico during Sibley's threat. He stayed to take over command of the department and kept it until war's end. (USAMHI)

North of New Mexico, in Nevada and Utah, Colonel Patrick E. Connor tried to control affairs in those territories, mainly keeping the mail and telegraph lines open to California and combatting occasional Indian outbreaks. It won him a major generalcy, as he appears here at the end of the war. (UTAH STATE HISTORICAL SOCIETY)

trade with the outside world. And as the U.S. Navy systematically sealed off the Confederacy's eastern ports in the last year of the war, the fast iron ships running the blockade found their way more and more to the Texas coast and Matamoros.

Free trade and the Trans-Mississippi's manufacturing made life in Texas more bearable than in the rest of the war-ravaged, poverty-stricken South. But farming steadily deteriorated as farmhands, draft animals, and equipment disappeared. Runaway inflation reduced the worth of government vouchers to the point that farmers and ranchers finally refused to accept them for their remaining livestock and produce. Commissary agents responded by appropriating horses, cattle, and crops without pay. The Trans-Mississippi, like the eastern Confederacy, was withering on the vine.

With Lee's surrender, strong Federal armies overwhelmed Confederate remnants in North Carolina, south Alabama, and western Louisiana. The last fight of the war flared in Texas, at Palmito Ranch outside Brownsville on May 13, 1865. Northern prisoners told the Texans they were the only ones left fighting. Two weeks later Kirby Smith surrendered the last Confederate army to the western Confederacy's old nemesis, Major General E. R. S. Canby.

Here in Colorado recruits of Company G, 1st Colorado Volunteers, muster on the main street of Empire in 1862. It was a long way to the war, but they would find it. (COLORADO HISTORICAL SOCIETY)

So would the 6th California Infantry, commanded by Colonel Henry M. Black. Their war would be one of few and brief Indian skirmishes. Most of their time they spent garrisoning an island in San Francisco Bay, Alcatraz. (USAMHI)

Up in faraway Oregon the Union had a general, too, Brigadier General Benjamin Alvord, who had nothing to do but keep the peace between settlers and the Nez Percé Indians. Out in the West it was largely a war of boredom for commanders who perhaps dreamed of the glory to be had in Virginia. (EUGENE WOODDELL)

Of course, there were those who had tried for glory in Virginia and failed, and the War Department looked to the West as a convenient place to shelve unsuccessful officers. Thus came Major General Irvin McDowell to command the Department of the Pacific. Defeat at Manassas in 1861 and again in 1862 had been too much for him to survive. He sat out the rest of the conflict in San Francisco. (USAMHI)

San Francisco was not such a bad place to sit. Here lay Fort Point, on the Golden Gate, one of the few casemated seacoast fortifications built before the war that never heard a hostile shot. (NA)

Its guns looked out upon a quiet, thriving harbor, with only a very occasional scare of Confederate sea raiders that never came. (THE BANCROFT LIBRARY)

If Confederates should come, McDowell's command would be ready for them. Artillery drill at the Presidio of San Francisco, during or just after the war. (THE BANCROFT LIBRARY)

Indeed, even the Navy would be ready for any Rebel foolhardy enough to sail into the harbor. In 1863 the Navy Department sent the Aquila *around the Horn, bearing a very heavy cargo for San Francisco—a dismantled monitor!* (COURTESY OF CHARLES S. SCHWARTZ)

Unfortunately, shortly after arrival the vessel sank at Hathaway's Wharf, with the ironclad still aboard. With enormous effort, the Aquila *was raised from the bottom.* (CSS)

Then began the work of assembling, piece by piece, the ironclad monitor Camanche. *Here proud workers stand on, and under, her bow as she sits in the ways. Local photographers Lawrence and Houseworth made these images, never before published.* (CSS)

In time the ship's hull and below decks were done, with always plenty of spectators around to gawk and get in the way. (NHC)

And finally she was ready to launch. On November 14, 1864, she rides the waves once more, still minus the distinctive turret of the monitor. (CSS)

That came next, as workmen with tools in their hands stand atop the installed gun turret and the pilot house above it. The projection from the top of the turret is perhaps some form of periscope, since no eye slits are visible on the tower itself. (CSS)

Finally, in January 1865, she was completed. The only trouble was, the war was almost over. (R. L. HAGUE)

Ready for her maiden voyage, an ironclad that would never see battle or fire a hostile shot, the Camanche *is about to leave the wharf at the foot of Third Street. She will finally be commissioned in August, months after the war is done.* (CSS)

It was a long way from the far West to the old Northwest, yet here, too, it was a war of little action and long waiting. No Confederate army ever threatened Fort Wayne, near Detroit, Michigan. For these overcoated soldiers, then, there was only garrison duty and, perhaps, the hope of being ordered off to Virginia. (BURTON HISTORICAL COLLECTION, DETROIT PUBLIC LIBRARY)

Even more removed was St. Paul, Minnesota, nestled peacefully on the bank of the Mississippi. (MHS)

Powerful Fort Snelling brooded over the mouth of the Minnesota River, assuring protection to the inhabitants. (MHS)

Soldiers and civilians and local Indians could pass the time together peacefully enough. (MHS)

It was even peaceful-looking enough out at Fort Ripley, near the Sioux reservations. (MHS)

In the frontier-like settlements such as Mendota, near Fort Snelling, there was no thought of threat or defense. (MHS)

But then in 1862 the Sioux arose in a bloody campaign that in the end took perhaps 500 white lives, and saw 38 Sioux leaders executed. These settlers rushed toward the forts and larger settlements to escape the Indians, who were enraged at being allowed to starve on their reservations. (MHS)

Within days the outbreak spread to South Dakota. These two women with their children were taken captive by a band of Santees and held prisoner for three months before being rescued by friendly Sioux called "Fool Soldiers." (SOUTH DAKOTA STATE HISTORICAL SOCIETY)

Over 1,000 Sioux were eventually captured and imprisoned here in this camp at Fort Snelling. Instead of drawing attention to their legitimate plight, the Sioux uprising only made their treatment more harsh. (MHS)

This is only one of the jails that held the captives, some of them huddling in their blankets before their guards, one of them, standing at left, an Indian himself. (MHS)

For the rest of the war, places like Fort Rice in the Dakota Territory were built to contain the Indians and prevent more outbreaks. (USAMHI)

Major Charles A. R. Dimon of the 1st U.S. Volunteers commanded the new Fort Rice and poses here with some of the local chiefs during a more tranquil time. They feared him for his harsh, trigger-happy, methods. (USAMHI)

Brigadier General Alfred Sully came to command the District of Dakota in 1863, and in the spring of 1865 made an attempt to make peace with the Indians at Fort Rice. Dimon, now a colonel, ruined his chances. (USAMHI)

And so Sully had to lead another campaign against them. Here the camp of the 6th Iowa Cavalry near Fort Berthold, where Sully hoped again to make terms. He failed, and the problems with the Sioux would go on for decades after the Civil War was done. (MHS)

It was a more conventional war a few hundred miles south of Dakota and Minnesota. Indeed, some of the earliest meetings of Blue and Gray came in Arkansas and Missouri. The first real Confederate hero of the West was Major General Earl Van Dorn, though he lost the Battle of Pea Ridge. A year later he would be murdered by a jealous husband. (MC)

The man who beat Van Dorn at Pea Ridge was Samuel Curtis, seated here in the center of his staff, wearing the uniform of a major general. He later commanded in Missouri, but never again fought a major battle. (MICHAEL J. HAMMERSON)

After Curtis left Arkansas, Major General Frederick Steele replaced him, and in his first act led a campaign that resulted in the capture of Little Rock. (USAMHI)

Curtis had already occupied Helena, Arkansas, and started the work of erecting Fort Curtis, shown here. And before Steele came, there would be other battles in the state. (LC)

Major General Thomas C. Hindman, commanding Confederate forces in the state, led his army against a much smaller Federal command in the northwest part of Arkansas at Prairie Grove. Here Hindman sits in uniform with his children on October 22, 1865. He would be assassinated a few years later. (RJY)

Hindman's army was made up of lean young Arkansas volunteers like these privates. (ARKANSAS HISTORY COMMISSION)

They were attacking the small command of Brigadier General James G. Blunt, a one-time Jayhawker and friend of John Brown of Kansas. (NA)

All that saved Blunt and his little army was the incredible march of Francis J. Herron and his two divisions, who covered 115 miles in three days to reach the battlefield and help defeat Hindman. He sits at center here with his staff, as a brigadier. After Prairie Grove he was promoted, becoming for a time the youngest major general in the war. Photograph by J. A. Scholten of St. Louis. (MICHAEL J. HAMMERSON)

After Prairie Grove, and Steele's capture of Little Rock the following year, Arkansas was made relatively safe for the Union, and Steele could begin the buildup of Little Rock into a major base and supply center. A view across the Arkansas River of several of his supply warehouses. (NA)

Warehouses No.'s 27 and 28 sat right on the river, next to an ice house and bakery. (NA)

The commissary department made its headquarters among a row of dry-goods and auction houses. These images, probably made by artist White of Little Rock, are so clear that the broadsides posted on the walls are legible. They have not been previously published. (NA)

It took a lot of employees to run Steele's quartermaster operation. They lived in these quarters, very comfortable by Civil War standards. The picnic table was a real extra. (NA)

The Federals also established a large general hospital to serve the department. It was, all told, a very well-organized and -constructed post that Steele established in Little Rock, and he needed it. (NA)

The state was never completely safe from Confederate raids. Besides the posts set up in the country, gunboats patrolled the rivers, particularly the Arkansas. The USS Fawn *appears here opposite Devall's Bluff on December 31, 1863, only weeks after a skirmish with Rebel raiders.* (NHC)

Even Porter's mighty flagship Black Hawk *sometimes ventured into Arkansas waters to protect river traffic.* (NHC)

Protecting the Federals' western flank, both in Missouri and Arkansas, was Fort Leavenworth out in Kansas. E. E. Henry's image was made around the end of the war. (USAMHI)

And protecting the department from threats within were prisons like this military penitentiary at Little Rock. No region in the country was more threatened by divided loyalties and civilian "treason." (NA)

Here in St. Charles, Missouri, on November 4, 1862, a group of suspected Confederate sympathizers pose for the camera. Missouri would cause more problems of civilian unrest and aid to the enemy than any other border state. (INTERNATIONAL MUSEUM OF PHOTOGRAPHY)

Among other things, the population often harbored or assisted daring and ruthless guerrillas, most notably the partisans led by William C. Quantrill. Here three of Quantrill's men sit for the camera. Fletcher Taylor stands at left. The other two are better known for their postwar deeds. Frank James sits in the center, obviously hamming for the camera with his flashy trousers and a major general's uniform blouse, though he never held any commission. And standing at right is his brother, Jesse James. Missouri was a training ground for their outlaw depredations. (STATE HISTORICAL SOCIETY OF MISSOURI)

Among those depredations was Quantrill's attack at Baxter Springs, Kansas, on October 6, 1863. He and his men brutally murdered scores of Federals in General James G. Blunt's headquarters band, which was with him. The instruments they carry in this image fell into Quantrill's hands, and every one of the bandsmen was killed. That was the warfare of the border. (KANSAS STATE HISTORICAL SOCIETY)

The Pacific House, on Fourth and Delaware in Kansas City, Missouri, was headquarters for Brigadier General Thomas Ewing in 1863. There, in an attempt to control the guerrillas, he issued his orders No. 10 and 11, which virtually depopulated four Missouri counties that had harbored Quantrill. A postwar image. (JACKSON COUNTY HISTORICAL SOCIETY)

But nothing but bullets and bars could finally control the Missouri raiders, many of whom used Confederate uniforms as only an excuse for outlawry. Here Jim Anderson, brother of "Bloody Bill" Anderson, sits subdued for a time by Yankee ball and chain. (COURTESY OF CARL BRIEHAN)

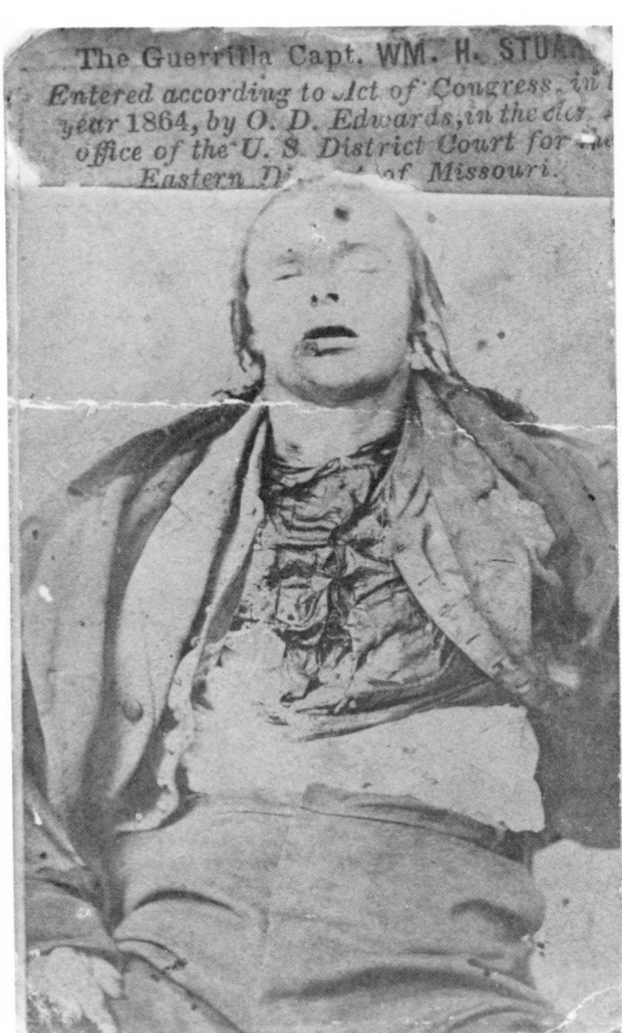

Those who could not be captured were often killed. Sometime in 1864 Federals caught up with Captain William H. Stuart. Photographer O. D. Edwards copyrighted and sold images of the guerrilla's bullet-riddled corpse. (COURTESY OF WILLIAM TEMPLEMAN)

A photographer was equally delighted to capture in death a last look at Bloody Bill Anderson, one of Quantrill's most feared and deadliest henchmen. (STATE HISTORICAL SOCIETY OF MISSOURI)

Still others survived the war and their own penchant for pillage. "Little Arch" Clements even took to wearing a crucifix. (LSU)

Undoubtedly part of the problem in controlling Missouri was that here, as in the far West, Washington sent officers who had failed into exile. In 1864, Major General William S. Rosecrans, disgraced after Chickamauga, took command of the Department of Missouri. (USAMHI)

He faced a formidable foe in command of the Confederate Trans-Mississippi Department, General E. Kirby Smith, veteran of First Manassas and the Kentucky campaign of 1862. He so organized and administered his department that it came in time to be called "Kirbysmithdom." (ATLANTA HISTORICAL SOCIETY)

And Smith was served by some able assistants, most notably Lieutenant General Simon B. Buckner, who came in 1864 to be his chief of staff. The bold Kentuckian would live until 1914, and would run for Vice President in 1896. His running mate was Union Major General John M. Palmer. (VM)

Also serving as chief of staff at times was Brigadier General William R. Boggs of Georgia. This portrait was made in 1864 at Smith's headquarters in Shreveport, Louisiana. (TU)

For the men who commanded out in the Trans-Mississippi, it was a war of too little with too few. Brigadier General Elkanah Greer of Texas had been commander of the pro-secession Knights of the Golden Circle before the war. His war service was as chief of conscription for Smith, a thankless task that netted him few recruits and many enemies. (COURTESY OF JACK T. GREER)

Richmond, too, looked upon the West as a dumping ground for officers who were in the way in Virginia. Major General Benjamin Huger of South Carolina was banished to the Trans-Mississippi on staff duties after his lackluster battlefield performance in the Seven Days' battles. (LSU)

And Smith also got his share of political appointees, though some proved to be happy choices. Henry W. Allen began the war as a Louisiana private. He was made a brigadier general in 1863, and the year later became governor of Louisiana. He proved a strong right arm to Smith in administering Louisiana. Unwilling to live in the United States after the war, he went to Mexico with thousands of other exiles and died there in 1866. An unpublished portrait of General Allen, made probably in 1864. (LSU)

A former governor of Louisiana was Paul O. Hébert, shown here as colonel of the 1st Louisiana Artillery in the summer of 1861. He became a brigadier and was sent for a time to command one of the most neglected places in the Confederacy, the Department of Texas. (VM)

He was later succeeded by Major General John B. Magruder, "Prince John" of Virginia, a little-appreciated officer who brought real talent to Texas and managed his undermanned department skillfully. (CWTI)

It was a state of small towns and modest cities, like Huntsville, where old Sam Houston died in 1863. F. B. Bailey of Navasota brought his camera here to record the court house square. Towns like this could produce only so many soldiers and so much supply, and too much of it was drained off to Virginia. (USAMHI)

With what was left them, however, the Texans did very well. One of the war's great heroes was Lieutenant Richard Dowling. Shown here as a major, the twenty-five-year-old Irishman defended Sabine Pass against four Yankee gunboats with only 47 men and two boats shielded with cotton bales. His victory was so needed and so spectacular that he and his men were awarded the only medals ever presented in the Confederacy. (LSU)

There were few photographers in Texas, and it is not surprising that little survives to show the war in the Lone Star State. Nevertheless, A. G. Wedge of Matamoros, Mexico, probably came to Brownsville on November 6, 1863, when the Confederates had to evacuate the town on the Rio Grande, and he left an important record of the event. (COURTESY OF GARY WRIGHT)

It was a border town as much Mexican as Confederate. (GW)

Brigadier General Hamilton Bee had a large supply of stores and cotton at Brownsville, and when superior forces of Federals approached, he packed up what he could take with him and destroyed the rest. (GW)

The riverfront was alive with activity, many people even loading their furniture to take it with them in the evacuation. Bee had only two steamers at his disposal, loading them with supplies to ferry over the Rio Grande to Matamoros, Mexico, for safety. (GW)

A pontoon bridge across the river helped to carry wagons across. (GW)

The photographer took his camera across the bridge to the Matamoros side to get this rare and somewhat blurred image of the bustle and confusion of the evacuation. Wagons and people are everywhere, and some are even trying to ferry themselves across on the skiff at left. Guards on the bridge are apparently holding it for military traffic alone. (TEXAS SOUTHWEST COLLEGE LIBRARY, BROWNSVILLE)

By the spring of 1864 the reserves of manpower in Texas were nearly exhausted. Here in Ellis County in late March or early April, First Lieutenant William J. Stokes could display for the camera just ten new recruits for his company. His veterans kneel in uniform, the new men standing behind in their civilian attire. Stokes himself is probably one of the three officers standing. They were all a part of the 4th Texas Cavalry, called the Arizona Brigade, and this rare image is the only one known to exist that shows Texans outdoors in their home state. Equally rare by 1864 are those sparkling new uniforms his veterans wear. (ELLIS COUNTY MUSEUM, INC.)

By late 1864 there were barely eleven depleted brigades in the whole department. Lower Louisiana was defended by just two brigades, one of them commanded by Brigadier General William P. Hardeman, a veteran of the Red River Campaign. (CWTI)

Many of the troops in the Confederate service claimed a Mexican or Spanish heritage, including these officers of the 3d Texas Cavalry. They are, from the left, Refugio Benavides, Atanacio Vidaurri, Cristobal Benavides, and John Z. Leyendecker. (URSALINE ACADEMY LIBRARY)

Helping them defend their homeland were colorful characters like the resplendent Captain Samuel J. Richardson, probably the only Confederate of the war outfitted in leopard skin. (MC)

The last real Confederate offensive of the war in the West somehow managed to come out of the beleaguered Trans-Mississippi. Its foundations were laid when the always incompetent Lieutenant General Theophilus H. Holmes resigned as commander of the District of Arkansas in the spring of 1864. (LC)

That made Major General Sterling Price of Missouri his successor. Kirby Smith had little use for Price, but in September he sent him with all the cavalry he could scrape together on a raid deep into Missouri. It would be the last Southern attempt to retake the state. (VM)

Major General Mosby Munroe Parsons of Missouri commanded one of Price's two infantry divisions on the advance into Missouri. He, like Price and many others, would go to Mexico after the war. There, on August 15, 1865, he was killed by guerrillas while apparently serving with Mexican Imperial forces. An unpublished portrait. (RJY)

Major General James F. Fagan of Kentucky led the Arkansas cavalry division on the raid. A handsome, capable officer, he commanded the rearguard just before the climactic Battle of Westport on October 23. In the battle itself, his division was scattered. (WRHS)

Colonel Archibald S. Dobbin led one of Fagan's brigades, and like the rest was soundly beaten in the battle. He later claimed to have been made a brigadier, and here wears the uniform of a general. (MC)

Along, too, for the campaign was another man who wore a general's blouse without ever being formally promoted, the "Swamp Fox" of Missouri, M. Jefferson Thompson. He had raised armies, commanded a gunboat fleet in battle on the Mississippi, and become one of the most engaging and ubiquitous characters of the Trans-Mississippi. (MC)

And by far the most talented and colorful of Price's generals was Brigadier General John Sappington Marmaduke, the magnificent Missourian leading the second cavalry division. Young, handsome, dashing, a daring horseman, he was also a skilled marksman. In 1863 he fought a duel with fellow General L. M. Walker and left his antagonist dying. Covering the rear of Price's retreating army after Westport, he was captured. While in prison he will be promoted to major general, the last such appointment in the Confederate Army. Twenty years later Missouri will elect him governor. (LSU)

It was one of those "shelved" generals from the East who defeated Price at Westport. Commanding the Federal cavalry, Major General Alfred Pleasonton struck Marmaduke in Price's rear and set off the rout of the Confederates. (P-M)

That was the last threat to the Union in the Trans-Mississippi. By the summer of 1865 the war in the West was over, the Confederates disbanded, and Federals like the band of the 4th Michigan could pose for the camera in San Antonio, Texas, ending the era of the war and beginning the occupation of the South that became Reconstruction. (COURTESY OF PAUL DE HAAN)

Private John J. Williams of the 34th Indiana would not be there to see it, however. On May 13, 1865, in a skirmish at Palmito Ranch, Texas, he became probably the last soldier killed in the Civil War. The first to die in any war are remembered—the poor man who is last is all too soon forgotten. Like the rugged frontier war he fought in out here in the West, Private Williams was doomed to obscurity. (USAMHI)

Abbreviations

CHS	Chicago Historical Society, Chicago
CSS	Charles S. Schwartz
CWTI	Civil War Times Illustrated
DAM, LSU	Department of Archives and Manuscripts, Louisiana State University, Baton Rouge
GDAH	Georgia Department of Archives and History, Atlanta
GW	Gary Wright
HP	Herb Peck, Jr.
KA	Kean Archives, Philadelphia
LC	Library of Congress, Washington, D.C.
MC	Museum of the Confederacy, Richmond
MHS	Minnesota Historical Society, St. Paul
NA	National Archives, Washington, D.C.
NHC	Naval Historical Center, Washington, D.C.
NYHS	New-York Historical Society, New York
P-M	War Library and Museum, MOLLUS-Pennsylvania, Philadelphia
RJY	Robert J. Younger
RP	Ronn Palm
SHC	Southern Historical Collection, University of North Carolina, Chapel Hill
TPO	Terence P. O'Leary
TU	Tulane University Library, Special Collections Division, New Orleans
USAMHI	U.S. Army Military History Institute, Carlisle Barracks, Pennsylvania
VM	Valentine Museum, Richmond, Virginia
WA	William A. Albaugh
WRHS	Western Reserve Historical Society, Cleveland, Ohio

The Contributors

EDWIN C. BEARSS is chief historian of the National Park Service and the author of many important books on the Civil War, including *Decision in Mississippi, Forrest at Brice's Cross Roads,* and *Hardluck Ironclad,* about the sinking and salvage of the Civil War ironclad *Cairo*. Mr. Bearss was a discoverer of the ironclad as she lay on the bottom of the Yazoo River, and spent years in the successful effort to raise her.

DR. FRANK J. MERLI has been for several years professor of history at Queens College, with a distinguished background that includes a year as a Fulbright scholar at King's College of the University of London. His book *Great Britain and the Confederate Navy 1861–1865* is one of the preeminent works of modern times on Civil War diplomacy and the much-neglected naval side of the conflict. He is currently working on a major history of the Confederate States Navy.

ROBERT K. KRICK is one of the most promising of the younger historians working in the Civil War field today. The author of several books on the Confederate Army, including *Lee's Colonels, A Biographical Register of the Field Officers of the Army of Northern Virginia,* and *Parker's Virginia Battery,* Mr. Krick is a noted bibliographer of the war as well. He is a historian with the National Park Service, working at the Fredericksburg National Military Park.

RICHARD M. MCMURRY was a student of the late Bell I. Wiley's and has followed in his path as a historian of the Civil War and the Confederacy. A graduate of the Virginia Military Institute and Emory University in Atlanta, he has specialized in the story of the war in Georgia. Among his books are *The Road Past Kennesaw: The Atlanta Campaign of 1864* and his recently published *John Bell Hood and the War for Southern Independence.*

EVERARD H. SMITH has long specialized in the story of the campaign for the Shenandoah Valley in 1864. A cum laude graduate from Yale, he took his Ph.D. at the University of North Carolina and is currently an instructor in history and political science at High Point College in North Carolina. He also maintains a serious interest in archival and manuscript work and in 1976 published *The Southern Historical Collection,* a supplementary guide to manuscripts at the University of North Carolina. Many images from that collection appear in this volume.

LUDWELL H. JOHNSON III, has been for many years a professor of history at the College of William and Mary and a noted specialist in the Civil War. His first book was *The Red River Campaign, Politics & Cotton in the Civil War,* and it is still regarded as the standard source. More recently he published *Division and Reunion: America 1848–1877,* a provocative and decidedly pro-Confederate history of the Civil War era which has challenged many long-accepted ideas about the conflict.

MAURICE MELTON has been a specialist in Confederate naval history for several years. His first book, *Confederate Ironclads,* was published when he was still a student. A graduate of the University of Georgia, with a doctorate from Emory University, Mr. Melton serves on the board of advisers for the Confederate Naval Museum at Columbus, Georgia, and makes his home at La Grange. He is currently regional manager for a southern industrial concern.

Index

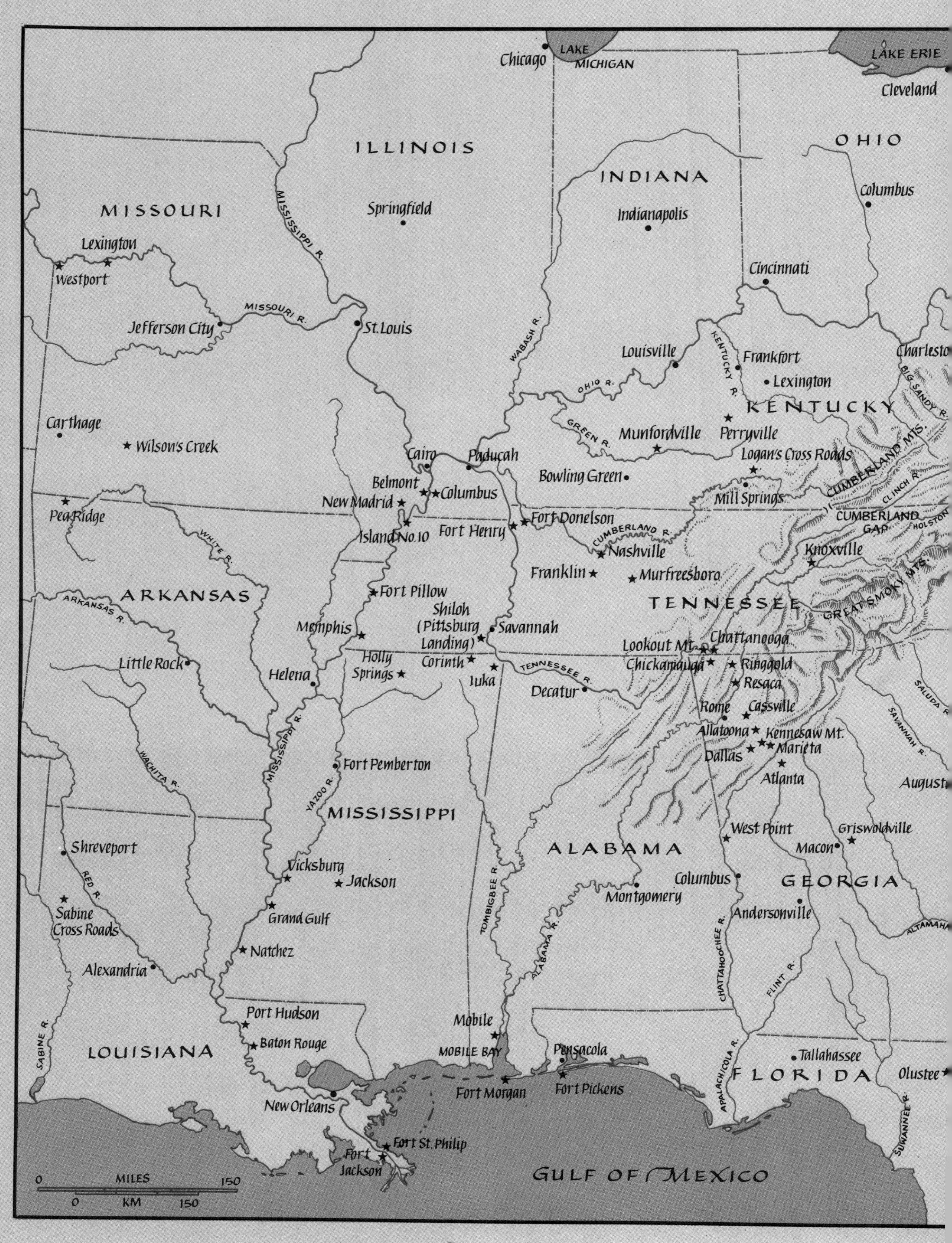

LAKE MICHIGAN
Chicago
LAKE ERIE
Cleveland
ILLINOIS
INDIANA
OHIO
MISSOURI
Springfield
Indianapolis
Columbus
MISSISSIPPI R.
Lexington
Westport
Cincinnati
MISSOURI R.
Jefferson City
St. Louis
WABASH R.
KENTUCKY R.
Louisville
Frankfort
Lexington
Charleston
BIG SANDY R.
OHIO R.
KENTUCKY
GREEN R.
Munfordville
Perryville
Carthage
Wilson's Creek
Cairo
Paducah
Logan's Cross Roads
CUMBERLAND MTS.
Bowling Green
Belmont
Columbus
Mill Springs
CLINCH R.
New Madrid
Pea Ridge
Fort Donelson
CUMBERLAND GAP
HOLSTON
Island No. 10
Fort Henry
CUMBERLAND R.
WHITE R.
Nashville
Knoxville
Franklin
Murfreesboro
GREAT SMOKY MTS.
ARKANSAS
Fort Pillow
ARKANSAS R.
TENNESSEE
Shiloh (Pittsburg Landing)
Savannah
Memphis
Lookout Mt.
Chattanooga
Holly Springs
Corinth
Chickamauga
Ringgold
Little Rock
Iuka
TENNESSEE R.
Helena
Resaca
Decatur
SALUDA R.
Rome
Cassville
Allatoona
Kennesaw Mt.
SAVANNAH R.
Dallas
Marietta
MISSISSIPPI R.
WACHITA R.
Fort Pemberton
Atlanta
Augusta
YAZOO R.
MISSISSIPPI
West Point
Griswoldville
Shreveport
ALABAMA
Macon
RED R.
Vicksburg
Jackson
TOMBIGBEE R.
Columbus
GEORGIA
Montgomery
Sabine Cross Roads
Grand Gulf
Andersonville
ALTAMAHA
ALABAMA R.
Natchez
Alexandria
CHATTAHOOCHEE R.
FLINT R.
Port Hudson
SABINE R.
Mobile
Baton Rouge
LOUISIANA
MOBILE BAY
Pensacola
Tallahassee
APALACHICOLA R.
FLORIDA
Olustee
Fort Morgan
Fort Pickens
New Orleans
SUWANNEE R.
Fort St. Philip
Fort Jackson
0 MILES 150
0 KM 150
GULF OF MEXICO